THE GIFT

Law Office of Laurence N. Kaldor
4613 N. University Dr, STE #238
Coral Springs, FL 33067-4602
www.laurencekaldorlaw.com

Copyright © 2023 by Laurence N. Kaldor

Printed in the United States of America

All rights reserved. No part of this book may be reproduced or used in any manner without written permission of the copyright owner except for the use of quotations in a book review.

For more information, address:
Info@LaurenceKaldorLaw.com

First hardcover edition 2023
First paperback edition 2023
First ebook edition 2023
First audiobook edition 2023

Edited by Barbara Joy D'Antonio
Book cover design by Laurence N. Kaldor

LIBRARY OF CONGRESS CATALOGING-IN-PUBLICATION DATA

ISBN 979-8-9880235-0-0 (hardcover)
ISBN 979-8-9880235-1-7 (paperback)
ISBN 979-8-9880235-2-4 (ebook)
ISBN 979-8-9880235-3-1 (audiobook)

www.thegiftthebook.com

1. Kaldor, Laurence N. 2. Self-help 3. Inspirational 4. Religious 5. Survival 6. Metaphysical

THE GIFT

LAURENCE N. KALDOR

Edited by
Barbara Joy D'Antonio

Laurence N. Kaldor, c. 2009

To my wife & kids for putting up with me while I wrote this book.
You are my love, my light, my everything!

To the medical staff that saved my life.

To my family, friends and everyone that supported & inspired me along the way.

To my mom.
Thank you!

To my dad.
You will live forever with me in the present!

THE GIFT

I

1

THE CRASH!

I'm not supposed to be here. Or so they tell me. It's curious. As the plane was going down, I knew I'd be okay. Don't ask me how I knew. I just knew. My dad would save us. And, we'd be okay. We had been in a multitude of precarious situations before which is the nature of flying small propeller driven aircraft. Every prop-pilot has his compendium of harrowing stories and near misses. However, the vast majority of ours occurred in less impressive, single engine fliers. Our new tricked out twin-engine Piper Chieftain was a stalwart, reliable puddle jumper. A plush, state-of-the-art, luxurious eight-seat, turbo-prop beauty, with ultramodern radar and high-tech navigation. Its powerful engines and lavish design provided an ideal shuttle for our weekend escapes. Unlike larger jet-engine aircraft, she was small enough to land in remote localities with short runways, and yet formidably spry enough to take us almost anywhere in the continental United States and across the Caribbean. Unfortunately, our baby was not designed to fly for extended lengths of time with only one engine, and definitely not in the middle of a tropical cyclone.

When we lost power to our right engine, mid-flight, en route to the Bahamas from New York, I was certain that my father's eighteen-year flight experience, military training, icy-cool temperament, and instilled confidence would be enough to bring this bird safely to the ground, despite Isidore's fury. Torrential gusts smashed into the hull from every conceivable angle, tossing us about like a paper airplane. With every jolt, I was mystified at my dad's ability to keep us aloft, and upright. Moments earlier, at his instruction, I informed the tower that we were no longer able to hold altitude. We were told to be patient and remain in a holding pattern. This was not an option. Our time was running out. Without waiting for control-tower-confirmation, and even if it meant cutting off other aircraft on approach, at my father's behest, into the small handheld microphone, my sixteen-year-old, post-pubescent voice crackled, "we are on final," and, "we're coming in whether we are cleared or not!"

We experienced a moment of eerie calm at three-thousand feet, as my dad lined up the runway for our emergency approach. For a microsecond we thought the turbulence had ceased, when suddenly a headwind slammed into the nose, lurching us forward in our seats, shoving the entire plane backwards, and stalling the left engine. The front of our craft pointed up, skyward, floated suspended for a moment, and then turned downward, beginning a perilous nosedive. As we descended, the floor dropped out, and I was plastered into my cockpit seat by immense G-forces. I immediately felt that familiar stomach-wrenching feeling of dropping instantly, as if on an amusement park rollercoaster. Sadly, I was cognoscente that we weren't mounted safely on rails. The sudden loss of altitude caused me to involuntarily hold my breath. The ground was coming up exceedingly fast. As the plane's pitch went vertical, the dark grey swirls of sky, that only seconds ago filled the cockpit windshield, were replaced with a murky green and brown patchwork from the swampy everglades below. Comforted only mildly by an acute awareness that my dad had the helm, I was otherwise paralyzed with terror and reverted to an adolescent survival mode. My anxiety was off the charts. We've been here before, yet this time was somehow different. While my dad was in control, it disconcertingly seemed as though the forces of nature were determined to challenge his command. In other words, I was scared out of my mind. I averted my eyes, too panicked to look out the front windshield. I turned my head away from the approaching swampland, twisting and rotating my upper body around in my chair. Contorting my torso and tightly wrapping my arms around the top portion of my seatback, now facing away from the front window, I burrowed my eyes into the stiff headrest, exhaling slowly into the stale pillow fabric. Shaking, I cowardly bear-hugged the seatback! My only coherent thought, "Let my father handle this."

Under normal circumstances the cacophony of ambient cockpit sounds inside any small-prop aircraft are considerable – from the massive roaring combustion engines, the whirring interior electronic equipment, the often-incoherent static-laced radio-tower-chatter on approach, to the outside wispy wind and ancillary weather. And, up until only a few moments ago those noises completely engulfed our cockpit. However, at this moment, they were all replaced by my pulsating heartbeat and repeated hyperventilating gasps for air.

These next few moments would turn out to be the most dramatic experience of my life, specifically regarding the "physical progression of time" and its virtual appearance to advance in slow motion. It wasn't my first involvement with relative time perception. For example, when I was six years old, I accidentally dropped a ceramic dinner plate and observed it fall in slow motion before shattering on the floor. On other occasions, I recall witnessing objects, such as baseballs, soccer balls, and even tennis balls slowing down during tournament games. I dismissed all these prior reflections as juvenile hallucinations. However, this authentic experience in the cockpit was seemingly the longest, intense, and most enlightening. At the time, I could not possibly imagine the cosmic and universal implications of these next few seconds.

Forgive the digression, but the ramifications of this understanding would prove to be life-altering. Allow me to simplify and explain using commonly accepted physical and gravitational principals – in general, an object will freefall at approximately two-hundred feet per second. Which means, from our present altitude we would only have approximately fourteen seconds before impact (give or take). It was the longest and scariest fourteen seconds of my life. However, as we plunged down from the heavens, for me, the passage of this brief time interval, nosediving towards earth, was experienced as a relative eternity.

Although, during those stressful few seconds, as explained above, my shocked auditory functions seemed to filter out all external noise, focusing on my internal pulse and respiration, while my other cognitive functions were alarmingly heightened. For example, I distinctly smelled the sour and pungent, rotten egg-like odor, coming from the hot oil, spewing from the right engine, just outside my window, combined with the familiar dull metallic and plastic scents wafting throughout the cockpit. Although my mouth was dry, I still tasted sweet remnants of red licorice bits trapped in my molars, coupled with the stale, bitter flavor of black coffee. The tips of my fingers found mundane comfort digging into the hard plastic of the smooth, cockpit seatback. The skin on my nose and cheeks were surprisingly pacified by the coarse texture of the headrest's rough synthetic fabric against my face, as I continued my feeble attempt to control my breathing. Although all these olfactory and tactile sensory inputs were providing merely an illusion of protection, remarkably, they did provide actual comfort in their distraction from the real and present danger rapidly approaching just outside the front windshield. Or more precisely, us towards it.

After what felt like an eternity of these sensations cascading in simultaneous synchronization, I wondered why we hadn't yet landed or crashed. Something should have happened by now. What on God's green earth was taking so long? While the righteous prophet Job would have been disappointed in my adolescent lack of patience, the great Harry Houdini would have been proud of my physical prowess and contortionist abilities at this particular moment. My left leg was outstretched, and remained tucked below the front instrument panel, compressed beneath the flight controls, with my sneakered foot providing support, anchored by my toes under the floor pedals. My right leg was bent at the knee, and raised, with my foot on the edge of the seat, allowing my thigh and calf to be wedged between the flight controls and my body. With only my left butt-cheek firmly planted on the cockpit chair, my torso was stretched and twisted, allowing me to tightly hug the upright seatback behind me. This half fetal position I was clamped into provided yet another irrational illusion of protection for my midsection and chest. Confused by our seemingly endless descent, I turned my head slightly to assess my surroundings, while maintaining my contorted vice grip, bear-hold, on the chair, only to discover that according to the cockpit's analog console clock, only a mere four seconds had transpired. Things were moving so slowly now that actual dust particles remained suspended inches from my face. How infuriating! Job would have indeed been truly disappointed in me.

I glanced over at my dad, who still had a firm grasp of the U-shaped flight controls. An ex-high school football letterman, an Air National Guardsman who fought in the U.S.-Korean Conflict, a self-made hands-on white-collar businessman, who maintained his rock-solid upper body strength by daily loading and unloading auto-parts alongside his workers in his Elmhurst, Queens' warehouse, was now flush, with sweat pouring down his otherwise pale face as he desperately tried to level off our twin-engine modern marvel. I had the presence of mind to know in that instance, that if we impacted the earth at our current vertical pitch-angle we would instantly be crushed and vaporized. I released my grip on the seat and turned back to a forward-facing seated position. I had to help. I had to do something. I began pulling on the co-pilot's secondary U-shaped flight controls in front of me. It was no use. They were frozen solid. The G-forces resulting from our nosedive were simply too much for me. I looked back over at my dad, the pilot, the captain, whose muscles were now bulging out of his completely sweat-soaked short sleeve cotton light blue button-down collared shirt. I continued to pull on the rudder to no avail. His arms began to shake. For the briefest moment, I thought he might actually pull the rudder off the console. His face was quivering, so intense and bloated, that I recall having the comical thought that his head might explode. The ground, the swamp, the tops of the trees, all becoming clearer and unnervingly closer.

I noticed his upper lip began to twitch, as he snarled and flared his teeth. I was still only able to hear my own heart beating, as if everything else was muffled by having cotton stuffed in my ears. But I knew him. I knew his mannerisms. I knew his many faces. I knew in this moment by his gestures and gesticulations that he was letting out a guttural and primordial scream. Even if in this muffled-slow-motion moment I could not hear it. I knew the scream. Like everything else in his life, he would never give up. It just wasn't in him to give up. As if by magic the flight controls that were frozen only moments ago, began slowly moving back towards me. Simultaneously, the nose of the plane began to rise in the windshield in front of me. Little bits of grey-sky-swirls began to form on the upper half of the front windshield. Suddenly, like a weight being lifted from my chest, for the first time in what seemed like a millennium it became easier to breath. To my chagrin, as the plane leveled off, we were still dropping rapidly, and began to glide like a missile over the treetops. Our speed actually accelerated as we horizontally flattened out from our nosedive. With one hand still firmly fixed to the rudder, my dad reached across me with his right hand turning dials and flipping switches. I was awestruck observing him. I knew that I was in the presence of greatness. Like a master craftsman, with instinctive precision he knew exactly what he was doing. Flaps fully down, gear down, nose up. Amidst the chaos of the moment he would maintain a semblance of control. I would learn years later, that during those final moments, he calmly turned off the engines and jettisoned any remaining fuel to clear the lines as best he could to avoid an explosion on impact.

As we continued to drift rapidly downward with only swamp, marsh, and trees in front of us, it was apparent for the first time that we were not going to touchdown anywhere near anything resembling an airport, a concrete runway, or any type of solid asphalt. We weren't even going to find an open road, highway, pasture, field, or clearing. That was it. We were in a dense swamp. A marshy forest. We were in it, and we were coming down. The vehemence of treetops scraping against the bottom of the plane was the first sound that I recall hearing over the reverberations of my own respiration and rapid heartbeat. Tap-tap-tap-tap-tap. In a crescendo, it brought back all other ambient sounds around me. As we began to fall below the tree line, the tops of the trees and their respective branches started smacking into the plexiglass windshield. Thwack-thwack-thwack. I glanced over at my dad one last time. He was flush now. Ashen. Exhausted, but still resolute. His partially bald head was exposed, as his one thick blonde thatch, that he otherwise utilized for his nineteen-seventies comb-over, hung down, flapping on the left side of his face by the window. The sound of the branches and glass intensified. Rat-tat-tat-tat-tat. He saw me looking at him in his periphery. Our eyes met. He reached over with his right paw and patted me with as much comfort as he could muster in the moment. He was my dad. Rat-tat-tat-tat-tat. He was my hero. Rat-tat-tat-tat-tat. He was going to save us.

Then, as the tree branches began to shatter the windshield only a few feet from my face, out of sheer panic, I gave up trying to help being co-pilot. I realized that he had been doing all the work anyway. I wasn't sixteen any longer. I was reduced to being a little boy in the protective hands of his father. And I was terrified! I reclaimed my contorted and twisted position, turning half-around, clutching the seat, burying myself back into the headrest, left leg anchored once again under the instrument panel with my toes locked under the foot pedals for support, with my right knee re-bent into a half-fetal position, foot planted on the edge of the seat, hoping that my right thigh and calf would somehow protect my midsection. All the while, my faith never wavered, knowing that my dad was going to save us. Rat-tat-tat-tat-tat. Everything was going to be okay. Any alternative negative thought was inconceivable. If only the wrenching sound of crushing metal would stop. Rat-tat-tat-tat-tat. Everything would be okay.

Then suddenly there was...nothing! There was a deafening quiet, coinciding with an eclipse into complete blackness. Dark. Calm. Silent.

In that obscurity I was unaware of what had happened. More precisely, I was unaware that everything would be okay. Despite my last fleeting memory, the juvenile belief in my father as savior, I was unaware that there are always higher powers at work. Not that there wouldn't be pain, suffering, death, and other life experiences. But merely that everything would be okay because it already was. I simply was not evolved enough to acknowledge it. This realization was not afforded to me prior to that terrifying free fall, nor during my engulfment into blackness. The plane crash was merely the beginning of my journey.

I'm not supposed to be here. That conclusion has been repeated to me hundreds of times over the years, from the rescue team that pulled our bodies from the wreckage in the swamp, to the myriad of surgeons who pieced me back together, to the scores of random strangers who heard about my traumatic experience, that, "people don't survive airplane crashes." Well, I did. Our plane crashed. Our beautiful, state-of-the-art *Navajo Chieftain* crashed into the Florida everglades barely three miles from Jacksonville Municipal Airport. And, I survived!

It's an amazing thing being told over and over again it's a miracle that you're here. "Your life is a result of a miraculous achievement," they would say. A miracle. An act of God. Divine intervention. That's a heavy burden for anyone to carry. I shouldn't be here. Yet, here I am. Since September twenty-eighth, nineteen eighty-four, every day, every minute, every second, has all been moments of borrowed, miraculous time. Heavy, right?

What if I told you, the whole thing, all of it, everything, is a miracle! Me, you, us, and them. The good, the bad, the pain, the pleasure, the hurt, the wonders, the joy, the trials, the tribulations, the suffering, the anguish, the torment, the overwhelming happiness, the success, the loss, and the love are all a part of the miracle that is life. More than likely, it is not the first time you are conceptualizing this. However, to many they are just words. Hyperbole. Expressions of idealistic grandeur. Most people spend the vast majority of their everyday lives never realizing how wonderful their lives can truly be. Always searching for the secrets. The answers. And, while they've heard these words before, for them it is just unrealistic. Impossible. Unattainable. Their lives, circumstances, and suffering are far too negative. Overwhelming. Even when they've perhaps witnessed other people doing it. Observed other people living it. Hearing from others how easy it is. Yet for them, it's an elusive pipe dream. For them, "life is hard." "Relationships are difficult, laborious work." They have myriad reasons as to why today they cannot achieve any level of lasting peace or sustained happiness. Obstacles are in their way. Always obstacles. Excuses. Always excuses. Regrets. Too many bad choices from earlier in their life. They're not smart enough. They're not pretty enough. Not handsome enough. Not tall enough. Not strong enough. Not wealthy enough. There is too much pain and suffering. Too much trauma. Too much drama. It's just too difficult. The mountain ahead is insurmountable. The valley too deep, the canyon too wide and the road too long and unyielding. They're unable to grasp the secret and harness their own inner power to unlock eternal happiness, peace, and prosperity.

Remember, I'm a ghost. Or a charmed spirit. I'm not supposed to be here. I died all those years ago. Others might say that I was reborn. Regardless as to your interpretation, after sharing my accounts, you'll make your own judgments. I'm merely sharing my own experiences, my own knowledge, and explaining how to utilize the tools that I've cultivated in my life, and continue to use every day since my discovery, to unlock one of the secrets of the universe in all its majesty and the key to outer success, prosperity, and achievement, as well as, to inner peace, happiness, and tranquility.

So, to say that I am fortunate is an understatement. To say that I am special is an understatement. However, the reality is that we are all fortunate. We are all special. We are all kindred spirits. Sadly, only a few of us are able to appreciate it. All of it! Many of you are already aware that "the present" is "The Gift." Perhaps you've even heard that before. "A Gift" that we are all given. Every moment, of every moment, of every moment! Well, if that's all there is, and that's the big secret, then this book should be over at the end of the first chapter. But, understanding "The Gift," unwrapping it and taking "the present" out of the box is only the beginning. Think about it like any gift you have ever been given. When you open it and put it out on the table, you often have to read the directions and learn how to use it. Sometimes it takes tools to assemble or operate it. And often it takes years to truly appreciate it, if at all. Sadly, some of us even entomb a present or a gift at the bottom of a storage closet, unacknowledged. But not today! Be patient. Take a deep breath. And let's explore "The Gift" together.

Through my narrative we will take the journey together. You will have an opportunity to learn how to best harness your own outer and inner strengths. Your own outer success. Your own inner happiness. Your own inner peace. This chronicle and the elements herein can be an allegory for you to relate things from your own life, as well as to learn directly from my experience. Within the pages ahead you will learn how to use your own essential tools to unlock the power of "The Gift." Your gift! And the best news is that you will not need to personally experience my level of pain and traumatic anguish to get there.

※※※ ※※※

But first, in order for us to continue forward, we have to go backward. Back to the silence and the darkness.

※※※ ※※※

Only moments ago, my father and I were rocketing downward in our small craft, cascading through the treetops into the everglades, careening beneath the tropical green canopies and branches, when suddenly I was cast silently adrift into utter blackness. A moment of calm. Peacefulness. However, that momentary respite was replaced by being raptured in agonizingly torturous, and perpetually searing misery. And just like that, my new reality was a shadowy abyss of unending pain.

———◆◇◆———

2

THE DARK

The pain! From the nothingness, excruciating and seemingly unending pain. Disoriented, and completely unaware of my situation, location, and surroundings. Adrift in blackness and aloft in time. My very identity was a mystery. Even that recent momentary interval of peaceful calm, just before the blackout, never existed here. There was no past, no future, only the present. The pain. And all I knew was the pain. Sharp, distressing and ostensibly stagnant, wrenching pain. No, not stagnant. Definitely not stagnant. Those thoughts regarding the progressive nature of time provided circumstantial evidence that my predicament was not stationary. Varying degrees of pain. Therefore, there was a future. There had to be. Because while the pain was continuous in nature, it ranged in intensity. Appearing to decrease slightly, then increased quickly in what felt like shooting waves. The agony. The pain.

Adrift in torturous darkness, my mind was racing to reconcile my dilemma. The pain was overwhelming. Just then, an inner voice whispered, "focus." Anything to distract from the anguish. The whisper prompted questions. Where was I? How did I get here? For that matter, who or what the hell was I? I was certain I existed. I had thoughts. I was communicating to myself through this narration. I was certain I had a past. I simply could not piece coherent considerations together. The whisper returned. "Focus!" But, the pain was all consuming. It was difficult to concentrate on anything but the pain.

It then occurred to me, I'm clearly a consciousness. "Put it together." A consciousness in pain. A suffering consciousness. The guidance continued, "more!"

Yes, there was more. More to me. More to the universe. A universe? Yes, a universe existed. I was simply being blocked or prohibited from piercing the murky veneer. Every thought was met with searing jolts of pain, as if to keep me off balance. Unfocused. Then, a new sensation. Frustration! Frustration...and pain! So, I was a frustrated consciousness in pain. A tortured consciousness. "Focus!" What was beyond the pain? There had to be more. More to the puzzle. There had to be. "More." I was provided clues which even prompted questions, but the information was being kept from me. By whom, or what?

Also, as I already concluded, since there was perceived forward momentum to my thoughts, logic dictated that there was not only a future but also a past. A recent past that I was suddenly acutely aware of. A recent past of tormenting pain. A past riddled with those previous, horrific waves of torture, albeit to varying degrees. "More!" Was there also a past that preceded the pain? Or was that everything? What a horrific thought. Had I always been an anguishing consciousness, engulfed in a nightmarish void? No, there was more! There had to be. I was just being prevented from seeing it. I was only afforded the pain, meshed with these random confused thoughts. And the nagging sensation that there was something else, outside that emptiness, only compounded my frustration.

⊱────── ──────⊰

In retrospect, during that period of unknown duration, I possessed no tangible memory of the plane, the crash, my own history, or of life outside of that quagmire. I lacked coherent or cogent specificity of almost everything, with a few very specific exceptions, that I began piecing together.

⊱────── ──────⊰

Curiously enough, and quite perplexing, was my certainty that regardless as to my absence of intelligible memory or empirical data, "I" was substantial. I was certain that I existed. *Cogito ergo sum!* I think, therefore I am! Other than the pain, I did believe that much. I existed. And even though not privy to any concrete answers, I held a firm belief that I not only existed then, but also in some form, at some time, outside that hellish purgatory. "More." Strangely enough, the frustration and quest for answers provided a distraction. A modicum of relief from the harrowing pain.

Additionally, and even more bewildering, was that my internal chronometer did not appear to be guided by physical laws or universal metrics, such as – seconds, minutes, or hours. The perceived passage of time was relatively obscured in that space. The painful jolts could have lasted for moments, hours, or even months. There was no way to judge duration, not without a fixed or stable reference point. There were even micro-moments that felt motionless, as if time itself were suspended. Therefore, traditional universal constructs, to which I instinctually grasped, appeared to have no meaning in this shadowy hollow.

And yet, there was "now." That very moment I was in.

That was my first awareness of "The Gift." That very moment. The present. It became the only substantive anchor amidst the morass. And somehow, my newfound awareness was of paramount importance to maintaining my sanity. I simply had no idea why. That was my fourth notion of instinctual certainty. First, I knew that I existed. Second, I was confident that there was more to my existence beyond that captivity. Third, I was acutely aware of the progressive nature of time. And fourth, I existed in the present, that very moment, which in and of itself, was a gift. However puerile my initial conjecture, it was a fundamental epiphany, nonetheless. Upon reflection, I humbly admit that I was eons away from realizing the magnitude, significance, and importance of what I had discovered.

My distraction was short lived, as the onslaught of pain continued. Its arrival, in powerful fluctuating degrees, again evidenced the progressive passage of time. And, since there was nothing else in this vacuous space, except for the pain and my random inquisitive thoughts, the former occupied the majority of my attention. The pain was the present. The pain was "The Gift." Sadly, the pain continually hindered my bewildered investigation. Focus was difficult. Focus was also the present. And therefore, focus was also part of "The Gift." The pain was impossible to ignore. Yet focus appeared to be a path to salvation. A battle began raging, within the present, to focus through the pain. A battle I knew I had to win!

Then I noticed that concentration was more manageable during waves of lesser intensity. I focused on the most recent past pain. I held onto that recent past, creating a new present. However, within my dysphoria there was no way to accurately judge how long my reprieve lasted before I was bombarded with a fresh onslaught of overpowering fire. Fortuitously, the memory of that reprieve resonated, even amidst the current inferno.

Within the present existed the memory of the reprieve. It was no longer in the recent past. Cognitively, I was aware that it was in the past, because it had occurred. And yet, I could still see it, in the present. I could sense it. Which meant, theoretically I could get back to it. How would that be possible? "Focus!" I concentrated on that feeling. On that moment. On that present, or "Gift," from the past. An interval where I was in less pain. I'll never know for certain exactly how it happened, but for a moment, I was back in that time of lesser intensity. There was still pain, but it was somewhat bearable. And then, just like that, I was yanked away, engulfed in flames once again.

The pain was relentless. I had to get back to that sanctuary. I concentrated again. I had to not only get back there, but also somehow figure out how to stay there. "Focus!" This time the memory was further away, yet still crystal clear. It didn't make any sense. But that didn't matter. Rationality was irrelevant. Anything to ease the suffering. The memory was there, with me, in the present. A moment from the past, a part of the present. I moved my energy inside that memory, back into the lesser intensity of pain. Logically, I was still in the present, even though I was simultaneously experiencing the past. I couldn't reconcile that strange phenomenon. I merely accepted the relief and wanted to extend it. I also became aware, that having been back there, in that interval of lesser intensity more than once, there was more than one memory of it. And with that awareness, I unlocked a myriad of memories of the same intervals of lesser intensity. I was quickly surrounded by them. Countless thousands of them. It then dawned on me that I may have been trapped in this vacuum of darkness for an eternity.

I don't know if that canon of memories provided a shield or some supernatural ability to maneuver within the chasm, but I quickly developed an aptitude at predicting impending pain and could ostensibly sidestep or dodge future intervals of searing torment by remaining in those memories. Additionally, I was able to foresee future painful jolts, and for the most part, avoid them. It appeared as though those severe radiances of pain existed simultaneously within the present, alongside the more tepid memories. Amazingly, it became a conscious choice where to focus my attention, and where to place my energy.

Being afforded a moment of composed reflection, I questioned whether my forecasts were mere guesses, or if I was actually seeing the future. Because if I was accurately prophesizing, then that would mean the past and the future were both contained within the present. "Stay focused." Was I clairvoyant? Or was I just lucky? No, it wasn't happenstance, I was actually able to see the future intense pain. It was just as clear as the past pain. And with that clarity came the ability to avoid it. It was marvelous. The past and future were in fact both there, simultaneously in the present.

That was an important revelation. However, I had to reconcile it with one of my erroneous conclusions. My recent conjecture may have been incorrect. In there, time not only appeared to be progressive, but also multidirectional. Possibly omnidirectional. How was that possible? "Stay focused." My awareness of the present anchored me. Centered me. "Focus on the present." Okay then, what is a present? A gift? Who gave it to me? Where did it come from? Where did I come from? So many questions. Meanwhile, the pain, at any level, made it difficult to concentrate.

All that mattered in the moment, was avoiding the excruciating brutality of the severest jolts. I could see them coming. And I knew that if a massive enough thunderbolt hit, I could be lost forever. My biggest nemesis was the future intense pain. It had to be avoided. Astonishingly enough, being able to see the waves made it possible to temporarily retreat within past moments of lesser severity that were all there in the present. For an unknown duration that method was working. When I felt a slight increase in pain within a memory, I would jump to another echo of the same memory where the past-pain level was bearable. However, the continuous onslaught, even to lesser degrees, was becoming maddening, and making it more difficult to focus. The battle was raging. Losing was not an option.

Remarkably, I began manipulating time at a microscopic level. I found micro-moments within the memories of lesser intensity and focused on them. Slowed them, to what appeared almost complete suspension. I found myself living in infinitesimal moments containing minimal amounts of pain. Was I gaining control of that environment? And if so, why couldn't I stop the pain entirely? Where was it coming from? Ultimately, if I were to prevail, I had to figure that out! Because, even at its lowest level its continuous nature was torturous. Eventually, psychosis would ensue and overtake me. My present would become insanity.

I knew I had to utilize those moments of clarity for introspection and discovery. "It's all in the present." I once again reverted to my query. What is a present? A present is a thing. It can be given or received. It has value. In an esoteric sense it doesn't need to be a physical thing. It can be a gesture or a showing. However, for the purposes of that analysis let's say it was a tangible thing – that very moment, or micro-moment, if you will. The immense pain was returning. It was becoming more challenging to fend it off. I had to continue my analysis, and quickly!

The first thing you do with a present is receive it. You become aware of it. You accept it. My gift was the pain. I was aware of the pain. I was aware of the present. It arrived in a metaphorical box. I was mindful of it. I acknowledged it. And then, I placed it on a proverbial table in front of me. Okay, that was Step One: Accept "The Gift." Become aware of it and receive it.

The throbbing pain continued. I was desperate to hang on. What would step two be? What is the second thing you do with a present? "Concentrate." You open it. You unwrap it. You unbox it. You explore and examine it. Often you must read the instructions, the warnings, the directions. Other times you merely admire it. In some cases, you try it on. Regardless, at the very least, you look it over and examine it. My present was the pain. Courageously, I took it out of the metaphorical box. The pain was massive. Enormous. I unpacked it and began to examine it. It was too big. I had to back away from it, in order to take it all in. Okay, Step Two sounds easy enough: Examine "The Gift."

Recognizing the urgency, my mind swiftly raced for answers through examination. The throbbing intensified. The burning. "Concentrate!" If I could manipulate time, why couldn't I stop the pain entirely? I studied the pain. There appeared to be something beyond the pain. "Yes, keep looking." There were memories, thoughts, experiences, but they were too far out of reach. They were being blocked by a massive wall of pain. Yet I sensed perceptions, memories, just beyond the wall, feeding my insight and intuition. But where did that present insight and intuition come from? I must have existed, in some form, before entry into that hole. "Focus." That self-examination again provided further evidence of a distant past or an alternative dimensional existence. "Yes." I was on to something but I still had so many fundamental questions. Who was I? What was I? "Concentrate!" Why couldn't I see past my earliest memory in that space? Who or what was blocking me? In order to stop the pain, I needed to address where it came from. Who gave it to me? Or, more precisely, who was inflicting it upon me? While I appeared to be alone in that black cavity, there had to be another entity. Someone or something causing the pain.

And just then, I sensed something else. I wasn't alone. A duality was created, whereby I was comforted by no longer feeling isolated, while simultaneously enraged at the prospect that this other entity was causing my torment. So, there I was, a prisoner in a dark crevasse somewhere in the corner of actuality, endlessly being tormented. But by whom? And why?

At the time during my initial period of suffering, I had no idea how close I was to unlocking the secrets of "The Gift." In reality I was being blocked from seeing the whole picture. Unbeknownst to me, that obfuscation was self-induced. The human mind and spirit possess astonishing and remarkable protective mental capabilities. We all have an autonomic ability to go into shock, or short circuit and shut down, as a self-preserving shield from traumatic pain – both physically and emotionally. These protective protocols are mechanisms that kick in to safeguard our ethos from intense horrors until we develop the tools to properly absorb and assimilate them. During that time period, and in those moments, my life force was no different. It was working overtime to protect me. Sheltering me, no matter how hard I tried to fight back to lucid coherence.

～～～～ ～～～～

No matter how hard I tried, in my examination of the present I could not investigate around the barrier and pierce my earliest memory of painful darkness. However, that intense deliberation uncovered minute cracks in the wall, summoning an image of my earthly self. I was correct, I did in fact exist in the past or on some other dimensional plane. My consciousness was part of a tangible being at some previous time or place. Although the imagery was obscured in white and yellow light, it was recognizable enough. It was me. A youthful human male. The more I focused, the larger the massive wall of agony grew. The cracks were sealed with more pain, preventing entry into those memories and a clear visualization of my prior self.

I therefore decided to explore other less painful areas of "The Gift." Since I was now aware that the future existed simultaneously there in the present, perhaps travel was possible forward in time. Unlike the solid painful obstruction in the past, the future contained powerful surges that I could manage to avoid. Astonishingly, this enabled me to see beyond the pain. I could witness my future, in the present.

Those forthcoming images, while terrestrial in nature, similar to my past conception, were bathed in bright white with yellow highlights. Accounts of my future self, surrounded by others. Encircled by love – husband, father, athlete, pilot, lawyer, prosecutor, judge, author, filmmaker, teacher, grandfather. They weren't laid out in a successive timeline. But rather scattered like a collage there in the present. How was I able to see that? It was me. I was so old. Were they premonitions, or possible futures? And, if I was no longer attached to my worldly form, how could I ever experience them? Did all possible futures exist in the present? "The Gift" now appeared complex. The more questions I answered, the more questions were created. "Focus!"

The assortment of images was comforting. While the past contained a massive impediment of pain, the future offered hope. I returned to that patchwork of visualizations individually. The feeling of love and warmth eased my suffering. Each endearing scenario contained inexplicable healing properties – caressing my wife's hand...my wife, deliberating in court, commanding actors on a set, playing with a dog...my dog, witnessing the birth of my children, and then I was somewhere entirely, looking down at the angelic face of my grandchild – which all began to wash away the surface of my agony.

And with that I was hit with a crushing wave of discomfort. Immeasurable. Off the charts! How was I unable to see it coming? The premonitions were all wiped away. I was radiating with heat, writhing in agony. And then...flash! I was instantly transported into a new paradigm altogether. Flash-flash. Blinding frosty light! Numbness. The pain was gone. The darkness was gone. The black void became a white cloud.

Flash! Flash-flash! A rush of oxygen filled my lungs. My chest heaved. I was unable to exhale. And yet it was surprisingly pleasant, albeit confusing. I was overcome with relief as the pain was gone. My query regarding "The Gift," and my need for escape seemed no longer relevant or required. I was inexplicably being filled with air. A new gift. A new present. A new moment. However, I could not exhale. It was one long continuous inhale.

Until that very moment, I hadn't given much thought to breathing. It's weird how much we take mundane autonomic life functions for granted. My distress was replaced with a dazed feeling of elevated euphoria. Fog. And the absence of pain instantly felt great! Relief! It all coincided with that flash of magnificent white light that seemed to swallow me whole. I was immersed in it, as though engulfed, numb, adrift inside a vapor. Aloft. Weightless. Floating. That was a new gift. A new present. The pain was all gone. However, this relief was not of my doing. Of that I was certain. There was an outside force at work. Who, what, where, how and why? All unknown.

My mind attempted to refocus. It was no longer easy to grasp the present. While the past was also hazy, the memory of the horrible pain still resonated. Only moments ago, I was doing something. I was controlling something. I was seeing visions. I was on the verge of calculating and discovering some vast cosmic deduction. Or I was on the verge of insanity. I couldn't remember. Pain. Pain? Yes, there was pain. I remember the thought of the pain and having the feeling of pain. Intense pain. Although, re-conjuring up the memory of it, was not enough to recreate the sensation of it. The pain was no longer there. I was merely aware that it did hurt at some point in the obscure past. "Focus!" It was clearly a new present. But wasn't the past included within the present? I couldn't reconcile. The black unpleasantness was replaced by a peaceful, white, nothingness.

And then…as though cotton was removed from ears, I heard sounds. New sounds? I couldn't be certain. Either the sounds were new, or the past pain was so intense that they had previously muted my auditory senses. But they were definite sounds. Whirring, beeping and mechanical resonances. Noises I could not specifically identify. And voices? I wasn't certain, because I couldn't discern language, but they distinctly sounded like muffled voices. Muffled and incoherent. And, they didn't appear to be speaking to me. However, it did appear to be a language – an intermittent pulse of responsive tones. And I was curious what they were saying. I was surrounded by a cacophony of new sensory inputs. I was taking it all in.

Having a respite from the pain, I was no longer aware of, nor was I appreciating the present. Additionally, even staying focused on the new sounds was problematic. The fog was obfuscating all attempts to concentrate. Every time I began a cogent idea, it evaporated before solidification. However, the auditory echoes, admittingly incoherent, were distinctive enough to channel towards a specific direction. Then, the whisper returned, "focus." In the absence of any other sensations, these noises were amplified and became my anchor in the moment. "Stay focused." But my curiosity, amidst the confusion was amplified as well. I was desperately probing these sounds for meaning.

The sounds were always slightly different. Modified. I found myself trying to anticipate the new noises, only to immediately forget what I was previously thinking about. My present became a fixation on the future. My awareness of the imminent noise appeared to give meaning to my otherwise whitewashed bewilderment. I had no sense of touch, taste or smell, virtually still no other feelings or sensations at all. And other than my heaving oxygen, from an involuntary never-ending inhalation, there were these new sounds. They were everything in the present. I had to follow them.

I tracked them right outside of my body. A body? Yes, I instantly became aware that I had a physical body as well. Dots were quickly being connected. Having a respite from the pain, the memories and future associations congealed in my mind. While my thoughts were apparently active, my physical body was not. In the darkness I had been a prisoner in an otherwise lethargic shell. Trapped. I yearned for movement. Release from that penitentiary. And somehow, by the sheer power of my will, my curiosity, in search of those new sounds, I transitioned outside of my own mortal form.

First, I floated around a modest-sized hospital intensive care unit. Then, drifted casually out into the corridor, and then back into a large, well-lit room, hovering above what appeared to be my hospital gurney. I observed myself, lying asleep. My likeness was familiar. A few people, that were perhaps nurses, were monitoring me and examining numerous technical devices affixed to my body by tubes and wires. While certain conclusions still alluded me, other ones became instantly apparent. That was clearly an out-of-body experience. Fascinating!

Over the many years since the plane crash, and that particular unexplained phantasm, I have subsequently encountered, read, and heard a myriad of stories of people who had similar "near-death" out-of-body experiences. While I cannot attest to the specificity or veracity of any of their personal experiences, I am relatively certain that my involvement was a medically-induced-narcotic-manifestation. Because, during that ghostly occurrence, as my non-corporeal form traversed the corridors of the hospital, and wafted above my physical being, I definitively observed, in meticulous detail, myself, unconscious, lying in bed...whole and intact. It doesn't mean I did not have the association. Rather it simply means the experience was most likely a hallucination. However, I yield all credence to other potential supernatural phenomena to a Higher Power.

I would later learn, from my own medical records and photos, that in those first few days of my year-long hospitalization, I was anything but whole and intact. Regardless, at that time, my drug-induced non-corporeal aberration, floating around the hospital, was still unaware, at least on a conscious level, of my true condition and the circumstances that resulted therein. Frankly speaking, until my recent sojourn flying above the corridors and suspended in my hospital room, I hadn't realized what had actually transpired in the aftermath of the plane crash. But for the time being it was just fun floating around the hospital.

Floating through the corridors provided another moment of clarity. Awareness! Through the bog I recalled many of my recent insights from the darkness. "Receive." Since my foggy awakening, I hadn't given "The Gift" a second thought. Because within that pain-free miasma, concentration was fleeting. Yet, the depiction of my listless body in the bed below brought back a cascade of pictures from my past. "The past is in the present." Yes, I had a past. For a moment I was able to cut through the mist and became raptured with a lifetime of imagery. Flash, flash, flash. Childhood, family, school, camp...flash, flash. Removal of the gigantic barrier of pain suddenly opened the floodgates of memories. My present was instantly filled with my entire life, up until that moment – My mother, father, sister, cousins, friends, home, adolescence, sports, school, pets, etc. It was all wonderful! "Focus!" Where was I? "Hospital." Yes, okay, a hospital made sense. How did I get here? "Receive." Okay, if I had a past, what was my last memory? "Concentrate." And just like that, within the present I was inundated with images of trees slapping windows. Slap-slap-slap. An airplane windshield. Rat-tat-tat-tat. A cockpit. Thwack-thwack-thwack! Our plane going down. Those memories were fragmented. Like an unassembled puzzle. I reasoned that the plane must have crashed. Had I perished on impact? From my perspective I didn't seem too badly injured. Unless I didn't survive, and I was observing my own postmortem corpse on that gurney.

※※※

Of course, as evidenced from this writing, I didn't perish on impact. However, I was anything but unscathed. As it turns out, after our small craft impacted the trees, slamming abruptly into the marshy everglades, I was physically ejected from my seat through a gaping hole torn into the ceiling. And, while the vast majority of my body departed the cockpit, a decent chunk of my left leg below my left knee remained under the instrument panel. The damage to my leg, however, was only a small fraction of my overall near-terminal injuries. Internally, I was mess. Every interior organ with the exception of my brain and my heart shut down, was in shock, or collapsed. Externally, my entire body was covered in open wounds and exposed flesh. My right eye was punctured, my jaw was shattered, my left eardrum eviscerated, and I had over eighty broken bones.

Over the years when people have heard my story, their first reaction is invariably "how lucky" I am to have survived a plane crash. "People don't survive airplane crashes," I'm often told. And while that adage is true enough, my typical response, tongue-in-cheek, is that, "lucky people don't endure airplane crashes in the first place." And that, "lucky folks land safely on the ground inside their airplanes." Which is customarily met with an uncomfortable laugh or an even more awkward silence. And then I smile to myself, at how easily and expectedly everyone walks right into that one.

Regardless, following my fortunate inevitability – my survival of the actual plane crash – the events that occurred during and immediately following impact were replete with numerous mathematical improbabilities, that some might interpret as lucky coincidences, while other faith-based folks likely define as miracles. As you recall, during our abrupt decent, being stifled by abject terror, I cowardly turned away from the dashboard, with my upper torso twisted, hugging the cockpit chair, so that my nose and forehead were buried in the seatback chair and my back was facing the instrument panel. Upon impact with the ground, the nose of the plane separated and broke off from the rear cabin. When the plane came to an abrupt stop, I was first thrust forward into the instrument panel, and then whipsawed backwards, propelled, like a cannonball, up and out of the newly formed hole in the cockpit ceiling. My virtually lifeless body flew across the swamp, glancing, scraping, and slicing through the dense tropical trees, branches, thorny vines, and thick brush until my limp, semiconscious hundred-thirty-pound body came to rest sixty yards behind the wreckage, face-up, on my back, in the thick mud.

Several amazing things had just occurred, without any one of which would have prematurely terminated my life. First, because of the cowardly way I was seated, the sudden jolt and immense force of the initial impact swung my body around so fast that only my chin, and not my face or top of my head slammed into the instrument panel. In technical terms my maxilla, frontal bone, parietal bone, and entire coronal suture – i.e. the part of my head and skull protecting my brain – were astonishingly unscathed by this disaster. Had I been seated normally, upright in the copilot's chair, I most likely would've experienced instant whiplash, terminal brain damage and died. Instead of snapping my neck and crushing my skull, I managed to only shatter my jawbone into pieces on the dashboard.

But that is only the beginning of the improbable sequence. After being ejected from the plane, as I traversed through the dense swampy everglades, my head – and more definitively, my brain – didn't come into direct contact with any tree trunks, or solid spear-like branches. Additionally, when my body finally succumbed to the gravitational forces, resting in the mud, if I had landed face down, I most certainly would have drowned. Also, because of all my open injuries, and exposed raw wounds, if not for the mud that I was immersed in, acting as an impacting coagulant, I most certainly would have bled to death. Furthermore, while Isidore was quite insolent and insistent in maintaining her stalwart tropical cyclone strength for over three hours delaying our rescue, the storm was gracious enough to frighten away any and all of the indigenous reptilian swamp-life – alligators and snakes – which otherwise could have been attracted to, and thereby greedily feasted on my remains. As I have been repeatedly affirmed by the vast multitudes of family, friends and strangers over the years... "lucky" me!

As you can see there is ample opportunity to *Pollyanna* my otherwise unfortunate aviation experience and conclude that I sure was "lucky" to have survived. For those who believe in chance. On the other hand, the faithful have interpreted the engine failure and resulting crash as either a wrathful punishment for youthful indiscretions by a vengeful deity, or miraculous salvation granted by the hand of divine compassion. While others have even chalked up the whole tragedy to mere coincidence.

At this stage, all these above interpretations are irrelevant, because they miss the point. It isn't practical to simply jump ahead to address "why" things happen. We will revisit these possible explanations when we get to Step Three. For now, we must spend considerably more time in the upcoming chapters exploring Step Two: The Examination Process. My initial supposition that scrutiny of the present could be achieved quickly was a solemn miscalculation, as was evidenced from my misperceptions of simple time principles. I had no idea how deep-rooted my engrained programming had been. My trauma shocked that subconscious indoctrination. Over the course of my recovery, and the years since, I would discover how faulty my entrenched conditioning was. The more I surveyed the landscape, the clearer the answers were revealed. The secrets of our existence and our universal power have always been there, in the present. That's "The Gift."

"The Gift" is right now. "The Gift" is your awareness of right now. "The Gift" is the present. "The Gift" here, my present to you, is the story of survival, success, awareness, deprogramming, and appreciation. And your "Present" to yourself is your ability to comprehend and receive it. To live in the moment with me. Therefore, "The Gift" is our collective awareness of this very moment, together.

After decades of helping others cope with their own exploration of the human condition, I can conclusively affirm and attest, emphatically, that you do not have to undergo an actual near-death experience or horrific physical or emotional trauma in order to raise your awareness and appreciation of your own gifts. You can take a deep breath now. We can use my tragedy as a shared experience and allegory for your own introspection and self-discovery. You simply need to be open to question your programming and address your own wiring. You have the benefit of my experience and testimonial. All the answers and tools are at your fingertips, right now, in the chapters ahead. It will take work. It will take focus. Your own personal deprogramming may even be painful. However, all that is required is practice, patience, and time. Along with serious introspection and an open mind. Like me, you probably have a long history of faulty programming that needs to be addressed. Possibly from your earliest memories. Many of your basic precepts are simply based on untruths and years of brainwashing. Take comfort that your success, happiness, liberation, and inner peace are close at hand.

If you are slightly off balance by learning new information that is contrary to your earliest belief systems, let not your heart be troubled, as we are on this journey together. Take comfort in the fact that my own early interpretations and assumptions were also incorrect, mostly because they were all based on preconceived notions of the universe and antiquated misunderstanding of our collective reality. In other words, you have my sincerest empathy because I had also been brainwashed since my conception.

Returning to my traumatic allegory and continuing the examination process, as I floated about the hospital above my mangled flesh, everything that happened next shocked and surprised me. As distressful as my excruciatingly painful rebirth was, it left me wholly unprepared for the horrors that came next.

3

THE DEATH

Unfortunately, the euphoric tranquility of my supernatural, floating, incorporeal experience was short lived, as I once again found myself cast into agonizing blackness. The dark abyss was awash with confusion and an onslaught of continuous searing discomfort. Upon return, I could not access any prior memory of the void nor any other elements from my past, which were again blocked by a massive wall of pain. Everything had to be rediscovered, including all those earthly perceptions of my future potential.

Guided again by whispers, I manufactured similar insights regarding the present, and how to best avoid serious surges of agony. After an exhaustive and lengthy, albeit indeterminant period in that torturous gorge, I was engulfed in another serene bog of brilliant, white light coinciding with a novel psychedelic out-of-body experience. That pattern persisted for countless repetitions – severe dark haunting episodes of aching, brief realizations, insights, and memories followed by repeated hallucinations and dull serenity. Each time was a dreadful fresh start.

Whenever I felt close to drawing any tangible conclusions or supposition's regarding my circumstances, I was always yanked away, back into either painful darkness or a bleary haze. There was seemingly no reprieve from that *Sisyphusian* cycle. Ineffectively, I struggled to break free. It was akin to being trapped in a temporal loop. Each interval began the same way. I was a dismembered consciousness, without memory, in a dismal dank abyss experiencing searing waves of pain. And at some point during the beginning of each interval I discovered a rudimentary awareness of "The Gift." Yet each discovery was experienced as if it were the first time. And interestingly, each of those painful discovery periods were followed by random periods of euphoric delirium. Frustratingly, any inferences or insights that were drawn during the painful darkness were muted by intervals of numbed, blurred and peaceful murkiness. My collective memory was repeatedly blocked by colossal barriers of impenetrable pain and diluted euphoria.

Mysteriously and fortuitously, hope materialized through the ether. Faint echoes of *déjà vu* from prior periods of painful darkness danced in the background. Somehow, during those cycles, I started to become aware that every interval was not a clean slate. Finally, a tangible constant. I didn't have to start fresh each time. I was able to retain insightful fragments from previous rotations. The whispers became more recognizable. They resonated a certain confidence. I had been there before. A determined piercing intuition festered just beneath the surface. Though the pain persisted, and increased, my optimism prevailed. The repeated message, "it's all in the present," materialized upon each re-arrival, and swiftly guided me into shelters within the chasm. It was combined with the echoes of, "more," which nourished my enthusiastic suspicion that there was something beyond that perdition.

However, after an uncounted return to the painful darkness without sustained relief, my optimism wavered. I was inundated with preset thoughts and feelings of earthly constraints. Limitations! I allowed the massive pain, and subsequent hazy euphoria, to constantly throw me off balance, unable to maintain focus for extended periods. Something other than that vicious repetition had to exist. If only prolonged emphasis were possible, I was certain release would be afforded. I interpreted this liberation to be "full consciousness." However, no matter how close I felt to the exit, escape eluded me. Subconsciously, I was inhibited by my own preconceived limitations. The insightful new whispers were trying to guide me, and I resisted them. Because of my programming I was trapped in both the relentless pain and the anesthetizing pacification. A seemingly endless and hopeless cycle.

In actuality, during those first few weeks, I was lying in a hospital bed on life support. The medical staff was amazed that I was still alive. Due to the extent of my injuries, everyone, including the chief of medicine at the facility, vocalized with certainty that my passing was inevitable, and "only a matter of time." Their programming ensured them that people do not live through plane crashes, and clearly not with the extent of my injuries.

Based on my own faulty conditioning, I concluded that I had not survived the crash. I surmised that this present incarceration – of pain, knowledge, and aberrations – was an afterlife transition. And for the time being I would not be permitted to full consciousness. At least not any time soon. But logically, there had to be a way out. A way forward. A way to get to whatever came next. Anything to get away from the agonizing pain. "Focus." I questioned the whispers – that everything was contained here in the moment. If that were true, then wouldn't my afterlife be here too? I simply didn't understand how this way station worked. But I had to try anything to stop the onslaught. "Concentrate." And then it dawned on me, that since I was no longer alive, and trapped here anyway, it was a phenomenal opportunity to explore the afterlife, here in the present. I could explore my death.

Okay, I was dead. Death was apparently a cycle of pain and euphoria. Hell and Heaven. Although, I was taught you either go to one or the other. Why was I experiencing both? Or was this just a way station test? Maybe the whispers were correct — everything, including Hell and Heaven were here in the present. I further examined this phase of the afterlife. I scanned the outer reaches and vastness of this black desert and suddenly became aware of my solitary isolation. I simply couldn't see beyond the emptiness. I observed that there was no jailor. No one bringing me sustenance. No food. No water. Yet nourishment, surprisingly, did not appear to be necessary. Apparently, the hereafter had no such earthly requirements. Within the confines of my preconceived notions of death, that made sense. I no longer had a need for these things. I merely existed here, unaccompanied. And, while I was alone, I was never lonely. My thoughts filled this space and comforted me.

I was once again struck by a passionate duality. I was isolated in this prison, but I wasn't alone. An indescribable impression of companionship consumed me. Yes, I was not alone. I had a sixth sense of another presence. Beyond my own thoughts. Another entity. An omni-presence. Something or someone vastly greater than myself. I felt so close to understanding it. A strength, a power, a grand insight, if only I could hold on. How could I be this isolated and yet still feel another presence? I felt so close to getting this. And then poof, it was gone. Once again, I was propelled into darkness by a massive thunderbolt of searing distress, followed by another stretch of dazed euphoria. The cycle continued.

Upon my return to the chasm, I precipitously concluded that death was dreadful! It wasn't for me. It was nothing that I had imagined. It was nothing that I was promised. Why the rotations? Why the pain? Why the torture? Unless this was Hell. In which case the misery at least made sense. But I couldn't reconcile damnation containing pleasing euphoric interludes. Okay, therefore definitely not Hell, and certainly not Heaven. Nothing here jived with my traditional teachings. Was this way station purgatory? Was I being tested? Was there something I needed to learn or witness before being allowed to move on? Regardless, I was unquestionably ready for the "more" echoing in the background.

The most confusing elements were the future representations. What was the purpose of forecasting life scenarios that were no longer possible? I can no longer enter the Airforce, become an attorney, be an actor or filmmaker, or even fall in love, procreate, and have a family. Death is death. Right? A finality.

Unless in my case it wasn't permanent. Perhaps there was still an opportunity to go back. Was existence a choice? The echo responded, "it's all in the present." Obviously, there was still more for me to figure out here. Ironically, the one thing this way station had in abundance was time. And if there was a chance, however remote, that I could return to earth, from the afterlife, at the very least the possibility required serious consideration.

※ ※

Forgive the digression, however, understanding and accepting mortality is an essential aspect of "The Gift." Therefore, several considerations about it are necessary to achieving inner peace. Many people have a fear-based, conditioned response to death. The mere mention of it triggers a cascade of unnecessary anxiety, which can detract from your own personal growth. We are also inhibited by our calibrated responses to stimuli, like my allegory. At least you can rest easy. In my case, as you are aware, I did not die, and was not experiencing the afterlife. Many of my assumptions, in the earliest stages of enlightenment, were based on my own misguided programming. Death was no exception. Your possible anxiety aside, there are a few preliminary axioms that require our mutual understanding. First, death comes for us all. Second, it often occurs suddenly, when least expected, even though rare-planned occasions exist. And third, and most importantly, its inevitability is our only human surety.

Let's briefly address basic childhood encoding regarding mortality. Most of us are taught that people have an instinctual fear of dying. For those of us with this precondition, it means we spend our lives in abject fear, on some level, often unconsciously, terrified of death. We will do anything to avoid it. The trepidation is buried deep within our psyche, far below the surface. That fear is often inflicted upon us as a mechanism for control by some Higher Authority. In fact, it's one of the easiest manipulation tools. People are known to voluntarily give up inalienable liberties in exchange for promises of security. Subliminally it occupies vast amounts of space in the present. This ever-present dread often limits our freedom, inhibiting our ability to fully appreciate the moment.

But what if you were no longer tethered to that pre-programmed trepidation? What if you could rewrite that initial database? By the end of this book, after learning to apply Step Three, your unhealthy habituated impulses will be minimized or completely rewritten, allowing you to embrace your mortality with a more welcome serenity.

One additional thought of preface on the subject is that nothing in this text is meant to suggest that your eternal existence, your soul, ends upon your death. The afterlife or the perpetuation of your essence is another "Gift" entirely which will be touched upon in future chapters.

As difficult as it is to accept, everyone wakes up at their own pace. Everyone evolves in their own time. I was, and am, no different. Even today I occasionally find myself both battling engrained unhealthy indoctrination, while ironically becoming embarrassingly intolerant of others who are still adversely affected and inhibited by their own conditioning. When it occurs, I welcome the opportunity to investigate the present and work to identify and overcome anomalies within my own makeup.

During the earliest days after the crash, despite the pain, thankfully I was experiencing this grand initial awakening, which ultimately saved my life. Becoming aware of the present, exploring the present, and finding safe harbors within the present was extraordinary. To recapitulate, just being open to the idea that 'everything is here in the present' allowed me to avoid sanity-breaking levels of pain. Using my recent past, I was able to find pockets of lesser pain and shelter in them. Soon I would learn to go back further and rest inside benevolent memories from my childhood. To be clear, I wasn't living in the past. These memories were here, with me, in the present. Using the future was even more fascinating. I wasn't clairvoyant. I was amazed to find elements of the future here in the present. This perception afforded me the ability to dodge predictable waves of intense pain and also to find shelter within visualizations of my future prosperity. Everything appeared to be here in the present. Therefore, applying Step Two, through a thorough examination of the moment, I was able to spend extended periods of time within these safe harbors, avoiding unbearable pain.

The pacifying sensation within these sanctuaries was extraordinary, especially considering that many of my earliest discoveries in the present were based purely on misperceptions from my defective coding. Mistakenly believing that I was experiencing life after death, I did not realize that I was subconsciously utilizing my investigation of the present, to accommodate my survival. Therefore, I still couldn't fathom why I was trapped within this vicious cycle.

Because I was not yet able to comprehend the true nature of my condition, I mistakenly believed that my out-of-body experiences were somehow connected to the intricacies of the afterlife. If there were clues in the hallways, my plan was to ferret them out. Also, I admit that it was a lot of fun to float freely about the hospital corridors. Flying was cool. It would be awhile before I pieced together the value of these illusions. Regardless as to their usefulness, it was most disappointing finding out that my incorporeal anesthetized travels were in fact hallucinations, because these trips were far more enjoyable than the educational sequences in the painful dark catacombs. The interesting news, which is also delightful, is that the memory of these experiences remain always with me, in the present.

The majority of my out-of-body sojourns were spent interacting with people from my early childhood, who happened to be visiting my intensive care unit. It was particularly thoughtful of them not to have aged. As they were all still five, seven and ten years younger, respectively. Exactly the way I had remembered them. Which was extremely comforting...and thoughtful.

These excursions took place in, or near, my hospital room. However, on several occasions I managed to transcend the confines of the hospital structure altogether and float about the community. No one seemed the least bit concerned, or put off, by my supernatural appearance. In retrospect, it is difficult for me to rationalize why, as a ghost, I would have any needs or even desires, to saunter down to the local big box stores. But they steadily proved to be an enjoyable change of scenery nonetheless.

My fondest hospital visit took place just down the hall, encountering my dad, who didn't appear at all concerned with our current surroundings. He was just there, in a light green medical gown, seated comfortably in a wheelchair. He looked as if he was waiting for me. I desperately wished this not to be an illusion. It was the serendipitous meeting I longed for. I used all my newfound abilities to cut through the marshy fog and anchor myself in the present. I was afforded a moment of abject clarity. With my toes inches off the ground, I was hovering upright, right in front of him, as we just silently took each other in.

In the absence of tactile sensation, I wasn't certain if my feet ever touched the ground. In this environment, neither vocal nor telepathic communication were possible. Yet, they also weren't necessary. I mouthed the question, "the plane crashed?" To which he subtly smiled, and silently nodded comfortingly. I added "are you okay?" To which he grinned, then lifted himself from the wheelchair and astonishingly rose. I quickly maneuvered right up against him and hugged him tighter than ever before. His bear-like arms wrapped around me and warmed my heart.

Logic then pierced the moment. Memories of the crash, coupled with realizations of my dark imprisonment, reminded me that I did not survive. I was a ghost. And therefore, if he were here, with me in the hallway, then he too did not survive. We had both perished in the wreckage. We were both ghosts. Which was even more disappointing because it really was nice to see him. To hug him. To be with him.

From his quiet jovial demeanor, he looked genuinely pleased to see me as well. The oddest part of our encounter was his eagerness to go back to work. I am not certain how I knew this. I simply knew it. The residue of his very life-essence was that of a workhorse. That was my dad. While I was infinitely more concerned with just being in his company, he was preoccupied by having more important places to go and things to do. I couldn't imagine what else could be so pressing, considering our circumstances. You know, being dead and all. Then for a brief moment we just looked intently into each other's eyes. And then he had that familiar expression, like he was late for something. I mouthed, "I love you dad." I tightly squeezed his giant right paw-of-a-hand with both of mine. Not wanting to let go. Hoping to keep him with me for all eternity. He smiled again, but this time I knew he had to go. He paused and mouthed back at me, "I love you too, son."

And, with that he turned and walked away, with his pale naked back partially exposed through his flimsy hospital gown. The distance between us began filling with white, chalky, smoke. Dead or alive, I greatly looked forward to our next encounter. Or at least hoped there would be one soon. I took comfort in knowing he was still with me. His presence always gave me strength.

After he departed from view, I was again given reassurance that I wasn't alone. But it clearly wasn't my dad's energy that I felt. It was something much greater. It was a feeling of energy and love. Otherwise, inconceivable power. Unfortunately, in my haze, I couldn't quite hold onto it long enough to identify the source before I was once again cast into darkness.

Insipidly, so many of my out-of-body explorations involved merely hovering in the corner of an intensive care unit, only a few yards from my physical body, lying on a hospital bed. I reasoned that these floating exultant phantasms had to be a part of a grander puzzle. Clues that required piecing together. Along with the other varied experiences in purgatory, I presumed that they were all elements of an overall vastly larger equation. I had so many questions, unfortunately, mostly based on my primitive programming. What would I discover if I could access full consciousness? I was now a ghost. I had somewhere to go. Ascending to heaven with God? Maybe. Rafting with the ferryman across the river Styx? Perhaps. Journeying alongside a bodhisattva guiding me to Nirvana? Conceivably. The intricate philosophies from my life were intriguing. At this point I had to be open to all possibilities, because life as I knew it had ended.

While my final destination was unclear, after spending what felt like an eternity trapped here, I was certain of two things: first, the ultimate goal for my immortal soul was not hovering in the corner of this room, floating aimlessly about a random medical facility, visiting family and childhood friends, nor spending eternity haunting the local big box chain stores; and second, transcendence to my penultimate destination would only be provided if I could stop these hellish cycles. I then capitulated and resolved that the answers had to be somewhere here in the present.

With that resolve, a new message materialized, "enter the crucial pain." Unlike the prior direction, this one horrified me. While I welcomed any additional guidance, all I wanted to do was escape the pain. Avoid it. I was exerting tremendous amounts of energy navigating away from it. Hiding from it. The echo responded emphatically to my hesitation, "enter."

I was confused and scared. I was already surrounded by pain. Consumed with it. Continually bombarded by it. Wasn't I already inside the pain? Or it inside of me? What was I missing? "Focus." I calmly resumed my Step Two examination of the present. While there remained a mountain of pain behind me, the most severe torment still appeared to arrive in waves in front of me. Mistakenly heeding my engrained programming, I believed that "it is always better to go forward than backward," so I resolved to soldier on.

I interpreted this guidance to mean that there was some crucial pain that I needed to enter in order to get past it. To get over it. I also optimistically rationalized that the future impressions were being provided to give me enough strength to help me overcome this crucial pain. Therefore, within the present, I assembled a collage of future visualizations. I focused on one of the warmest and brightest segments closest to me and like a flash, I was in a hospital. But not this hospital. It was a different hospital than the one I had been haunting. I was much older, and I was crying...but I wasn't sad. I was happy, wearing medical scrubs and crying tears of joy, cradling a small female newborn child. My child. My beautiful baby girl. I questioned how this was possible. "Stay open." I was intensely conflicted, yet...I fought against my programming and tenderly rocked this little girl in my arms. I focused on her angelic face. Her eyes filled me with comfort and strength as affectionate tears ran gently down my cheeks. And from this safe harbor I was able to shelter myself from the inferno of anguish surrounding me.

Observing seemingly endless waves of pain on the horizon I knew these sanctuaries were temporary. All these future aberrations were momentarily pleasing, but they weren't providing adequate shelter from the raging storm. As wonderful as they were, they weren't going to be enough. And the pain, while horrific, was in no way crucial. I had to figure out the meaning of the message. I had to break the cycle. I was mentally and physically exhausted.

And then, as if sensing my frustration, the whisper offered renewed guidance, "the past is in the present." I instantaneously knew that my predisposition to go forward was incorrect. This crucial pain and the answers to ending this viscous cycle must be in the past. "Focus."

※※※※ ※※※※

Crucial pain. What did that mean? I was making progress. I knew I was. Think. "Stay open." Perhaps I was misinterpreting intensity for importance. While the extreme and intense waves were attacking from the future, that massive wall behind me was too painful to penetrate. Too painful? Maybe crucially painful. Come on, put it together. "Enter." Was the gargantuan barrier impenetrable because of its strength, or rather because of its significance? "Enter." I cautiously inched closer to investigate. The pain increased as I approached the impact of the plane crash. What if the resolution to get out of here rested in the way I came in? The accident itself? Conceivably this was the most crucial pain I needed to explore. The thought of absorbing that much pain horrified me. Why would I want to re-experience the pain of the crash? The cause of my death! Hearing the illogic of my own thoughts gave me pause. "Stay open." And then I thought, I'm already dead. What's the worst that could happen? Right?

The penultimate goal was to get out of here. Learn the lessons I needed to learn and finally be set free. I had already endured such horrific agony. If re-entering the accident was the only way out, then so be it. No matter how devastating a task, it had to be accomplished. I didn't understand that I was being reconditioned, or what purpose that would serve, considering I was already dead. Within the confines of this new paradigm, it made it easier to accept that everything was here in the present. Whatever this present was. Now, all I needed to do was find the plane crash enmeshed within that enormous mountain of pain and maneuver inside. Easy enough.

Okay, I have to focus. Why did we crash? What happened? "Concentrate." Flash-flash. Trees smacking into the front windshield. Thwack, thwack-thwack! Flash. My dad next to me. These memories were bitterly painful. "Back further." Concentrate! Flash-flash-flash. The plane nosediving like a missile towards the ground. The pain was relentless. "Back further." Flash. Rain. Wind. Flash-flash. My dad and I bouncing around the cockpit in wild turbulence. The pain was a little less, but still distressing. "Further." Come on focus. There you go. I was able to reach through it. We were safely on the ground. It was the night before. All was calm. The pain here was minimal. Tolerable.

We were in a modest, dimly lit, airport motel room. I was back in the past. The past here in the present. My dad was with me. And somehow this was not a hallucination. This was a memory. He was very much alive. He wasn't a ghost in a hospital corridor. And astonishingly, the pain was gone.

My father was right in front of me, reclining on a bed, fully clothed, in his blue jeans and un-tucked cotton button-down blue shirt, watching the news on a small, cheap, old television. Specifically, he was fixated on a fairly new cable channel that broadcast the weather. A familiar sight on these short excursions – my dad, intently viewing the weather on TV. My goodness. I was overcome by the sheer thrill of it all. I assure you that nothing was less fascinating to a healthy sixteen-year-old boy than watching the weather on a small box.

My dad sighed as he sat up and lumbered slowly off the neatly made bed. Turning his body, he placed his feet on the floor, revealing the untidy pillows scrunched in a pile that were supporting his back against the headboard. Outside, lightning flickered and illuminated our otherwise shadowy room, as several palm tree branches bent over and tapped against the sliding glass door. Rat-tap-tap. The trees were tilted, pressed against the glass by the severe storm winds, as the long, dark, wispy, green leaves rattled endlessly on the patio. Rat, tap-tap-tap. Rain poured noisily down in heaps, as puddles collected in the curvature of the outside courtyard floor. The room was dank and musty from the humidity, yet surprisingly cozy.

My father picked up an aviation book on the end of the bed, along with a few neatly folded flight charts. He tossed them all into a medium-sized hard plastic dark grey briefcase that was ajar on a small circular table in the corner. Then he returned to the edge of the bed, sat back down, transfixed by the televised weather. As if the intensity of his gaze would magically alter the forecast, moving the stormfront away, and clearing our path to the Bahamas.

I was famished. I asked him if he wanted something to eat. Ignoring my question, he responded by relaying the news that the tropical storm assuredly was not developing into a hurricane. He added, in his thick Bronx accent, "It will most likely dissipate into a depression." Additionally, he was optimistic that the gulf stream would carry the severest weather over the Gulf of Mexico, and up the west coast of Florida. I waited silently, wide-eyed, stomach growling, holding out and gesturing a small, laminated hotel take-out menu, while my father continued with his conclusion that we should expect a clearing and plan to depart first thing in the morning. To which I dryly replied, "So, I'll bring you back a sandwich and a bowl of soup then?"

My dad's attention to the TV did not waver for a second. While I stood there, he then began a rant about how annoyed he was that Ronald Reagan, his hero, had fired all the air traffic controllers and that, "all the damn airports were understaffed." Still waiting for an answer, I quietly waved the plastic menu, hoping the annoying elastic warble would prompt a response. As my stomach gurgled with intermittent pangs of hunger, my father continued his explanation that Reagan had made the right decision, but, at the moment, we were paying the price for, "those damn workers who had no right to strike." I gave up.

I marveled at how the ambient room light flickered across his face, as the rain and lightning filled the otherwise subdued atmosphere. Following my own heavy sigh, I capitulated, deadpan, "huh, so you'll be having just soup then." His gaze never left the boob-tube. I checked my right front pocket, making certain I had a crisp ten-dollar bill. After feeling the crumpled smooth paper between my fingers, I exited coolly, hearing the heavy hotel room door quickly swing closed behind me.

Everything was wet. Soaking wet. The small Jacksonville airport hotel's tropical architecture was similar to many hospitality establishments in Florida, whereby the hallways were open with only a ceiling and few support beams for shelter. The long passages that connected the rooms to the lobby, the dining area, and even the pool area, were all aerated and exposed. And of course, our room was all the way on the other side, at the furthest distance from the lobby and cafeteria. While I otherwise appreciated our privacy, I was greatly inconvenienced by the distance I needed to traverse in this torrential wind and rain.

The outdoor hallway was also replete with a generous array of indigenous tropical flora and fauna. It was lined with beautiful trees, vegetation, and exotic plants. Normally, when it rained, which it did in Florida nearly every day during hurricane season, it was actually quite refreshing. Over the years, I enjoyed the otherwise pleasant experience of being surrounded by the moisture and mist during a sultry downpour. However, during a severe thunderstorm these open accessways offered little protection. The floor was wet, the walls were wet, and somehow the ceiling was even saturated with condensation.

After a swift and expeditious visit to the dining room, I returned to brave the open corridor, completely drenched, carrying our hot dinner, on a brown hard plastic hospitality room-service tray, with our meals covered by small metallic flimsy lids. On my way back, I was again taken by the majestic tropical beauty adorning this otherwise unexciting place. The contrast was striking. What was more fascinating was the realization as to the sharpness of my memory. I didn't pay special attention to any of these specific details the night that I had actually lived through them the first time. And yet here they were, in pristine clarity.

At the time, my enlightenment was still in its infancy, weighed down by my own faulty wiring. Unable to comprehend why I was being afforded this second opportunity to experience these memories, in all their splendor. I had so many questions. Why were only some of those memories of the accident painful? More importantly, why were others so benevolent? Some even appeared essential. I couldn't figure it out. And, why couldn't I simply jump to the end? I rationalized that it was too soon to draw any conclusions. For now, I simply needed to remain sheltered here, and continue examining the moment.

Everything was so beautiful in the rain. The windblown streams of water sparkled in the floodlights as the moisture reflected off the giant palm and banana leaves. I was also taken by the lack of people at this relatively early evening hour. I pictured them all huddled safely, and dry, inside their rooms. While I was out here soaked. Then I thought perhaps the establishment was virtually empty. Most folks, unlike us, were probably smart enough to stay home and avoid traveling in this harsh weather altogether. I quickened my pace as the relentless wind gusts increased, whereby the raindrops began stinging my eyes like tiny grains of sand.

Making the last turn down that final stretch along the open-air walkway towards our room, I noticed a young blonde teenage girl, about my age, standing in her half-opened doorway, deciding whether or not to venture out. She was adorable. Naturally pretty with a wholesome southern charm. As I bounded toward and past her, I comically remarked, "I wouldn't do it if I were you! Go back in! Save yourself!"

She stood in her doorway watching me as I passed. Her smile and courtesy-fake-laugh gave me confidence to continue my flirtatious routine. In the sweetest southern accent I had ever heard, she asked me, "Where's the cafeteria?" Which I optimistically interpreted as her feeble attempt at small talk, because she had to know where the dining room was. The entire motel was smaller than a football field and she would have passed the café upon check-in. In reality, the place was so small that if not for the wind and rain, the dining room was clearly visible from where we were standing. Also, throughout my vastly unsuccessful teenage dating years I had come to truly appreciate these rare opportunities where I had no formidable competition. This isolated stormy scenario greatly strengthened the veneer of my awkward bravado. Alone, in a tempestuous outdoor hallway, in my mind, I was the equivalent to being the last man on earth. And with a young lady this attractive I figured it increased my odds of success to at least, say...fifty-fifty.

Arriving at my front door, buying time, I pretended to fumble for my bulky metallic room key. I motioned with my elbow and explained, "It's just to the right of the lobby. You can't miss it." As she hesitated, and opened a magazine to cover her head, I added, "It isn't worth it. There's a guy leading pairs of animals onto a giant wooden boat in the parking lot. Go back inside. Save yourself!" Internally, I groaned at my pitiful attempt at metaphoric humor.

However, being with the last man on earth, she chortled, "I love boats and animals. Especially in pairs. I look forward to seeing it." Then she smiled adding "My parents are starving. I have to go get them some food. You have a good night, you hear."

I smiled back, then glanced down to work my bulky oversized gold-plated hotel key into the door. When I turned around a moment later she was already racing away, down the open tree-lined path, splashing puddles, as she jogged toward the lobby, with confidence and youthful athletic coordination. Adorably, the open magazine she held over her head barely provided any protection. Just after she made that first turn at the end of our hallway, she glanced back, and caught me, through the shrubbery, watching her run. We made eye-contact. I was busted. She paused, grinned, and blushed slightly, and then kept running. I then thought to myself, it wouldn't be so bad if the weather trapped us here another day. It would be fun to make conversation with her in the morning over pancakes. I entered my room, had a quick dinner with my dad and let my adolescent fantasies carry me off to sleep.

Rising at about four-thirty that next morning was a blur, which was typically the case whenever we had to "beat the weather." It was interesting that while certain aspects of this memory contained minute clarity, it would appear as though the physical exhaustion from that morning inhibited complete and immaculate recollection. Most of the events of that morning were hazy, while there were distinct moments of lucidity. For example, I distinctly recall cramming as many quarters as possible into an overpriced hotel vending machine to stock up on *Twizzlers'* strawberry licorice. Over the years that corn-syrup and fructose delight had become my go-to junk food on those puddle-jumper flights.

The rest of the early morning was a smattering of sleepy, scattered images, all muddled together. Packing. Rain. The coins and the *Twizzlers*. Waiting for my dad to confirm our departure. The weather on TV. More rain. Waiting for my dad to finish his new flight-plan. And even more rain. While I'm certain at some point we actually checked out of the hotel and took a short golf cart taxi-ride to the small, private, terminal entrance, in reality, I may have sleepwalked through all of that. My semi-coherent thoughts drifted back to the young rain-soaked girl from the previous night. Amorous feelings were outweighed by jealously, that in all likelihood she was probably dry, comfy and still asleep in her hotel bed. "Lucky her," I thought. Then I wondered if she liked *Twizzlers*.

Once on the tarmac, I distinctly remember the mist gently blowing against my face, waking me up again. I recall standing behind the tail of the plane, visually inspecting it with my dad. When flying a small private craft, it is the pilot's job – and the co-pilot's – to inspect their own plane, looking for any abnormalities before takeoff. I was always fascinated at this. What the heck was I looking for? "Any abnormalities?!" What in the world constituted an abnormality? I wasn't an engineer. I never built, worked on, or constructed an aircraft. My mechanical experience, beyond childhood plastic connecting blocks and model trains, consisted of rebuilding a zee-fifty model dirt-bike with a Tecumseh two-cycle engine in Junior High school shop class. And, while that small feat may sound impressive to some, I assure you that it wasn't. For one thing a couple of friends had to help me construct that dirt bike. And for another, I only received a B on the project.

My digression aside, what in the world did I know about airplane abnormalities? Regardless, I did my job. As always, I looked. I inspected. I looked down every crack and crevasse. All of the screws appeared fastened. The bolts were attached. The wings felt strong. The flaps were solid. I followed my dad around the plane in a counterclockwise circle pretending to know what I was looking for, mimicking his observations and behaviors. He tapped the wing, so I tapped the wing. He tested the flaps, so I tested the flaps. And so on. Ultimately, I gave him the usual thumbs up. Yup, in my expert opinion as a sixteen-year-old co-pilot, and B-average Junior Highschool shop student, we were good to go.

The wind had calmed and there were actual pockets of clear sky through the thick clouds. Welcome to Florida. If you don't like the weather, just wait ten minutes. You could be standing in the rain on one side of the street bewildered by the stark dryness across the road. Me, I was taken by the patches of light-blue early morning sky, while concurrently being drenched by the rain. My jeans were soaking through. I loaded our stuff into the plane's back cabin and climbed on board while my dad chatted with a local mechanic. A real mechanic, who stereotypically looked the part – heavyset, unshaven, slicked-back silver hair, wearing grease-covered grey polyester overalls – and had an air of confidence that he, unlike me, was a true expert in his field. Most astonishingly, he was filthy at five-thirty in the morning. And he probably received an A-plus in his Junior Highschool shop class. All-in-all, he convincingly carried himself like a man who knew his aircraft.

Inside our small turbo-prop plane, I quickly changed into dry sweatpants, draping my saturated jeans over the far back seat. I then stowed our luggage and arranged our belongings for the short three-to-four-hour trip. I knew exactly where my dad liked our things stowed during these flights. I may not have been mechanically inclined, but I was an estimable first mate. While getting settled inside the cabin, I observed them through the co-pilot's window conversing outside. I knew they were discussing our recent injector valve repair, which had caused our initial delay out of New York two days earlier. Though I couldn't hear their conversation, I witnessed them both nodding approvingly and referencing the right wing.

This memory was chock full of fascinating details – like the grease-covered middle-aged mechanic's overalls and scruffy face, the rain turning into light mist, the picturesque pockets of sky and light that pierced the thick gray morning clouds, that blond girl's luminous smile as she ran down the hallway away from me, and the sweet waxy strawberry taste of those *Twizzlers*. Then...finally, with my dad seated next to me, on my left, in his pilot's chair, we were cleared for take-off.

Flying, itself, is an amazing experience. However, there is nothing quite like the rush of lift-off. The moment the plane takes flight. The power. The control. Only moments before, our plane was motionless as we waited impatiently for our turn at the end of the taxiway. Today's taxi and pre-flight were unremarkable. I pontificated that the very last time you do something it should be special. But alas it was the same mundane, routine experience.

There was that quiet moment just after the tower issued our clearance. We visually checked for incoming air traffic and noted that it was all clear to proceed. My dad applied a small amount of thrust rolling carefully onto the runway and turning us into position. We focused on the seemingly endless tarmac extended in front of us. Interestingly enough, I always savored those moments, rolling slowly over enlarged airport call numbers and positioning the plane before the uncountable centered dash-lines stretched out on the pavement in front of us. One last exhale. This is the part that was always exciting. At my father's direction, as co-pilot, I pushed the throttle all the way forward, instantly feeling the thrust in my palm. The engine roared, the G-forces pushed us back into our chairs as the plane started forward. The small round throttle knob vibrated in my hand. Takeoff always felt slow at first, as the deafening sound of the engines distracted from the initial movement. The tiny craft tilted slightly forward off its back wheel as we quickly gained speed. My dad put his sturdy hand on top of mine, cautiously, making certain the throttle was all the way forward. Focusing on the horizon out the front windshield, I glanced quickly down at our speedometer. As we rapidly approached fifty miles per hour, I knew it would be any second now. Fifty-five, sixty, sixty-five...my dad and I each applied forward pressure to the U-shaped flight controls in front of our respective seats in order to hold the plane down...sixty-six, seventy, seventy-two...and then, the magic happened, as it always did. The front wheels lifted off the ground. Instantaneously, we were weightless. Climbing! Defying gravity. Exhilarating! This was followed by the wondrous rush of rising higher and higher into the air. We each pulled back on the yoke, banking into our initial turn, and climbing toward our ultimate cruising altitude.

On this particular day, as we climbed, piercing the initial low-level cloud cover, the sky ahead was surprisingly tranquil and clear. The sun was just about to rise. I glanced at the radar. Confirmed! The storm was moving away from our direction. And we from it. As my father guided us on course, he gave me the green light to begin our in-flight entertainment. I happily switched on my oversized boom box cassette player and instantly blared out *"You're the Inspiration"* by Chicago, of course. As we soared upward, we both joyfully sang, off key, along with the soothing voice of Peter Cetera to the *Chicago 17* soundtrack. The bad weather was now behind us. Nothing but blue skies ahead...and plenty of *Twizzlers*.

Then the sunrise burst through the front windshield. I had to avert my eyes. This fresh brilliant white light was blinding. I was then immediately aware that the light wasn't coming from the sun, and I was no longer on the plane. The brightness flickered for a second and then resumed its blistering intensity. This was not a memory. I was not floating anesthetized. I was not adrift in painful darkness. There was nowhere to hide. This was not my doing. Outside forces were definitely at play. The cycle had finally been broken, and I was now consumed by this new shining light. If only it wasn't so excruciatingly uncomfortable and wickedly painful.

※※※—※※※

At the time, I had no idea what the outside illumination was, or what it represented. In reality, I was physically still a disaster, barely subsisting on life support. Psychologically however, I had just experienced several amazing things. Most importantly, a newfound awareness of the present and its multifaceted properties, fortuitously affording me shelters within my psyche, maintaining my sanity. Also, I suddenly became aware of myriad intricate details encompassed within the present, that went entirely unappreciated during my original experiences. Because of my faulty programming, for the first sixteen years of my life, I was unaware of the present. Life was essentially passing me by.

Additionally, using the present to overcome physical pain is one thing. But could this new awareness work to overcome emotional pain as well? And would any of these principles work in the real world? Upon reflection, it was easy and logical to accept that the accident resulted in severe physical pain, yet I was unaware of the emotional baggage that this horrific trauma had created. This is all in addition to the deep-rooted garbage accumulated from an indoctrinated childhood. The greatest lesson I had yet to realize would be that emotional pain is infinitely more challenging to contend with than physical pain.

At the time, I believed I had passed away in the crash and was passing through an afterlife way station. What I didn't realize was that I was somehow being provided survival insight which required a rewriting of sixteen years of initial encoding. In actuality, I wasn't perceiving the end of my physical mortality, but rather the death of my programming. Ironically, my survival depended on killing or erasing the irrational waste accumulated from over a decade and a half of brainwashing. Survival meant starting over. I was assured, by my programming, as were the doctors, that people who sustain my magnitude of injuries do not survive plane crashes. I was also taught, as many of you were, that in general, life and death are outside the ambit of our control. Therefore, the only chance I had to endure was to erase and rewrite that entire code.

Regardless, despite my impatience, I had to go slowly because everyone wakes up at their own pace. The awareness is otherwise too shocking. My fragile psyche was no different. Then I thought, even if I could come back, even if it were possible, did I want to return? Did I want to face all that pain, both physically and emotionally? Why choose life? Death, and the quiet tranquility it offered seemed a preferable alternative. Fascinatingly, during this next phase, right after my metaphorical death, I was in no way prepared for the depths of anguish and difficulty that lay ahead.

Unable to shield my eyes from the light, I instantly realized that I was no longer in the plane with my dad. Also, this uncomfortable irritation wasn't part of the familiar anesthetizing haze nor was it emanating from the painful darkness. This was new. This wasn't my doing. This was coming from outside of me. Outside of my thoughts. I was correct, the cycle had in fact finally been broken. Was this the hand of God? And if so, how could I show this much cowardice? Despite the irritation and pain, I steadied myself the best I could. I calmed myself. I was ready. I braced myself for ascension into whatever was coming next. Unfortunately, I had no idea that this next phase would present new unimaginable horrors along with the biggest single challenge and choice of my life.

4

THE LIGHT

The sudden burst of harsh illumination was blinding. Relentless. Unnerving! Despite my every effort to close my eyes, they remained wrenched open by some unknown outside force. Squinting or shying away was impossible. They began hurting terribly. I was desperate to close them, as the fierce sunlike radiance persisted. Piercing. Burning. No matter how much effort I exerted, they remained unnaturally exposed and opened by intense pressure applied to my upper cheek and forehead. I was suddenly acutely aware of my face. I had a face?

The uncovered surface of my eyeball membrane filled with fluid, which I was unable to clear. If I still had hands, I could not feel or use them. This was by far the strangest, and most torturous hallucination to date. But it felt so real. And, during this brutalization, oddly enough, I was back inside my own body. I couldn't feel the rest of me. Was my entire body now my face? I was peeking out into the world from my earthly self. Or so I surmised, from my vantage point and visual perspective. I was disoriented and confused to say the least.

Quickly piecing things together, as a way of diverting attention from the unrelenting scorching light, I reasoned that I was back on an observation bed or table. I couldn't tell which. Regardless, I was woefully disappointed that I did not appear to be meeting God. My other senses remained muted. No taste, no touch, and no smell. Only mechanical muffled sounds and this blinding imagery. And, while I was given free range of movement within the confines of my mind, I was devoid of all other external physical motion. Thankfully, and surprisingly, I was then distracted by a new alternative influence. A voice. Not my voice. Not my internal whispers. An outer voice. A deep masculine tone dispassionately declaring, "He's following the light." The voice was clear. It was English, and it had intention. The pressure on my eyes was released. Then, mercifully, the white light was removed, which afforded me immediate relief. In its place was a smattering of distant blurred shapes in a variety of shades across an otherwise colorless greyscale. The same deep-throated speech continued, "Blink twice if you can understand me."

I blinked twice and then struggled to keep my eyes open, so as to assure my communication was received. My compliance appeared to be of paramount importance. Everything was visually fuzzy, but, distinguishable from my previously cloudy, euphoric out-of-body experiences. This was different. This had an earthly realism to it. This was either the terrestrial world reaching back out to me, or it was finally the afterlife getting ready to receive me. Either way, I wanted to be ready. Remember, I only had my faulty programming with which to draw conclusions. And regardless, any alternative existence was preferable to my agonizing captivity. Whether it was heaven or hell, I was ready. Bring it on!

I was befuddled by these new stimuli and frustrated by my inability to communicate effectively. My frustration was exacerbated by not being able to utilize three of my senses. Why were only sight and hearing permitted? Regardless, this new experience had a tangible quality to it. "Gosh," I thought, "I really should have paid better attention during my parochial studies as a child." I felt utterly unprepared for the hereafter. Then it dawned on me how grateful I was that at least sarcasm transcended into the afterlife.

This was also distinctly dissimilar from other recent experiences within the cycle because of my utter lack of control. Aside from my thoughts, there was clearly an outside force or authority. Internally, within the cycle, I was learning how to navigate the painful darkness and hallucinogenic haze. For the most part, in those other environments, I was able to travel at will, within my collective memory, occasionally being offered a jumbled glimpse into my future reality, or even allowed to waft about at my leisure as an anesthetized poltergeist. But now, it was as if I were being restrained or held back in some way. I was being introduced to a new paradigm entirely.

This was the first time since the plane crash that I was experiencing life from the vantage point of my earthly self. My body. Not as a floating manifestation. In other words, this was the first time in weeks that my perspective felt real. Because it was real! I was touching humanity again. Or more apropos, humanity was reaching out and touching me. In my befuddlement, still believing that I had passed on, I decided that the afterlife was not very comforting or inviting.

"Now close your eyes, and keep them closed," the masculine voice commanded. I obeyed, closing my eyes. Outside pressure was applied to my eyelids, wiping away moisture and tears. There was no other tactile sensation. Only the pressure and subsequent relief, having my eyes cleared and dried. "Now, open your eyes slowly. It may be very bright." When I opened them, I was able to distinctly observe my surroundings. The ambient light was dim. I saw people. Well, heads of whom I presumed were people. Three floating heads to be exact, without the apparent necessity for physical bodies. Two female and one male. I ascribed these gender assumptions based solely on anthropological stereotypes regarding shape, tone, texture, and oral tenor. All three were extremely close, obstructing my view to anything else. Each of the three levitating heads were almost completely covered, except for their eyes. They appeared human enough. That is to say, they each had humanoid shapes and characteristics. Also, they wore tight white coverings on their skulls and faces.

My field of vision appeared shallow. When one of the heads moved, all I could make out was a dimly lit grey wall, and possibly a white ceiling in the background. This denoted that I was in some type of enclosure. I had no idea if I was looking at a partition or the floor in the background. For all I knew, I could have been upside-down in zero gravity, pinned to the ceiling. Nothing in the enclosure had any rich color or texture, just muted grey tones. From my perspective it appeared to be a finite space. Mentally, I was preparing myself for whatever was coming next. The afterlife just became really interesting!

"Good, now let's see if you can follow my finger," the deep voice requested, from behind his mask. Then a huge blurry, large, pale, straight, finger-like object appeared in front of me, obstructing my entire view. I followed it from left to right and up and down. "Incredible," the voice bellowed. "Excellent!"

Okay, this was clearly English, I concluded. Or at least I understood the words to be English. Perhaps these floating heads used a universal communication device, and I was merely interpreting English. Or, perhaps I simply watched far too many science fiction programs. I also observed that this creature had dismembered fingers, unattached to a physical body, with no other noticeable appendages. Humanoid, but not human.

I followed the finger through a few more passes. Then it was removed and replaced with the masculine head again, observing me, as if looking into my eyes for something specific. I mustered all my energy to speak, to communicate, to wave my arms. To no avail. At this moment, I did not appear to have any limbs, or physical body either. No mouth. No tongue. No hands or fingers. Only eyes, ears, and my mind. Perhaps there was no need in the afterlife for terrestrial bodies, or useless appendages. Maybe that's why wealthy eccentrics like Walt Disney had their heads cryogenically frozen. And after my recent experience in this observation room it now kind of made sense.

However, Walt Disney aside, a few glaring inconsistencies resonated within these new circumstances. Why wasn't I able to communicate? They could speak. Why couldn't I? They could move. Why couldn't I? I struggled with the contradictions. Then, before I could reconcile anything, the fog returned, and the small enclosure was filled with white smoke. The heads were gone, or at least I could no longer see them. I closed my eyes for a moment to regain focus, and when I reopened them, the smoke had cleared. I was back up, and outside of my body, hovering peacefully along the hospital hallway. I glanced down at my own hands. I was again fully intact – arms, legs, all my senses, etc. However, even though I retained my personal perspective, the experience lost the realism from the observation room. I was once again a phantom, floating in the corridor.

This environment was familiar. And now that I was whole again, communication could be better facilitated. I frantically searched to find the orb-like individuals. I searched countless rooms, including the one containing my physical body. Nothing! The disembodied heads were nowhere to be found. Actually, I then noticed that no one seemed to be around. The hospital appeared abandoned. I didn't care. Now that I had my body back and I could communicate, I had to find those floating heads. I even scoured a few of the local big box chain stores. But alas, they weren't there either. Everything, everywhere, was desolate and deserted. I was abandoned and alone. I then looked back down at my hands and wiggled my digits. As a small consolation in the moment I thought, at least I had regained my fingers, and they were attached to my arms. The concept of dismembered heads now seemed preposterous. Was that experience with the alien heads just another elaborate hallucination?

No, in fact that experience was real. I was not imagining it. I was merely confused by what I was seeing, and my body and mind were simply not ready to fully wake up yet. I still had a massive amount of re-programming to go. And sadly, for the time being, the agonizing cycle resumed.

On the one hand I was convincing myself that I had merely imagined the entire flashing light, floating head experience. On the other hand, it had contained an inexplicable degree of clarity and sharpness. The acuity gave me pause. Whatever it was, felt so real. So different from these other two environments to which I had recently grown accustomed. I concluded that even if real, they couldn't be human. No such beings ever existed on Earth. Therefore, assuming they were real, the question was, were they angels, interstellar aliens, or interdimensional beings? Was I being studied or tested? My curiosity was piqued. I would need to be ready for my next encounter with whatever they were.

After my current euphoric interlude ended, I was cast back into the agonizing abyss. This time I found shelter in the memory of my brief interaction with the orbs because of course, that experience too, was here in the present. My programming was successfully being rewritten. I was unquestionably learning focus and discipline, greatly reducing the intensity of my physical pain. However, revisiting all universal laws – of physics, time, and space – deconstructing my primary coding, and discovering the vastness, value and splendor of the moment was going to take time.

Studying the memory of the heads prompted another interesting digression contemplating my cumulative experiences from the time of my perceived death. There was an overwhelming sense of individuality. I was the one going through this. My dreams. My illusions. My memories. These were my experiences, and mine alone. I never lost my first-person perspective. Not for a moment. This brought me tremendous comfort. It reassured me that I existed. Whether or not I was being studied or tested, it was all me. My gift. A most fascinating epiphany.

My introspection was then abruptly, and rudely, interrupted by an overwhelming barrage of intense pain, as though my entire existence, my very soul, were on fire. I could only image that it was akin to being electrocuted or struck by lightning. I was ablaze, in agony. And then oddly enough, it felt cold. Excruciatingly cold. Painfully freezing. I couldn't reconcile the contradictory sensations of hellfire while simultaneously being so bitterly cold. I had come so far, learned so much. Why couldn't I see this wave coming? Then I put it together. Like the exterior sounds and the floating orbs, this sharp, stinging sensation was being induced by an outside influence. I was being tortured. But why? Were the orbs punishing me for my insights? I needed to refocus. Find my tools. First, I had to locate and identify this icy-hot pain and accept it here in the present. "Concentrate." Then, I needed to become aware of future waves of intensity and avoid them altogether. "Focus." This pain was the most excruciating thus far. Nothing was comparable.

Thankfully it was working. Concentration was difficult but possible. I was able to find refuge in my past and future shelters. However, this new revelation that the pain was being inflicted by an outside entity was devastating to my overall morale. Why was someone or something intentionally hurting me? Has this entire experience been a slow premeditated torture? Despite my successful maneuvering into otherwise safe spaces, I was overcome with grief and sadness. Depression set in.

In reality, what I was experiencing were my bi-daily bandage dressing changes. At the time, sixty percent of my body was an open wound. Countless nerve endings were severed. And during dressing changes, the areas needed to be cleaned, sanitized, and disinfected. This exposed those severed nerves to the open air as well as the alkaline based disinfectants. Externally the medical staff was doing their best to keep my physical body alive. While, internally, I was doing my best to physically, psychologically and emotionally survive. While I was learning and growing, I was also just trying to hang on.

To overcome my depression, I needed to make sense of my conflagration. I had to learn to get over the pain and sadness. "Love." Drawing on my preconceived notions of evolved beings, I envisioned that the orbs would respond positively to strong, genuine feelings of love. Reviewing my catalog of memories, from my otherwise short lifetime, I concluded that I was not a bad person. While my memories ran the gambit of emotions, including hate, jealousy, rage, envy, and anger, my overall life essence was filled with an abundance of love.

I tapped into that love in an attempt to overcome my emotional doldrums and misery. It was working, whereby the severest torment was dissipated by my strongest and sincerest memories of affection. My optimism returned. I was eager to show this love to the orbs. I would bring it with me. I was convinced that they would be so overwhelmed by my virtuousness that they would end the torture and deliver me salvation. Love had to be the answer, and I'd be ready for our next encounter.

During my meditative contemplation, a new stimulus was introduced. Faintly, in the distance, I heard music. At first, I believed that I was creating the music, from memory. However, the harmonic sounds weren't coming from inside the void. Similar to the experience with the orbs, these melodies had a different feel. They were emanating from outside. And while I couldn't make out the song, they were strikingly sharp, crisp, and real. This reinvigorated my enthusiasm. A taste of life outside my incarceration. Like a window in a prison cell. Hope!

The music was pleasant and familiar. The only logical conclusion was that the orbs were providing it. Why? And how could they have access to human music? I then performed mental gymnastics, applying science fiction rationality. Chalk it up to fourteen years of watching hours of television daily. There's a reason they refer to it as programming. Regardless it was a primary source for my subconscious to tap into. Therefore, I merely accepted that as superior beings they had both access to Earth's pop-music, and the ability to telepathically choose selections that I would find soothing. Adding further nonsensical justification, I was now being rewarded for turning my focus to love.

Then the familiar whisper advised, "enter the crucial pain." Irrespective of my apprehension, I had now come to respect this inner voice. I reflected on the events leading up to the crash, focusing on where I had left off. Almost as if on cue, from the exterior periphery, I heard the familiar opening rift to "*You're the Inspiration*" by *Chicago*. Da-nah-nah, nah-nah, nah, da. Like watching a movie, I saw my dad, next to me, in the cockpit of our plane. I altered my assumptions regarding the floating heads. Perhaps they weren't torturing me after all, but rather helping me navigate my way out. Or conceivably they were unaware of the physical pain being inflicted on me. And the music was a means to an end. A tool. A beacon. My internal echo was providing direction, while my captors were providing support. It then occurred to me that we were working together. Working together to save my immortal soul.

<hr>

My conjecture, despite my defective programming, wasn't that far off. While I still had yet to grasp where or how the whisper was being generated, the music was emanating from a small portable radio at the intensive care unit's nurses' station. They used it to entertain themselves and sooth the patients. I had correctly deduced that we were in fact working in tandem. Outside they were doing everything medically practicable while, internally, I was learning how to endure.

<hr>

The assuasive tenor of Peter Cetera's voice brought with it the cacophony of garbled mechanical engine noise. And just like that, I was once again there, chewing on a sweet strawberry flavored stick of licorice, seated comfortably next to my dad, in our compact airplane cockpit on our way to the tropics. I was once again raptured by the intricate details within the memory. It was, however, strikingly distinguishable from the cold realism experienced recently with the dismembered-head creatures. Unlike that surreal observation area, this was clearly a memory – it was meticulous, vibrant, and warm.

With the severe weather behind us, the flight thus far had been unremarkable and uneventful. From the perch of the copilot's seat, soaring thousands of feet in the air, I had at least five miles of unobstructed visibility, clear blue skies above and nothing but endless picturesque Atlantic Ocean on the horizon. The music joyfully blared as I butchered, "You bring feeling to my life. You're the inspiration."

I noticed the first sign of trouble when the plane jerked momentarily, causing the right engine to abnormally sputter for a few seconds, before resuming its normal rhythm. Usually, mild turbulence, or even air pockets, while jarring, are reasonably common during most flights. But this short lurch was different. It was atypical because our flight thus far had been exceedingly smooth and, more precisely, the issue appeared to emanate from the engine, not the wind. While my dad expressed little to no concern, or at least hid any apprehension, it drew my attention to, and scrutiny of, the propeller and engine just outside my window.

Regarding these smaller aircraft, I was always fascinated by the close proximity of prop-engines to the cockpit. As opposed to larger commercial jetliners, with expansive wings, whereby the massive engines are much further away from the nearest window. In these light aircraft, you could literally reach outside your door or window and touch the engines, which were merely only three or four feet away.

A few minutes after that first jolt the right engine sputtered again. To my horror seconds later it began spewing a thick black liquid, that leaked out from the sides of its bulky metal casing. A murky black streamline immediately formed, trailing behind the right wing. The engine continued sputtering as the oil flow increased. Soon, the entire white metal engine was concealed in a sheath of black goo. Inappropriately, I imagined how amazing it must have looked from the ground. Yet, the alarm created by the circumstances snapped me back to reality. And, although I lacked any substantive aviation-engine acumen,

I knew this wasn't good. Then I wondered what that silver-haired, airport mechanic would think. Upon farther reflection, I was soundly convinced he would determine that this wasn't very good either.

I knew my dad was still unaware of the situation. I quickly glanced at him, still flying intently, and then stared back out my window. Stunned and unable to speak, I reached back and repeatedly tapped his right forearm, prompting his annoyance. One of the cardinal rules that had been instilled in me since childhood was that when anyone is operating a vehicle it is never acceptable to manhandle them or interfere with their steering. However, I felt this exception warranted an abrupt and immediate interruption. I slowly looked over to observe his facial expression. His initial annoyance passed instantaneously as his face became pale, validating my anxiety and sense of urgency. I shouldn't have looked back at his expression. It turns out that I didn't need the airport mechanic's endorsement after all. Engine, spewing black liquid, very, very, bad! Got it!

My father's demeanor also promptly adjusted. He transformed from stoic and relaxed to stoic and serious. Instead of emulating my panic, he paused. Where I wanted to scream, he took a deep breath. I could see his eyes vibrating, doing a multitude of calculations. It was amazing to witness. Cool and calm under pressure. Was he instinctually aware of "The Gift? And if so, why did he never share this insight with me when we were alive? Perhaps he understood "The Gift" on a subconscious level. Regardless, that was my dad. He truly was the one you wanted at your side in an emergency. Everything he had taught me, and lectured me about, and trained me regarding emergency protocols and procedures were all reaffirmed in this moment, by this man.

He calmly but firmly inquired as to my observations of our current circumstances. "Did you hear anything? What did you hear? How long has the oil been coming out? When did you first notice it?" While I gave him these one- and two-word answers to each of his queries, he was multitasking – turning knobs and tapping on gauges while simultaneously absorbing all of the relevant data in the aggregate. "Just hold her steady for a second and stay on course," he assertively instructed. With that, I grabbed hold of the U-shaped flight controls in front of me, steadied my feet, specifically my toes, against the pitch, roll, and yaw controls on the floor. In these smaller aircraft you adjust the aeronautical elements with both your hand controls and your foot controls – or floor pedals. Even though the engine continued sputtering intermittently, thankfully the pristine weather made it fairly easy to keep the plane steady.

He leaned over me to visually inspect the damage just outside my window. He settled back into his seat, clasping his fingers together, sitting calmly with his elbows leaning on his armrests. My nerves were completely rattled, while he peacefully extended his two erect index fingers and pressed them firmly together against his lips. It looked as though his head and face were being supported by his clasped hands and two stalwart fingers. He was quietly assessing, while I was bursting out of my skin. It took all my effort to maintain any outward composure.

"*Oy vey*, I think we have to go back," he muttered. Then he looked at me, nodding his head, resolutely, "Fudge, I think we have to go back." He reached for and pulled out a small map book that was wedged in between his seat and the center console armrest. Flipping hurriedly through the pages he found two airstrips that we had just passed maybe twenty minutes earlier. "I need you to get me the specs for these two airfields from the smaller map book." My hesitation prompted his immediate clarification. Still speaking slowly, clearly and with a resolute calm, he added, "it's in the rear sleeve of my flight case."

While I climbed between the seats and into the back of the aircraft, I heard my father radio a nearby control tower. He requested an update on the storm front we had left behind earlier this morning. Having the map book in hand, I returned to the front of the plane and slid back into my seat. I once again took the flight controls as my dad began calculating distances with a pencil, and a protractor, on a partially unfolded glossy paper map that now obscured the totality of the pilot's side of the dashboard. He proceeded to fully open the map, which literally enclosed him, partitioning the cockpit. Through the wax paper, I could see his silhouette feverishly working out a flight plan. There were no great options. Just bad news followed by even more bad news. The radio tower informed us that Tropical Storm Isidore had now formed into a tropical cyclone.

The worse news was that while Isidore's eye was currently over Central Florida, it now appeared to be unpredictably heading back inland, away from the Gulf Coast and potentially back towards the East Coast, directly in our current path.

My dad jotted down a few directional points on the yellow pad and double checked his work, referencing the sprawled-out map in front of him. He scrunched the map into a ball and passed it to me, with a directive to fold it properly. I immediately complied and began to uncrumple it. Then, he put the pencil in his mouth, like a dog carrying a bone. "Hold on to something," he casually cautioned, slightly muffled due to the small piece of wood lodged between his teeth. The plane banked hard to the left, throwing me off balance. I steadied myself by clutching a small leather safety loop that was mounted and hanging above my window. Holding on for dear life, I re-crumpled the map and tossed it over my shoulder onto one of the seats in the back of the plane. I promised myself I would refold it properly later when we landed. Within about twenty seconds we leveled off, heading back the way we came.

"Where are we going?" I asked. "Wouldn't it make more sense to continue to the Bahamas? There wasn't a cloud in the sky back in that direction. And there's a really big monster storm now in front of us."

He either ignored me or didn't hear me. As the plane calmed and our flight steadied, he took the pencil from his mouth and slid it above his right ear, wedging it in place. "Did you pull up those two airports like I asked?" He gestured toward the map book that was seated loosely on my lap. I had. After passing him the map book, he immediately saw that there were paperclips acting as bookmarks for each of the two individual airport pages as he taught me to do. He hated dog-earring or tearing books if it wasn't an absolute necessity. That came from a long-standing belief or superstition that books are sacred, and one should never deface or damage books in any way. To this day I still have difficulty taking notes or writing in the margins of any bound literature that isn't a designated workbook.

Needless to say, it was exceptionally unsettling when my father proceeded to tear out those two individual pages, paperclips and all. These were unprecedented times indeed! Then using the paperclips, he affixed the torn-out map pages to his yellow pad to facilitate examination. He handed me back the now desecrated map book and instructed me to put it with the map ball. Which I promptly did, by flinging it carelessly over my shoulder into the back of the plane. Unprecedented times called for unprecedented measures. I made another "note to self" that later, I would have to put that neatly away as well. Most disconcerting, and alarming, was that my meticulous militant father didn't seem to care about his cabin being untidy or unkempt. On the one hand it further heightened my anxiety regarding the serious nature of our situation, while on the other hand it was comforting to know that his preoccupation was on our safety.

Essentially talking to himself, he ultimately answered my earlier query, "If we turn around again and land in the Bahamas, they will not be able to fix the plane. Which means we would have to put her on a barge and haul her back to Miami. And that's going to cost a fortune and probably take months." He continued, "we've only been up for forty...forty-five minutes. Which means we should be able to hit one of the smaller airstrips and be on the ground in about fifteen to twenty minutes." And then he glanced over in my direction, as though confiding in me and seeking my approval. However, I knew in his heart that he had already made up his mind.

I nodded, as though the plan sounded reasonable. I solemnly looked into the distance at the thick dark clouds occupying the entire horizon. The clear blue panorama was now well behind us. As unnerving as our condition appeared, I was surprisingly not terrified. My father's demeanor had successfully dissipated my anxiety. We had been through so many close calls during our years of aviation together that I just assumed my dad would take care of it. He always had before. I reassured myself that I was in good hands. The best!

Over the next few minutes, each of us persistently glimpsed at the right engine, amazed that the propeller was still spinning. The oil flow continued and now covered my entire half of the plane. Further rationalizing his decision, he expounded, "yeah, this is the best way to go. There would be no way to fix this plane outside of the United States. And I'd much rather be over land than water." With the tip of his index finger, he gestured toward our small monochrome instrument weather panel. He tapped on the square screen, located in the center of the co-pilot's side of the cockpit dashboard. "Keep your eye on the storm and keep the monitor on the maximum distance setting."

I adjusted the view of our state-of-the-art weather instrumentation so that we could observe the furthest distance possible via satellite. On the upper left periphery of the screen was a swirling, growing solid green mass. I inquired, "Is that...?"

"Yeah, I'm pretty sure that's Isidore." He cut me off.

Concerned, I clarified that only twenty minutes ago, the control tower informed us that this storm was still over Central Florida and a pretty far distance from our current position. In fact, when we departed this morning, we expected the storm to push out west and dissipate over the Gulf of Mexico, and then most likely head north up the West Coast of Florida. However, according to our instruments, if I was reading them correctly, the green mass was getting bigger and rapidly traversing the top of our screen, heading smack into our flight path. My dad merely nodded concurring with my interpretation, as he slowly exhaled. "These storms move pretty darn quick," he added.

He radioed the closest small airport regarding our approach. Their reply was devastatingly unfortunate. Their larger runway was closed for repairs. "Repairs!? What the Sam Hill?" He flipped the map over, glanced at his notes and frustratingly muttered, "Mother jumper! This is not good! Their other runway is too short for us." With that, he crumpled up the map page into a ball and tossed it over his shoulder. That seemed to be the appropriate and acceptable way to file things during this flight.

Then, after glancing at the specs on the second map page, he said, "No, this one's no good either. We're just too darn heavy. We've got to go back to Jacksonville." He then crumpled up the second map into a ball and tossed it over his shoulder as well. We both looked at the weather radar screen, which now was more than half-filled with the dark green mass. Trying to console me he confidently affirmed, "don't worry, we'll be on the ground before she gets here," indicating with his index finger our ultimate destination on the radar, just under, and to the right of the solid green mass. Then, pointing to the yellow pad still on his lap, referring to his scribble-scrabble notation, releasing an enormous sigh of exacerbation, he added, "Okay, just a little over twenty more minutes, give or take."

A quick glance outside revealed that our plane had now entered and was completely engulfed by low level and dark shaded cloud cover. The blue skies were completely gone. Not even pockets were visible. The turbulence was continuous now, like driving on an unpaved road amidst a plethora of potholes. Sprinkles of precipitation began pelting our windshield, as small thin streaks of water raced in narrow lines across the plexiglass. And with that, the looming monochrome green mass on our radar screen inched slightly down and to the right, directly in our path, closing in on our ultimate destination. In order to land safely we would have to enter the storm.

Suddenly, the front windshield was overwhelmed by another blinding white light that completely obscured my vision. It was as if the dashboard and the windshield were replaced by the sun. I covered my face with my arm, trying desperately to avert my eyes. I was disoriented to say the least. This sunlight didn't make any sense inside the cockpit.

✽✽✽ ✽✽✽

Once again, I couldn't look away. The light was extraordinary. And then my arm was gone. My dad was gone. There was only this blistering light obstructing my view in all directions. All the ambient noise from inside the cockpit was replaced with the now familiar mechanical whirring and beeping sounds from my captivity. And with that, the muffled voices returned. I was back on a bed or a table, in the same confined observation enclosure as before, in the company of the same three disembodied floating head creatures.

Why was I yanked away again? Why couldn't I continue within the memory of the plane crash? I had not yet reached the crucial pain. What about that memory was so excruciating that they were preventing me from seeing it? I thought I was ready. Apparently, I wasn't. I quickly had to reorient myself for this next encounter. The gatekeepers to the nexus had returned. The blinding light had returned. I was not prepared.

How could I be?

5

THE CHOICE

The pain from the light was intense. My eyes were again burning. "Can you hear me?" asked the familiar deep voice. The light was removed. My eyes watered. My vision blurred. From behind the floating mask he repeated, "Can you hear me?" The question prompted a renewed sense of urgency. While I longed to remain with my dad in the cockpit, this was the opportunity I had anticipated, and I was not going to allow this connection to pass. They were reaching out again. I had to respond. I wasn't prepared. I had to reorient myself.

This encounter with the orbs had an increased level of significance and pressure. I had no idea why I interpreted that contact to be so vital. However, I concretely felt the tension, prominence, and immense gravity of the moment.

I was instinctually correct. Either my sixth sense had subconsciously kicked in, or perhaps while unconscious, I overheard medical staff discussing the dire nature of my condition. Regardless, this interaction was imperative. Their medical experience, and deficient preconditioning, assured them that people do not survive plane crashes. Had I been unresponsive, at this moment, they were prepared to take me off life support...and give up on me.

⁂

"Blink if you can hear me." Upon hearing the command, I fluttered my eyelids repeatedly. I had eyelids...and I could move them. Oddly enough, I was also able to slightly move my head. A most remarkable sensation. Movement. This was even more noteworthy because I didn't have a perceivable neck or body. I couldn't understand how I was able to move my head. I just did it.

"Nod, if you understand me." I nodded ever so slightly. Prompting the suspended male sphere to respond, "I don't believe it. Astonishing!"

"Well, that made two of us," I thought.

Anthropomorphizing, I imagined him smiling behind the mask. "Nod gently or blink if you can feel this." And then an even more amazing thing happened. Tactile sensation. Small precise pressure being applied to my face. I blinked again. Then I felt small precise pressure applied to various other parts of my earthly body. Wait!? Other parts of my body? I was more than just a head? And then, like a whirlwind, my other senses were returning. I was able to see, hear and feel. My palms were poked. I felt it. My fingers were poked. I felt it. My toes were poked. I felt it. My chest was poked. I felt it. And with each of these pinpoint pressurizations I either blinked slightly or nodded my head affirmatively. While movement was restricted, it wasn't completely inhibited.

Then, my chest filled with air. I could feel my lungs. Strange, I couldn't exhale, as if my nose and mouth still didn't exist. I recalled, during many previous painful cycles in the darkness, having this particular sensation – being filled with air, like a balloon. But this was different, experiencing the inhalation from this new perspective. It was all so real.

Also, I couldn't move the muscles in my cheeks, nose, or my jaw, but I did feel the pressure being applied to my face. Therefore, while movement was narrow, I clearly had the sensation of touch and compression. And, although all of this may have been in my imagination, I'd swear my olfactory sense had returned. I fancied a dull, metallic, muted aroma. It was faint, and nondescript, but it appeared to be a scent, nonetheless.

Then, I had control of my extremities and appendages. Or at least I believed I did. I wiggled my fingers and toes. While tactile sensation was limited, I could feel pressure and had the ability of movement. Inexplicably, everything was numb, apart from my left hand. I was somehow able to feel a soft cloth-like substance between my fingers. I caressed the smooth fabric. Amazingly, I appeared to be an intact being after all. Or at least mostly intact. Thus began the journey of my body waking up.

Seemingly satisfied and pleasantly impressed by my responses, the male head hovered away. His positive reaction alleviated my tension and sense of urgency. And with his giant head no longer obstructing my view I now had a pristine opportunity to better take in my surroundings. From my position, moving my head slightly, I observed that I was, in fact lying on a bed. The room was still colorless yet contained plenty of shadows and gray tones. Unfortunately, my range of motion was still extremely limited. I rotated my head slightly to the left and looked up at the only orb that remained in my company. Apparently, the male head, and other female head, had left the enclosure.

The remaining female head was preoccupied. She was scrutinizing things that were either affixed to my bed or hanging near it. And occasionally she would look down at me and make eye contact. I recognized the importance of capitalizing on this opportunity. My left hand was free. How could that be useful? Unfortunately, my arm was numb, immobile and useless. Then it occurred to me, communication might be possible after all. I snapped my fingers a few times, which was enough to get the female head's attention. She looked at me, and then looked at my hand. Even though she was masked, I knew she was expressing acknowledgment because her eyes widened. It had worked! Communication was possible.

Hoping and relying on universal symbols, I pantomimed "writing," by making small cursive swirls in the air with my thumb and index finger tightly pressed together. She noticed my improvisation, and, floated away. Thankfully, she floated almost immediately back. Mystically, levitating next to her was a recognizable writing implement and a small piece of parchment. She clearly understood my intention.

Seeing these two familiar items simultaneously created both excitement and anxiety. I was motivated by the familiarity of seeing a pen and paper, and the prospect of what they represented. But I was nervous because it provided me the first opportunity to effectively communicate my questions, which meant that I was now at the threshold of answers. I was immediately cautioned by Aesop's maxim, "Be careful what you wish for. You may get it." All I had wanted were answers. And yet, finally confronting the penultimate revelations of my own mortality was both awesome and terrifying.

The paper and pen somehow materialized under my hand. Taking the pen, I began to scribble and noticed that the paper was being held in place for me. Unfortunately, it also became exceedingly apparent, that as a "righty" my left-handed penmanship was mechanically deficient. Was this also a test? Would being merely dextral prove to be an impediment in the hereafter? Regardless, I focused. I proceeded slowly. I formulated and crafted each letter as best I could. Ultimately, I scribbled my three-word question. I then maneuvered the paper counterclockwise ever so slightly to indicate that I was finished. She looked at the paper, and then back at me. Then back at the paper. Her response seemed to take an eternity. And this pause caused me great consternation, because using my left hand, I am not even certain what I wrote was legible. I craned my head as best I could, struggling to simultaneously tilt the paper up and in the direction of my limited eye line. I could barely see the tiny scrap of paper at all from my awkward angle. After exerting tremendous effort, I was able to glance at my squiggles and make out that it was legible. In chicken scratch, I had successfully, albeit sloppily, sketched the question, "Am I dead?"

Why was there no reaction? Perhaps this creature couldn't read or understand English after all. "Get the male head back here!" I futilely thought. Finally, she looked down at me. There was a long pause. Her eyes became filled with tender emotion. Gentle pressure caressed and comforted my left hand, and matter-of-factly in a very sweet and nurturing female voice, she simply replied, "No." And she floated away. There was no extended explanation and no extensive conversation. Just plain, "no."

No!? Not dead? Well, I sure as heck wasn't alive. At least not the way I remember life. It wasn't as rewarding an answer as I had expected. And, if I wasn't dead, where was I? What was this place? What was happening to me? And what was to come? I was incredulous, prompting a plethora of follow-up questions. Hundreds of thoughts colliding and cascading at once. And yet, I knew my communicative abilities were extremely hampered – considering my inability to verbalize, coupled with my ambidextrous mechanical deficiency. If only I remembered morse code or had ever learned sign language. I then became anxious again, not knowing how much longer this conversation would be permitted to continue.

Regardless, as to the limitations, this was still the best opportunity, thus far, for me to obtain answers. I had to maximize this opening. I had to prioritize. What information was most important? If I am afforded only one more question, what would it be? And I knew I had to be succinct. Precise. Brief. Sadly, brevity was never one of my strengths. Another test, perhaps? I had to think! Quickly! Focus!

And then, for the first time within the confines of this paradigm, with the head-creatures, I heard my now-familiar inner whisper "family." While it was surreal to hear the whisper in this environment, as with previous messages, I intuitively knew what it meant. I was imbibing information. Reprogramming. Then, astonishingly, images of two distinct infants appeared, floating in the ether. They were the faces of my daughters. This was another first. I was experiencing future images enmeshed within this new paradigm. Like this observation room, these images felt so vivid and real. How could this be? I didn't have any children. However, I recognized them, even though I had not met them yet. My conditioning told me this was impossible. I was convinced that it was all just an elaborate hallucination — the floating heads, the observation room , my children, all of it. As if responding to me, the echo repeated, "family."

Then the visualization morphed, kaleidoscopically, revealing the angelic eyes of my beautiful wife. Wife!? And children? Well, at least a wife made sense. That's where the children must have come from. It was difficult to reconcile this fantasy within the arcane parameters of my traditional encoding. However, because my internal voice was so emphatic, instead of dismissing those images, I allowed the feelings of intimacy and love to wash over me. It was amazing.

I further contemplated the significance of procreation with respect to my current state. At the time of the plane crash, when I was still alive, I was a virgin. I had never experienced sexual intercourse. I was saving myself for marriage. And yet, I died a virgin. But, no! The floating-head-lady said I wasn't dead. Or at least I wasn't dead, yet. Or I wasn't dead anymore. This required clarification. However, a prerequisite to that clarification seemed to be my progeny. While I had always accepted adoption as a viable means of creating a family, this prophecy I was just presented with clearly presented offspring containing my genes. They were visualizations of familial connections, intimacy, and love. I struggled with the formulation of a simple cogent query for the floating head lady. One question to clarify both the status of my current existence as well as finding a potential purpose for living.

⁂

In actuality, I was barely still alive. At that time, the mutilated, mangled, and scarred husk of my body remained in critical condition, and on life support. My preoccupation with my future family was setting the stage for an impending assessment. Did I even want to come back? Or would it just be easier to give up and move on?

Based on the guidance of my inner voice I concluded that procreation, intimacy, and love were going to be of paramount importance in my decision-making process. The thoughts and images of family overshadowed the patchwork of my ancillary future experiences, accomplishments, and achievements. Therefore, my terrestrial existence, my will to live, and my very survival depended on the answer to my next question.

I snapped my fingers to again attract my levitating female companion's attention. She floated back. I repeated my pantomime for writing. As if by magic, the paper and pen reappeared under my hand. My inquiry required succinctness of both words and characters. Brevity and precision. Again, both not my strongest suits. I carefully, albeit sloppily scribbled the question, "Does it work?" And then proceeded to draw an arrow pointing to where I perceived my genitalia to be, assuming my supine position and intact prior human form. Unexpectedly, at the time, this question proved to be more fundamental than my first. I eagerly awaited her response.

In retrospect, there were countless better questions, and more sophisticated thoughts that I could have communicated in order to help weigh my circumstances and guide my motivations. Because of my programming, and my age, I had mis-associated sex, as the primary conduit for intimacy. However, in my adolescent immaturity, that was what I had come up with.

I'd swear, I heard a chortle from under the floating-head's mask, as she reviewed my inquiry. Nodding and chuckling, she responded, "yes, it would appear that it still does." The snickering continued as she floated away. This time out of the enclosure entirely. I could hear the giggles from outside my captivity.

Perhaps I should have been embarrassed. However, quite the opposite. There was a lot to process. But embarrassment was not a consideration. For one thing, I thought I was communicating with a superior being who would be above childish, earthly, foolishness. And for another, more importantly, it was wonderful to get the information. It would be extremely vital in my decision-making process. I was overcome with feelings of love, embracing the totality of affection that existed in the moment. I was emboldened. Comforted. I was going to have a family. Or I was going to possibly have a family. Or, because everything existed here in the present, I already had a family, in the future. I admit it was very confusing...and very exciting!

And then, to my surprise, as if that experience with the orbs couldn't get any stranger, this time the male head returned with three female heads in tow. The four of them formed a semi-circle around me. The newest head took a position closest to me, on my left side. As this novel female orb came into focus her appearance was different from the others. She wasn't wearing a head covering or a mask, allowing her long, auburn hair to hang down below, and along, the sides of her face.

As she moved closer, our gazes met, and I instantly recognized the contours of her face. I knew those eyes. I knew that face! Yes, I knew that face well! Unexpectedly and jubilantly, I welcomed the facade belonging to that of my mother. It didn't matter if it made sense or not. It was my mom's face. And it was wonderful!

As our eyes locked in silence, it momentarily felt as though we were the only two beings in existence. My gift was my mom. She looked down at me, and I up at her. The joy of seeing her collided with the illogic of the situation. How could she have been there? In that place? Why was she presented as a floating head? Despite the substantive nature and realism, she was either an elaborate delusion or an image created by a grand entity for my benefit. Logic obfuscated the incongruity of that encounter and my visual perception.

And then, I felt a comforting pressure, that I'd swear were two hands, clasping tightly around my left hand. However, no one in that enclosure, except for me, had any limbs. Whether it was real or not didn't seem to matter. The interaction was having a profound effect on me. The warmth and pleasure of the moment was overwhelming. Was this related to my current preoccupation with family?

Again, tapping into my exhaustive cannon of science fiction lore, I concluded that either these creatures recreated my mother from my own memory or they were somehow able to teleport her essence to this very way station. Regardless, it made sense, in the moment, allowing me to brush aside the illogic and incongruity. I therefore accepted that the floating head and two hands belonged to that of my mother. At the very least, this is who the creatures wanted me to interact with. And I could not deny the pleasure and contentment that I was experiencing. Their maternal facsimile was flawless.

My mother's eyes overflowed with water, as tears streamed down her face. My heart ached. If there was even a chance that I was communicating with my real mother back on Earth, I wanted her to know, I needed her to know, that I was okay. I was ready for whatever awaited me. I definitely did not want her to know about the pain. Facsimile or not, I wanted to comfort her. Despite my effort, she did not seem to receive my telepathic attempts at pacification. She just continued to cry, sobbing uncontrollably.

I then theorized that my confinement was at a crossroads. A transition. Two paths extended by this maternal aberration or residue from my prior life. An echo, reaching out to me. One option appeared to be an invitation guiding me back to Earth. The alternative offered a warmhearted consolation, easing me forward, mourning my passing, and welcoming me into the hereafter.

Accepting my premise as feasible, that this image of my mother was chosen to be my guide, I attempted to communicate. Staring into my mother's watery eyes prompted only one question. If I were somehow re-connecting with my prior life, the plane crash and my crucial pain, there was something else I needed to know. I once again, recreated the international symbol for writing by swirling my fingers in the air. Mystically, I again felt a piece of paper and a writing implement under my left hand. With my grossly inadequate left-handed writing skills, I slowly etched out three capital letters and a solitary punctuation.

My mom glanced at the scrap-paper containing my one-word question in all capital letters, "DAD?" Comfortingly she responded, "Yes, he's fine. He's in the other room resting. He's not strong enough to get up right now. But you'll see him soon." Aberration or not, that was clearly my mother's loving voice. They had nailed it!

It was interesting though, in my mind, how one question led to a flood of other questions. I wasn't certain if that meant that he had also died and was recovering in the same way station with me. Or, if they were giving him a similar opportunity to return. I thought it odd that I had to wait to see him though. I had a lot to reconcile and process. And then coherence began fading. I felt myself drifting further away, transported back to the familiar euphoric space. As the area filled with white smoke, it was difficult to know what was real and what was imaginary.

That familial interaction was not an illusion. It was with my mom. She was real. She was there at my bedside. However, her description of my father's condition was a fabrication. He was not in the other room resting, nor was he fine. Through their own faulty programming, many people mistakenly believe that fabrications can be innocent and beneficial. Deception is often justified as a means to protect people, especially loved ones, or patients, from harsh realities. They erroneously believe that grim truth is too painful — that people aren't strong enough to handle the truth. Some even inaccurately convince themselves that actuality is subjective. One of the most difficult aspects of my own re-conditioning was acknowledging the value of honesty and veracity, which is discussed at length in Chapter Nine. Suffice it to say, one of my most valued lessons was that everything is in the present, and the present always contains the objective, absolute truth. Without this realization and understanding, it is otherwise impossible to ever utilize Step Three and truly appreciate "The Gift."

※※※

The fog returned, and fleetingly consumed me. The small enclosure was once again obscured with white chalk-like dust. The heads were gone. My mom was gone. The residue of her touch, and love, stayed with me. I soared peacefully for a short while through the hospital corridors before being cast back into agonizing darkness. Even though the torturous cycle resumed, I was fortunately able to find contemplative asylum within the memory of my recent maternal interaction.

Comforted by the vision of familial feelings and the sensation of love, I decided that I was ready. Ready for whatever was next. I was ready to either return to earth or move on with death. I scanned the present, in the darkness. I still couldn't visualize what was next. No matter how far into the future I looked I could not see past my old age. But "I was ready," I thought. Why wasn't that enough? What was keeping me here in purgatory? What else did I need to do?

The guidance returned once again, reminding me to "enter the crucial pain." The assistance was little different this time. There was an additional message. The word "enter" was overlapping with the expression "embrace." And following the repeated echo was an overwhelming feeling to "decide." Enter, embrace, and decide. There was also this comforting feeling that I was nearing the end. I was finally at the crossroads. I felt it. There was some grand austere pain I had to face, and somehow welcome. Some demon that was waiting for me.

Some terror to be grappled with in order to finally be permitted transition. And somehow my decision-making capability, my free will, was in play. At this point I accepted that liberation could only be chosen from elements I couldn't yet see or comprehend. There was pain that needed to be entered and embraced. And I was so close. Everything was leading me back to the plane and the moments before the darkness.

While struggling psychologically, my vitals were declining. I was dying. If my body did not begin to heal, death was imminent. The doctors had done all they could.

I looked into the abyss behind me, at the massive wall of pain. I was ready. I slid back into the co-pilot's seat. Instantly, the rhythmic whirring, humming, and beeping from the darkness was replaced with the ambient sounds from the cockpit and the disconcerting clatter of our sputtering right turbo prop engine. My father's voice cut through the white noise, "Say again, repeat, over?" I was back in the plane. Back in the storm. I looked to my left, and watched my dad navigate us toward Jacksonville Municipal Airport in the distance. Despite our engine difficulties, we were preparing to land, hopefully safely. And not a moment too soon.

A youthful male voice on the radio boomed, "adjust heading to three-nine-seven and enter the holding pattern at the middle marker using your V.F.R." "V.F.R." is an aeronautical term referring to using "Visual Flight Rules." As opposed to "I.F.R." which refers to using "Instrument Flight Rules." We had been using our instruments to navigate since entering the overcast cloud cover, with close to zero visibility. However, as we just dropped below the clouds, we had to exercise extreme caution, because of the congested air-traffic. Passing the outer marker, we could already count at least six other aircraft close by, already in a holding pattern, waiting for their turn to land. From here on, our instruments were not sufficient. We also had to rely on what we could see out of our windows.

My dad followed the instructions and began to change our heading to three-nine-seven. As the plane banked to the right, he gently handed me the radio mic. He was annoyed, muttering, "A holding pattern? This putz is putting us in a God damn holding pattern?! What kind of a wet-behind-the-ears idiot they got in this tower?!" The last twenty minutes of our flight had become exceedingly difficult, riddled with severe unpredictable turbulence, similar to a gut-wrenching carnival ride. The reality was that we were in the clutches of a massive cyclone, while suffering terminal mechanical engine failure. It was maddening. To make matters worse, the young soldier in the control tower was inexperienced, overwhelmed, and ill-equipped to run the tower under emergency weather conditions. We should never have been added to a holding pattern. Due to our perilous mechanical troubles, we should have been flagged for an emergency landing in first position priority.

We then entered another patch of, unavoidable low-level cloud cover. Once again, we had zero visibility and had to rely solely on our instruments. Suddenly, everything fell silent. Progressive time was suspended. Like pausing a movie. Through the motionless streaks of water on the windshield, I witnessed a panoply of shades, textures, and twisted configurations outside. The view was quite breathtaking. We were in the thicket of Isidore's most tumultuous and violent gusts. Yet, the overlapping mix of swirls and shades spanning the grayscale spectrum was a miraculous spectacle. A true feat of nature. There were literally clouds inside of clouds, protruding from inside other clouds. I imagined that it resembled being inside a giant ball of cotton candy. I don't recall appreciating any of those details from my actual experience.

What was even more extraordinary was that I appeared to be the one augmenting the environment, regulating the progression of the memory. Because of my fear, I had inadvertently stopped time for a moment, giving me an opportunity to assess my surroundings. Even zoom in on minute details. I could go slowly forward or backward. It was all here in the present. I then proceeded to adjust time forward in slow motion. The wind was astonishingly multi-directional. Wisps of cloud vapor were being pulled and stretched haphazardly, as well as jolting and smashing into the plane on all sides. I allowed time to progress normally. Wham! Nature whipped across the nose and the wings. And then, boom! Wind slammed abruptly into our craft from the right side. Then, randomly from the left side. I slowed everything down again. With each impact, the plane was thrashed from side to side, left to right, right to left, and up and down, like a toy being tossed about. At any speed I was awestruck by the sheer magnitude of it all. My panic dissipated, and I resumed time at a customary speed.

At the middle marker we carefully entered a holding pattern with four other aircraft. I watched my dad maneuver the plane like a master craftsman. Whatever nature threw at us he had a counter move. I had no idea how he kept us upright. The veins in his biceps and forearms were bulging. He was struggling. Using all his strength and years of aeronautical training to fight the elements.

I reflected on how much better off we would have been continuing on to the Bahamas. Of course, it would have cost time and money to get home, but at least there was no storm. I knew better than to vocalize this. I glanced at the weather radar, shaking my head in disbelief. The entire screen, at the closest setting, was now completely covered by the green mass. We were churning deep inside Isidore's bowels. At three-thousand feet, we could see the runway parallel to our position, less than a few miles away. I felt like I could reach out and touch it.

We followed the group of other planes in a large circle just east of the airport, enviously watching other craft touching down on the runway. In the distance, other smaller holding patterns had formed, as new arrivals had to wait their turn. It then occurred to me that Isidore had taken many aviators off guard. Her surge in both strength and intensity and sudden change of direction forced a myriad of aircraft back to Jacksonville in hopes of finding safe harbor. We watched, helplessly, jealously, as other planes safely landed, while envisioning that we too would soon be on the ground.

With every turbulent jolt that either raised, dropped, or swatted us around like paper, I thought again about those clear calm skies over the ocean, the Bahamas, and even chancing one of those other two smaller runways we had passed only twenty minutes earlier. I even fantasized us trying to land on the highway. But no, my dad knew better. He had somehow gotten us back to the airport. "We are so close," I thought. "If only we could get clearance for final approach."

And just then, the engine sputtering outside my window became a clunking sound. The plane jerked hard to the right. I could see the individual silver propeller blades slowing down. Clunk! Small amounts of black smoke wafted from the engine casing. Clunk! Clunk-clunk! My dad immediately shut down the right engine. Clunk-clunk-clunk! Wide-eyed, I watched the propeller slowing. In mid-air. Nothing could be more horrifying. The shiny silver propeller blades of the right engine stopped cold.

My dad had me read him the fuel gauges, which were located on my side of the cockpit. And calm as a cucumber he said, "In order to keep us level I need to rebalance the fuel, and we don't want to catch fire." Then, as was his instinctive comedic personality, he deadpanned, "fire, at this point, would be bad." I mustered the most uncomfortable smile imaginable. After the fuel had been rebalanced, with equal amounts in each tank, I didn't notice an appreciable difference. We were still bouncing around wildly.

Apparently, our fuel balance was only one factor. It was exceedingly more difficult for my dad to keep the plane steady with a solitary propeller. My father explained, "This plane wasn't meant to fly with only one engine." He continued, "Sure, she's been tested and certified, and does great in ideal conditions. But unlike a twinjet, these twin-props weren't meant to fly in any degree of inclement weather. There's no way we can keep this baby up much longer. We have to get on the ground."

He reached into my lap and forcefully grabbed the microphone. The tenor of his voice had completely changed, "Tower, this is Lima-Five-Niner-Whiskey-Fox-Trot. We have mechanical failure in the right engine. We can no longer hold in pattern. Clear other traffic! We're coming down. Over!" Then he muttered under his breath with the microphone off, "with or without your damn permission!"

He tossed me back the mic fixated on keeping the plane steady. "I can't believe that Isidore made it back this fast." He told me that from now on, until we're on the ground, "you talk to them. I'm going to land this bird." He then sternly commanded, "I need you to repeatedly squawk and call in the mayday. The tower will see where we are, and…" After a momentary pause, "everyone else will have to clear a path."

"Squawking" is an aviation term for pressing the transponder button, which causes each individual aircraft's unique call sign – i.e. identifying numbers and letters – to flash on the air traffic controllers' board. It also allows the controllers to know and verify an aircraft's current position. Since my earliest memory of flying, squawking was always one of the funniest things to do, as it was standard procedure during typical landings. However, under normal circumstances, you only "squawked" a couple of times or as directed by the tower. Here, in our emergency, I was continually pressing the transponder every few seconds, during our decent. Everything about this landing was atypical, and this time there was no joy in the task. Also, throughout my father's entire piloting career, this was the first occasion and need to call in a mayday.

My dad broke the holding pattern formation, heading directly away from the airport. I continued to squawk, pressing the transponder button repeatedly. I was consumed with questions as we maneuvered away, continuing to bounce around like we were riding a mechanical bull. I swallowed hard and internalized my questions. Why were we heading so far away? Only moments ago, we were parallel to the runway. If we would have banked hard-right, and descended, we could have been on the ground already. And then about twenty seconds later, our plane banked hard into a descending right semicircle, revealing the airport and the runway lining up in the distance. I internally questioned why we were so far away though.

Responding, as if by telepathy, my dad explained, "the weather is so rough, and our plane is so unresponsive. If I would have tried to force a landing so close, the odds are that, either the wind aloft would've pushed us away from the runway, or worse, we could have collided into another plane already on approach. By us moving out a little further, and you continuing to squawk, it gives the tower and the other pilots time to get the hell out of our way." He then asked, "do you see the runway?" Without taking his focus away from landing, in his periphery, he saw me nod and acknowledge. "then, call it in. Let them know we're coming. And don't stop squawking."

I did just that. "Mayday, Mayday. Lima-Five-Nine-Whiskey-Fox-Trot. We are on emergency final approach. Over?!" I pressed the button. Squawk! My voice crackled with elevated anxiety, "mayday, mayday, repeat El-5-9-Whiskey-Fox-Trot...we are on final...we are coming in whether we are cleared or not, mayday, mayday." Squawk-squawk! The tower may have responded. I don't know. I wasn't even certain if I ever let go of the microphone call-button, which would have made hearing the tower's response impossible. Other planes speckled the sky at varying altitudes. However, my dad's strategy was effective, as there were no other aircrafts in our direct path.

This grudge match between my dad and Mother Nature proved to be the heavyweight prize fight of the century. We were in the fifteenth round now. As terrified as I was, my money was on my dad. With every crushing blow Isidore landed – left, right, uppercut, jab, jab, hook, cross, etc. – my dad had a block and a counter punch. Furiously turning knobs, correcting dials, and adjusting the U-shaped flight controls, he was visibly sweating now and exhausted.

Suddenly, we entered a patch of low-level fog which momentarily, and completely, obstructed our view of the runway. Then over the crackling radio boomed an adult deep, mature male voice, not to be confused with the adolescent private that we had been communicating with up until now, "This is Colonel Wilson, I have assumed command of the Jacksonville Tower. Whiskey-Fox-Trot, we roger your emergency mayday, you are clean and green to land. Copy?"

Hearing the Colonel's voice gave us renewed hope. There was now, finally, a competent experienced adult in charge of the tower. We had a fighting chance. We emerged from the low cloud cover, only to see more patches of fog ahead, affording us only a splotchy and obstructed view of the runway, still in the distance. As we continued our rapid decent, we entered yet another all-encompassing blotch of grey haze, that gusted into our path.

The laws of physics and aerodynamics were working against us. An airplane of our size and weight, will maintain loft – or flight – between sixty-five to seventy-five knots per hour. Our maximum airspeed with one turbo-prop engine was approximately one hundred forty knots per hour. While crosswinds provide friction, they are usually only a marginal drag, and do not dramatically affect airspeed. In general, a tailwind essentially increases your airspeed by the amount of the tailwind. Conversely, a headwind reduces your speed accordingly. If your headwind is greater than the amount needed to provide or maintain lift, you descend. Despite my father's best efforts, our minuscule craft, with only one functional engine, was proving to be no match against the gale force winds.

Unfortunately, less than three miles from the southwest runway at Jacksonville Municipal Airport, Isidore landed a devastating blow. She unleashed a continuous gust greater than fifty miles per hour, completely negating our forward momentum. It felt as though we were being pushed backwards. Then, the left engine sputtered, and the left propeller began moving so slowly that I could actually see the blades turning like a child's pinwheel. In the background, Peter Cetera, who had become a part of the ambient white noise, continued to serenade us.

At that moment, we were like a paper airplane being tossed into a fan. The nose of the plane went almost straight up, practically vertical. We paused, in an upright position, virtually motionless and weightless, then proceeded straight down into a nosedive. My dad and I were both thrust backwards and pinned to our seats. Through streaks of rainwater the ground encompassed our entire front view.

As the canopy of treetops drew closer, I turned myself around, hugging the copilot's seat in abject terror. *Chicago 17*, which had been playing softly in a continuous loop, was once again restarting the opening piano riff to *You're the Inspiration*. Da-nah, nah, nah-nah, nah, nah, nah, nah, nah. With all my heart I was certain that my dad would save us. And once on the ground, I vowed to unfold those crumpled up map balls and put them, and the map books, properly back where they belonged.

My father, my hero, was going to land this plane safely, somehow.

~~~~~~~~~~

But as you are unmistakably aware, he didn't. He couldn't, despite his resilience. During the descent however, he was miraculously able to level us off, just above the treetops, averting a nose-first ground collision. Additionally, he maintained the presence of mind to shut down the left engine, and jettison any remaining fuel, thereby clearing the lines and stopping the oil and gas flow. Thus, lessoning the chances of an explosion. Unfortunately, a few moments after we leveled off, careening across the treetops, we crashed into the Florida Everglades, less than three miles from the airport runway. My father suffered whiplash and died instantly upon impact. My body was ejected from the plane, landing approximately sixty yards behind the wreckage. My hero had never given up. He saved my life.

And then I saw the crucial pain. It was all around me. Everywhere. Physical pain. Emotional pain. Primal anger manifesting itself into insurmountable masses of searing pain and torment. As bad as the physical pain was, the emotional anguish overshadowed it. It was all there in the present. The truth. There I was, barely alive, praising the recent memory of my father, whom I loved and respected dearly. Yet, whom I knew was primarily responsible for this terrible tragedy. I was angry at him for causing my injuries. I was incensed at him for recklessly endangering us in the first place. And I was furious at him for passing away.

~~~~~~~~~~

And then two doors materialized, opening slowly in front of me. One contained this wonderful long life, filled with family, love, and prosperity, juxtaposed with this massive, almost insurmountable pain – crucial emotional pain, along with years of arduous physical struggles through recovery and rehabilitation. In addition, I was also acutely aware of a lifetime of emotional baggage from my childhood. I was instantly granted enough clarity to visualize the long, and often tumultuous road ahead.

Overcoming the crucial pain was not possible in the world that I had come from. Since I was born, I was taught that there were severe limits regarding the control I had over so many aspects of my life and destiny. Most things happen to me, rather than because of me. That old life came with so many boundaries, restrictions, and absolutes, like people not being able to survive plane crashes. Therefore, in order to survive, all my programming would have to be rewritten. Redesigned. Recoded. How much control did I actually have to facilitate this? How much different, better, liberating, would existence be, untarnished by a lifetime of brainwashing? How could I possibly know, having never experienced it, aside from the visualizations here in the way station?

Beyond the other door was death. And while death offered a peaceful tranquility, it was a clear finite end to my mortality. Upon reflection, I wasn't frightened of either door. Each offered an end to the cyclical misery. Eternal rest seemed like a conceivable, viable option. I had suffered enough. I was tired. Reprogramming my entire life and starting over seemed exhausting.

And there it was. My choice. As I observed both open doors, I was overwhelmed by a feeling of profound significance and purpose. It wasn't a whisper of direction. I wasn't given any specific guidance. Instead, I experienced an indescribable, awe-inspiring sensation. My life, if I wished to return to it, would have meaning and infinite potential.

Each doorway beckoned for me to "choose." I contemplated my options. I made my decision.

6

THE AWAKENING

The rush of warm water was exhilarating. My vision was blurred. I was suddenly thrust into crystal clear consciousness, like waking up from a dream. Completely submerged, and engulfed, in liquid. And I was breathing. Yet, I was underwater. I struggled to reconcile my surroundings. Nothing made sense. This could not be the airplane wreckage. We didn't crash into the ocean. I was not in the swampy Everglades or impacted in mud. I was merely encased in some type of fluid. It wasn't cold or hot. It was the perfect temperature. It felt amazing. Invigorating! Was this my reincarnation? My rebirth? Could I possibly be in utero, inside a womb? After my long internment in purgatory, was I ultimately being allowed to come back to life? And if so, where was I going? Regardless, this was finally it. And I was ready.

My perpetual essence, or sense of self, was intact. Which led me to quickly conclude that Eastern religions had been correct all along. Since my eternal soul, and memories endured, this must be a form of re-embodiment. I was being afforded the opportunity to bring my past life into the next one. How exciting! And I was ready!

I was further intrigued to return as one of myriad different animals – lion, insect, whale, bird, zebra, etc. Will I get to choose? Or will my return-animal-form be chosen for me? I began concentrating on an image of a majestic soaring eagle, as if my intent would somehow influence my cosmic destiny. And with that, my imagination and delusions of rebirth were violently interrupted by a cacophony of mechanical sounds, coinciding with high-pressure jets blowing bubbles in my face and across my entire body. This was not a reincarnation. I wasn't an eagle. I was back in my former earthly skin. And I was disappointed.

So much for my premature Eastern-philosophical speculation. My senses were on overdrive. All my tactile perceptions returned at once. My entire body instantly had feeling. All of my senses were alive. I could even see ambient light, although it was blurred and out of focus. Despite my disorientation, and overcoming my initial disappointment in not returning as a bird of prey, it was wonderful to be back!

The water jets abruptly ceased, and I was involuntarily moving upward on a metallic slab. I emerged quickly from a vat of water, on a mechanical platform, completely restrained. While my individual senses were returning, I was still deprived freedom of physical movement. And just like that, the pleasant comforting sensations were all taken away. Replaced by searing hellfire. This was awful!

Every nerve ending was aflame! As the water quickly receded, this new environment came into focus. If I still had limbs and a head, they were all restrained in some way by some foreign force. The pain was maddening. I was being artificially lifted slowly into the air. The only distraction from the pain was an incessant noisy mechanical crankshaft whirring as I rose higher and higher. It too, was annoying. In my restrained physical position, I could only see several flat neon light panels affixed to a ceiling.

The pain was excruciating. I appeared to be fully conscious, back inside my body. The pain was even more intense than the stress I had experienced while unconscious in the darkness. Yes, I remembered everything. And yes, I recall believing it impossible to fathom greater torment. And yet, I was incorrect again. I wanted desperately to audibly scream, but still had no voice.

My mind was racing for relief. Through the haze, I remembered discovering new tools to deal with this. "Concentrate!" It brought me tremendous comfort to hear the echo. I greatly hoped that these tools were legitimate and that they would work in this fully conscious environment. "Focus!"

It was difficult to center myself amidst the agony. Step One, receive the gift. I quickly accepted the present. I was alive, and I was in pain. That was easy.

As horrible as it was, the massive pain was my present. Step Two, exploration. Discovery. Investigation. The pain was relentless. Concentrate! Examine the present. Focus! Examine the moment. Where was I? What or who was causing the pain? And where was it coming from? What was in the present? Stay Focused!

Astonishingly, the tools kicked in. Progressive time slowed, and then nearly stopped. I was then aware of the pain, but it didn't appear to adversely affect me at this speed. This provided me a unique opportunity to take in my surroundings and explore the details. Things that I used to overlook or take for granted — you know…details.

My eyes still had complete freedom and even my neck could slightly move. The room was bright. Reflective and glaring. This was clearly a hospital-type facility. Everything identifiable in the room was mechanical and sterile. So much metal. So many machines. Cold. Antiseptic. Most of the machines didn't appear to attach or connect to anything. This was a hospital! I was in a plane crash, and this was a hospital.

The room was small. Or smaller than I otherwise imagined it to be. The ceiling was fairly close to my face, which indicated that I was suspended in an elevated state. The unimpressive white, flat, foam, rectangular ceiling tiles connected to even cheaper-looking plastic, frosted, rectangular sheets, which covered florescent, white, ultraviolet tube lights.

There were other people in the room. They appeared to be under me. As I craned my neck ever so slightly, to take in the room below, several things happened. First, the people, who were virtually motionless a moment ago, began moving at a normal pace. And second, my movement seemingly caused an inordinate amount of shooting pain. The source appeared to emanate from multiple places throughout my body, and apparently, the slightest bit of movement in this environment was wrought with searing agony.

Slowing time back down, and remaining still, eased the pain. And my vantage point had improved. Apparently they moved me a few inches adjusting my angle. I could see more of the room. These individuals were likely medical personnel, or technicians. Not floating orbs. These were whole human beings.

Complete with heads, torsos, and all their respective appendages. My cognitive abilities were much clearer. I was awake. Everything about this experience was real. It was substantial. This new environment was reality. This tangibility was the present. I was a patient, being treated in a hospital. But I couldn't get off this device. I reasoned that my injuries must have been considerable.

Once again, I allowed time to resume at a more normal speed. These attendants seemed to be part of the machinery. They didn't pay much attention to me. Their movements as well as their intentions appeared to be mechanical. While they looked human, they could have been robots or androids for all I knew. I concluded this wasn't an illusion, and I wasn't in a science fiction movie. These were people. Human beings. And this was unmistakably a medical facility of some kind. I counted three rather large muscular male figures, completely adorned in white uniforms, white gloves, white masks, and sky-blue skullcaps. In addition, there were two female attendants, or nurses, wearing similar medical protective gear. Remaining still, the pain was tolerable.

Just then, the two females and one of the larger males removed their masks and gloves, deposited them into a large plastic blue barrel and exited the room without a word. The two remaining males continued to perform seemingly monotonous tasks on random equipment throughout the room. While they worked, I remained suspended, wet, and bitterly cold. Staying completely and utterly motionless was the only way to avoid the seemingly intolerable waves of pain. This was my present. This was my discovery. I was a patient in a medical facility. I was severely injured. Motion caused pain. Stillness provided relief.

Taking further advantage of the calm reprieve, I continued my investigation. Aside from my cognitive awareness, my other senses seemed to have also returned. Which meant that my brain and nervous system were functioning. Additionally, the ability to receive pain, while agonizing, meant my spinal cord was most likely intact and functioning. A silver lining perhaps, all things considered. And then I recalled, only moments earlier, being submerged in warm water, and feeling immense pleasure. Accessing that recent memory, I was reminded, "everything is here in the present." If I could figure out how to utilize those other tools, recollection of the water would provide a decent shelter.

Then, one of the orderlies covered me with a blanket. Instantly, I was raptured with shooting pain throughout my body. Thankfully, it passed quickly. Stillness once again minimized my suffering, and I was grateful for the warmth the cloth provided. The cold had been agonizing. I was frustrated with my apparent lack of control over outside influences, which hampered my ability to remain focused. This was a serious consideration regarding dominion over my life, especially during this period of reprogramming. "Concentrate!"

Remaining as still as possible allowed me to continue my exploration of the present. While my external movement was restricted, my internal muscles could flinch and contract. I slightly wiggled all ten of my fingers, all ten of my toes, and flexed the muscles in my arms, legs, forehead, cheeks, chest, shoulders, and neck. I could feel the soft fabric on the skin of my forearms and thighs. Interestingly, this minor flinching and flexing didn't cause any severe pain, only slight discomfort. Certain areas of my body appeared numb, as if there were gaps in my nervous system. I conjectured that knowledge of those gaps would provide useful information later. At that time, it was merely noted.

Thankfully, all five senses had returned. Vision, hearing, and touch were obviously functional. Additionally, my olfactory sense had also been restored. Everything smelled like sterile cotton. It wasn't good. It wasn't bad. It was simply dull and muted. However, in the absence of any scent at all, this was a welcome cognizance. Taste was also revived, and it was awful, stale, and metallic. My throat muscles were operating. I could swallow. My mouth and jaw were virtually immobile, yet my tongue did have movement. I was clearly alive.

My mouth, like my nose, appeared full or stuffed with metal and plastic, limiting my tongue's normal range of motion. Surprisingly, these modest self-manipulations of my tongue, eyes, and muscles, did not cause tremendous pain as opposed to the sudden jolts or even minute movement created by outside forces. The present was accepted and being investigated. Conclusions were being drawn. While these extrapolations seemed arbitrary, they were not trivial.

Relative time meant little while I was unconscious. I had no idea that four days had already transpired between the written interaction with the heads and waking up in the water therapy room. During that time, several important things had occurred. From the doctor's perspective it was an enormous milestone for me to engage in those written communications. However, within mere hours of those scribblings, my vital signs rapidly deteriorated. Despite my receptivity, the medical staff was compassionately convincing my mother to let me go. Remember, based on the totality of my injuries, my limited responsiveness, and the statistics regarding aviation accident survival rates, all indications pointed to my inevitable and imminent demise. Based on their programming, it would be cruel to continue keeping me alive artificially.

Unbeknownst to them, I had made a monumental decision. I chose life. Specifically, life with purpose. Internally, upon crossing the threshold, I began my own arduous, slow, meticulous process of self-healing. It required erasing all my prior programming. Survival depended on removal of all doubt. Trying was not an option. Success required absolute certainty and confidence. A person can survive a plane crash.

I resolved to put myself back together, from the inside. I started by slowly controlling my heart rate and blood flow — steadying my breathing. Adrift on a metaphorical raft I followed my arteries and veins throughout my body, cleansing my plasma, tossing out contaminants, infections, and waste. I visualized repairing broken vessels and arteries. However, echoes of my prior indoctrination continually fought with me. It required strict discipline. Surfacing thoughts of illogic and impossibility were continually purged, like viruses from defective software. Calmly applying focus, concentration, and discipline, I continued to heal.

The medical staff was astonished by my seemingly miraculous recovery and attributed it to either an "act of God" or "pure luck." Regardless, acknowledging my turn around, they decided to change their approach from a passive hospice-type care to an active intensive surgical and rehabilitative regiment. This included almost daily surgeries, organ repair, suturing, and skin grafting. They also began water submersion therapy to cleanse my wounds, exercise my muscle atrophy, and stimulate my autonomic systems. Without knowing it, and in spite of their programming, we were working in tandem.

Upon waking up in the water, beginning my third week in the hospital, I instantly recognized the biggest obstacle was extrapolating how much control I had over the outside world. Internal, psychological control was one thing, but outside forces were another. Having only the whispers to guide me I was hoping more information was forthcoming. It was a little daunting having to relearn everything myself. Amazingly, I received a new message. But it wasn't a whisper. It was rather a concise thought "no restrictions." The idea filled me. Motivated me. Could I write an utterly new program with no restrictions? My memories, past and future, were all still with me, in the present, as well as everything I had experienced in the painful darkness. It wasn't all an illusion. In the present I accepted my surroundings, and my abilities, and rejected antiquated restrictions and limitations. But logically there had to be some limitations. I surmised that I would figure them out as I went along. Interacting with outside elements, opinions, forces, and stimuli presented an interesting challenge especially the influences still based on arcane principles and philosophies. Regardless, the resonance of that new message propelled me forward with "no restrictions." Imagine that — life, without limitations.

✣ ✣

Back in the water therapy room, affixed to that machine, my investigation was interrupted when the suspension device abruptly shifted, sending shockwaves through me. Again, I was set aflame by an outside stimulus! The machine jerked, as the device swung me around tilting my body forward, and upward slightly, revealing my lower extremities and facilitating a bird's-eye view of the room. Slowing time again, successfully easing the pain, allowed me an opportunity to better take in my surroundings.

I was covered and wrapped from the neck down in an off-white cotton blanket. While I couldn't see my flesh, I appeared intact. In my periphery, to my right, I could see the shiny silver metallic tub that I was in moments ago. It was much less impressive than I had imagined. Curiously, I wondered about my appearance. If only I could catch a glimpse of my reflection. Any attempts to unwrap the cloth were thwarted by my artificial constraints. Apparently this environment still possessed limitations. I was also quickly reminded that the slightest physical undertaking delivered maddening shockwaves. I was exerting considerable effort to remain motionless.

Then the mechanism lurched again. The pain snapped me back into real time. I screamed inside my head. No one could hear me. I struggled against my bonds, yet there was no reprieve. I was overwhelmed by conscious pain, and there was seemingly no escape. I was frantically searching the present for any salvation. The radiance became unbearable, and everything suddenly went black.

In what felt like an instant, I blinked or was reawakened by another wave of shooting pain. I have no idea how long I had been unconscious. However, it didn't appear to be that lengthy a respite because I was still suspended, affixed to that machine, which was abruptly lowering me down and over onto a table. Every aspect of that experience was torturous. There was no peace. I was unable to slow time. There were no moments of stillness. No place to hide. There was nothing to hang onto. The pain was just too much. Scrambling to find my safe harbors, I blacked out again.

That time I must have been out slightly longer, because when the torrential painful electricity-like jolt woke me up, I was on my back being adjusted onto a soft padded table, by muscular human arms and hands. As my vision refocused, I was still in the water therapy room next to the long mechanical swing-arm, only a few feet away. I simply was no longer attached to it.

The only distraction from the agonizing movements were my observations. Lying on my back, with my head slightly elevated, I was able to see more of this makeshift gurney. Curiously, there was a metal apparatus above me, suspending my legs in the air. The mobile table had metal bars raised on each side, like a baby's crib, to which my arms and hands were affixed, completely restraining me. While the medical minions worked on securing the portable bed, every bump, jolt, and touch sent me reeling in agony. Not being afforded the ability to breathe freely, there was never an opportunity to exhale or relax. The pain was also exhausting. And once again, everything went black.

The motion of the medical bed shocked me back to consciousness. My internal screams were replaced by uncontrolled sobbing. I longed for a moment's peace. Yearning for stillness. Any chance to reorient myself and escape to safety. Without focus, my attempts to augment time failed. "Please," I begged God, The Universe, or any Higher Power that would listen. "Please, just stop moving!"

Instead, my pleadings were ignored and unanswered. The gurney bounded down the hallway, unabated. Wheels bouncing and careening wildly. I felt every single crack and crevasse in the uneven floor tiles. And with every moment, of every moment, of every moment, shockwaves of searing, fiery pain engulfed my entire essence.

I tried to accept the present and take in my surroundings. The hallway appeared devoid of other life. Staying focused was momentarily working. More details. The ceiling was a patterned mixture of more uninteresting white foam rectangles, separated by endless rows of flat, frosted, plastic florescent lights. Sadly, the pain obfuscated my investigation. Observing the present was not going to be enough. It simply wasn't providing sufficient relief. I concluded that these outside forces were never going to stop. No one was coming to save me. It was entirely up to me. I closed my eyes. Thankfully, my whisper returned. "Focus!" I wasn't going to let them beat me. "Everything is here in the present." A shockwave forced my eyes open. The pain was overpowering. And, once more, blackness.

This period of darkness was different. I wasn't unconscious. And there was virtually no pain. Amazingly, I was inside my body. Specifically, I was inside my heart muscle. I was rhythmically being pacified by its steady beating. Apparently, I had used the memory of self-healing to get back inside. Focus! No restrictions. This wasn't a memory. I was living in real time. I was aware of the pain outside. I was aware of the hospital, and even the hallway. The outer noises were distant and stifled. Muffled. So much pain out there.

In the darkness, I concentrated on the soothing tempo of my pulse. It was working. I was calm. I was safe. Fascinatingly, in the present, I could exist intellectually within the confines of my mind, past and future, and also, within my physical body. That was new.

Within the darkness, I witnessed a massive shockwave of pain try to snatch me back outside. Instead of avoiding or dodging it, I embraced it, absorbing it, allowing it to dissipate in a river of plasma and energy. Then, I merely released the residue as I exhaled. Evidently, I could exhale in here. That was also new. I no longer questioned how I was doing it, or if it was even possible. I merely accepted that I could do it. And succeeded in the process. Until I saw the waves of pain no longer being inflicted, I refused to go back outside.

Restrictions and limitations? I had to accept that I could only control my own thoughts, emotions, and feelings. Apparently, I had no control over the outside elements and forces. While my physical body bounced over every pothole in that hellish hospital hallway, I remained secure in my internal sanctuary, focusing on my breathing and the mollifying rhythm of my slowed heartbeat and assuasive blood flow. Additionally, I used that period in the darkness to continue to heal.

※※※

And then suddenly, all was suspended. Time, space, everything, everywhere. Intriguingly, the spatial anomaly wasn't generated by me. I was overcome by a powerful presence. All around me. Everywhere! Something, someone, or some great entity had paused time. I had experienced similar feelings on a few rare occasions throughout my life, but never to this degree. This was way more intense that the whispers and messages. And on some level I had attributed them to being self-generated – like my conscience. This spoke directly to my faulty programming. I had been incorrect about so many things. This was bigger than anything I had ever experienced. This wasn't coming from me. This was being given to me. This was extreme. Almost indescribable. The closest comparison would be pure energy, like a massive rush of adrenaline, simultaneously infused with an overwhelming sensation of love.

And most importantly, there was one more element. There was an intellectual component as well. Information, or new coding, was provided. I didn't see a person or hear a voice. I just knew the information. For one thing, I knew I was being taken care of. I wasn't alone. I have never been, and would never be, alone. I also knew that, despite my desire or instinct, I did not need to control every aspect of my recovery and reprogramming. I didn't know where this information came from. I merely knew it to be true. The source seemed important. I couldn't quite put my finger on it.

Everyone wakes up at their own pace. I was no different. And the most important, comforting, knowledge conveyed was that all my questions would be answered when I was ready.

I opened my eyes. Time appeared to have resumed its typical forward progression. In my stillness, the pain outside had subsided. Largely because my body was no longer moving. I wasn't on a gurney anymore. I was resting on a stationary bed, in a modestly lit private room. Two male attendants and a slender female nurse exited the room and turned out the overhead light. I was alone. Alone with my thoughts. And yet, comfortingly, I knew I wasn't alone.

My physical body was finally at rest. Immobilized and restrained. Although I was still unaware of the extent of my physical injuries, my mind was at ease. This was the present. The moment. My gift. I had chosen life. And here I was, having just experienced something paranormal, unexplainable, and glorious. Moving forward, I knew for certain that each present contained that unexplained, reassuring energy source, as well as internal, external, emotional, and intellectual components. All equally important.

I was exhausted. I was at peace. I closed my eyes, drifting off to sleep, piecing together how I got here and accepting that there was a tremendous amount of work ahead of me. For the first time in weeks, I slept.

~~~~~~ ~~~~~~

Cerebrally, I was still unaware of the events that transpired during those first three weeks since the accident. My only memories were internal, from my semi-conscious perspective. Many of the details were not revealed with specificity or accuracy for years.

After my father leveled us off, coming out of the nosedive, I was still hugging the cockpit seatback. I could feel the bottom of the plane cascade across the treetops. We continued to descend rapidly. Branches forcefully collided with all sides of the aircraft. Huge leaves smashed into the front windshield. Still descending. I snuck a peak and watched the glass crack in several places. I turned away again, burying my head into the seat's headrest. That was the last thing I remember before being cast into darkness. Unconscious! Black!

My father never turned away. He had never given up. Once leveling off, he continued to navigate our Piper Navajo Chieftain's uncontrolled descent into the Florida everglades, three miles short of the Jacksonville Municipal Airport runway. Our small twin-turbo-engine craft, call sign L-5-9-W-F-T, shredded into pieces as it rocketed through the trees tearing the wings clean off. When it finally came to rest, that last jolt cleanly separated the nose, containing the cockpit, from the rear passenger cabin.

My father, who was firmly seated in the pilot's chair suffered whiplash, dying instantly upon that final impact. His body passed through the flimsy seatbelt, and he remained face down against the dashboard, half afloat in the marshy swamp. Rain and wind poured down on his pale corpse through the newly created opening that separated the cockpit from the main cabin.

Because of my awkward position, twisted, half-turned and hugging the seat, upon that same impact, I was flung forward by massive gravitational forces, also piercing through my flimsy seat belt, toward the control panel. However, because I was not seated properly, forward facing in my chair, instead of suffering whiplash like my dad, my head and upper torso snapped around quickly, smashing my chin, not the top of my skull, into the cockpit dashboard, completely shattering my jaw and cracking more than two-thirds of my teeth.

The stopping-force recoil then violently whipped me backward, up, and out of the newly formed opening in the ceiling and tossed me like a rag doll approximately sixty yards behind the wreckage, through the dense shrubbery and across the marsh. Before exiting the craft, my hands, feet, and legs were exposed to several quarts of scorching hot oil that erupted from the cracked fuselage and was violently dispersed.

Also, upon my abrupt exit, a huge chunk of my left leg was carved out, between my knee and ankle, by the sharp metal instrument panel. As my limp body flew through the air it was miraculous that my head did not ricochet off a tree trunk or get decapitated by a spear-like branch. Traversing the mire, I did incur scores of minuscule cuts from the dense trees, shrubbery, vines, leaves, and branches. The mud that I ultimately landed in saved my life by acting as a coagulating agent, sealing, and impacting my wounds, preventing me from bleeding out. The soft soil even soothed many of my harshest oil burns.

Thankfully, when my body came to rest, it did so face up. Had I landed facedown, I most likely would have drowned, or at the very least suffocated. Also, the thick dense foliage, large palms, and oversized banana leaves, provided protection from the tropical cyclone conditions.

Because of my incessant and continual radio squawking, up until our terminal descent, Emergency First Responders easily triangulated and pinpointed our wreckage within the thick murky swamp. Storm conditions delayed any rescue attempt for approximately three hours. Isidore's trajectory had once again changed, as she reversed back northwest towards the Gulf of Mexico, up and over to the Florida panhandle. As soon as the weather dissipated enough, a medical evacuation helicopter arrived on scene with four of the most capable, heroic, and professional first responders ever to don the uniforms.

They hovered over the wreckage, unable to find an adequate clearing to safely land. Two of the paramedics lowered themselves down a retractable cable into the crash site, while the pilot and a third emergency medical technician remained on board. The pilot was utilizing all his years of Air Force training and practical experience to keep his bird steady amidst the unpredictable winds and sporadic rain. Even though the strongest gusts were moving away, storm conditions remained hazardous.

Inside the wreckage, or what was left of our crumpled tin-can, the paramedics performed emergency rescue triage. One para-emergency medical technician noticed my father lying face down in the mud, leaning against the cockpit dashboard. The other swore he heard me crying out, wailing in pain, moaning, from about a football field's distance, through the dense foliage. Double checking my dad's vitals, and confirming his expiration, they both decided to leave him for the moment and attempt to locate and rescue me.

Without missing a beat these two heroes went into action. One of them switched on his helmet flashlight and took out a machete-like blade and trudged off into the shallow marsh in the direction of my groans. The other, reattached himself to the dangling cable and was carried up, just above the tree canopy to improve his searchable vantage position. Within minutes the EMT on the ground found me. His companion dropped down to assist.

Instantaneously, the cable retracted, and almost as quickly as it rose, it reappeared with an emergency orange and blue rescue stretcher attached. With the precision and skill of their collective years of training they masterfully secured me to the stretcher for extraction. Once we were all back on their craft, the three of them looked at each other, and then back through the dense branches and massive trees. In the far-off distance, they could see shiny metal fragments of our wreckage. They could not believe the distance I had traveled – up, out, and through the trees. To their collective astonishment, I was still alive.

They then returned to the crash site to retrieve my dad. On the way, the remaining EMT was reviewing notes on a clipboard, evaluating me for his report. The other two were already back outside dangling from the cable on their way down. Moments later they brought up my father's lifeless body and rested it against the back wall of the copter's cabin. After everyone was on board the pilot asked for the "all clear." The EMT with the clipboard requested thirty more seconds to capture a few last photographic images of the site. He utilized his handheld thirty-five-millimeter camera and flashed a few last aerial pictures of the wreckage.

Pocketing the camera in his jacket side-pouch, the medic secured the side copter door. The other two EMTs were already strapped in and double-checked that my stretcher was properly fortified to the base-plate hooks. Tapping loudly on the back of the cockpit chair, "All clear, let's return to base!" The pilot simply responded in a monotone voice, "roger that." And the copter rose quickly, swiveled one-hundred-eighty degrees, banked left, and departed the scene.

Everyone in the helicopter was lost in thought. Breaking the silence, the EMT who retrieved my father inquired as to my condition. The medic with the clipboard had a penlight in his mouth and was shining it into each of my eyes. He slid the small torch into one of his jacket pockets and responded, "two bodies recovered. one male, Caucasian, mid-forties, found dead, on scene. Body bagged and tagged. One male, Caucasian, teen, alive, vitals weak, non-responsive, in shock, multiple contusions, burns, lacerations, and abrasions..." He then paused and glanced back out the window at the wreckage site getting further away in the distance.

The medic with the clipboard re-read the next question to himself, "Condition Upon Hospital Arrival?" He then looked up at the pilot, his commanding officer, who he could clearly see in profile from across the cabin, and asked, "how long until we get to JMH?" The pilot responded, "touchdown in less than seventeen minutes." They looked at each other knowingly, as the helicopter speed accelerated. The medic looked down at me, observing the extent of my injuries. He simply marked an "X" in the box labeled D.O.A. Which in layman terms meant that even though I was alive when they found me, by the time we disembarked at the hospital, he assumed that I would be "Dead on Arrival."

Thankfully, I did not die on arrival. Even more gratefully, Memorial Hospital Jacksonville was one of the best, top-rated trauma hospitals in the United States, if not the world. Triage decisions were made with split-second fastidiousness on a daily basis. As I was wheeled into the Emergency Room, the attending emergency surgical assistant had an amputation saw in his hand, next to several sterile tables occupied with neat rows of precision tools, positioned close to my supine body.

They moved me into the center of the room, under hanging lights. Several additional nurses were already busy cutting away the remnants of my sweatpants, tee-shirt and underwear, applying oxygen, fluids, and anesthesia. The assistant was still awaiting instructions from the chief surgeon in the room. Out of respect, no inquiry was ever spoken out loud, however, everyone in the Emergency Room was in suspense, simultaneously wondering, "What are we waiting for?"

The chief surgeon, Doctor Harold Johnson, did a number of calculations, taking in the totality of my injuries and my circumstances. Drawing on seven years of military medical field training coupled with eleven years of trauma surgery, he responded with a one-word answer, "No," while simultaneously placing his hand gently on the attending physician's arm containing the saw. This immediately paused the room's call to action. The pungent odor and greenish-yellow color of my wounds clearly indicated massive infection.

The Chief surgeon addressed his assistant, "We're not going to amputate. Let's open up a trach, get an N.G.T. started, clean him up, and open up the chest cavity to stop any internal bleeding." The assistant didn't question the chief's instructions, and Johnson was never one to explain himself. Technical operating procedural instructions, or orders, with specified doses and amounts were quickly called out by the chief. For posterity, he added, "we'll patch him up, keep him alive, and as comfortable as possible, for whatever time he has left."

As additional storm and unrelated trauma patients continued to arrive, filling adjacent tables and rooms, it was ultimately the chief surgeon's triage decisions over life and death. All his years of experience, and his jaded programming, led him to a similar conclusion reached by the para-rescue EMT, that airplane crash victims, suffering the extent of my injuries, do not survive. And even if their bodies miraculously endured for a short stint, terminal brain damage was a certainty. My case was an easy assessment. I was a disaster. My vitals were low, and I had lost a tremendous amount of blood. All my major organs had failed, or were in shock, except for my heart and brain. I was catatonic and riddled with infection. If the decision had been to aggressively try to save me, both legs, my left arm, and my right eye would have been amputated immediately.

He had other patients to save. He would honor his duty as well as his Hippocratic Oath, and "do no harm." Based on his indoctrination, and an overwhelming sense of compassion, he just wanted me to be as comfortable as possible, in the short time he calculated I had remaining. He verbalized his conclusion to his younger assistant and the nurses present, "It was a plane crash for God's sakes. He's only a little kid. I'm not going to hack him up into pieces forcing the family to have a closed casket..." He paused, displaying an atypical, momentary exposition of emotion, rarely shown to his subordinates, "...this is someone's baby." He quickly collected himself and went to work cutting me open.

As Dr. Johnson observed, all my vital organs had stopped functioning, with the exception of my brain and my heart. One lung was punctured by a broken rib, while the other lung had collapsed requiring the need for an artificial respirator. Many of my other organs required reparative surgery, stimulation, minor suturing, or were bypassed by various mechanical devices and tubes. Both of my legs were mangled and much of the flesh exposed. My left forearm was also crushed and torn open. My left eardrum was ruptured. My jaw was completely shattered, exposing the flesh and bone underneath. My right eyeball had become dislodged from its socket and showed no responsive cognitive function.

After working on me for several hours, the head nurse observed, "He's stabilized, Doctor."

Dr. Johnson responded, deadpan, "Close for me. We stave off infection and keep him alive as best we can." His words hung in the air. He glanced at the vast machinery surrounding me, "I don't know how he is still with us. It'll be a miracle if this kid is still alive in the morning...or even at the end of my shift." He was led away by a nurse to tend a gunshot-wound victim brought in on an adjacent table.

※※※

Meanwhile, in Melville, Long Island, my mother received the call. Without even packing an overnight bag, she left work and caught the last commuter flight out of New York's John F. Kennedy Airport to Jacksonville. She arrived at the hospital in the early evening with a friend who came with her for support. On her way into the intensive care unit, adjacent to the emergency room, she was verbally being prepared by an attending ER nurse to "expect the worst."

No parent can ever be prepared for what my mom witnessed. My body was on display in the intensive care unit adjacent to the Emergency Operating Room. I was attached to a seemingly endless array of lifesaving machinery. My mother, still trembling in shock, with her open hand covering her mouth, blurted out, "Okay, I can identify him. That's Ronnie, my husband. Where's my son?" She continued looking around, searching for other operating tables. Apparently, the airplane crash, the shock, the fluids, the injuries as well as the several hours of surgery, had inflated my hundred-and-twenty-pound adolescent body to the swollen appearance of my two-hundred-ten-pound father.

The nurse calmly corrected, "Ma'am, this isn't your husband."

However, my mom rejected that information, "No-no-no, that's Ronnie." She studied my face. If it wasn't her husband, it had to be... "No. No. No, no, no. That's not..." she trailed off finding it difficult to breath.

"Ma'am, can you identify him? Is this your son?" the attendant gently reiterated.

My mom refocused and was now able to see remnants of my face through the bandages, tubes, and wires. It was me. Her son. Her baby. Her mangled baby.

She couldn't breathe. Her legs gave out. Both the friend that brought her to the hospital and the nurse caught her, holding her upright.

"Ma'am," The nurse asked again in the calmest, gentlest voice, already knowing the answer by my mom's reaction, "can you identify him?" My mom was sobbing and nodded affirmatively. The nurse paused. She needed to hear it verbally for her medical records.

In a barely audible crackle, beneath pangs of anguish, my mom replied, "yes, that's..." and her voice trailed off. My mother stumbled backwards and collapsed into a nearby wooden chair, crying, trying desperately to catch her breath. Another nurse came over after a few minutes and led her back out to the nurse's station. Eventually, she made her way downstairs to the basement morgue to identify my father's body, after which she returned to the ICU waiting room and sat by a window, staring out into the night in disbelief, unable to stop shaking.

Early the next morning, at the conclusion of a marathon twenty-hour shift, the chief surgeon, Dr. Johnson, brought my mother a cup of black coffee. He confessed his surprise that I had survived the night. He explained that due to the severity of my condition, the extenuating circumstances of my trauma, compounded by my unresponsiveness, that should I somehow survive, at best I would be rendered a vegetative invalid. He further explained that due to the multitude of my lacerated and exposed nerve endings, that I was most likely suffering immeasurable pain. Statistically, my limited quality of life and outlook were dreadful. In his opinion, the most humane thing to do was to continue providing sustenance, both intravenously and nasogastrically, along with anesthesia, while simultaneously disconnecting all the life-saving machines and allowing me to peacefully pass away.

Having nothing but a mother's instinct, hope and prayer, and perhaps desperation, she decided not to "pull the plug." She refused to sign any order that would aide in the euthanization of her son. She clarified, "Doctor, you do whatever you have to do to keep him alive! As long as you God damn well can!" She exhaled, and continued weeping.

He shrugged and nodded, as if to nonverbally indicate, "okay." Dispassionately, he turned to go clean up after a long grueling day in the E.R.

Pleadingly, choking back tears, my mom softly added, "Please!"

He turned his head, and this time audibly replied, "okay." Taking in my mother's devastation, and despair, he stopped, exhaled, nodded his head affirmatively and loudly repeated, "okay!" He then continued walking away, disappearing through two oversized Emergency Room doors, leaving her alone in the waiting area.

Sixteen days later, and after scores of minor medical procedures, an attending physician called for my mother to come to my bedside, with a sense of urgency and excitement. Up until this point, I had been completely unresponsive. The personnel from the Intensive Care Unit, clinging to their misguided notions regarding the limits of the universe, were amazed that I was still alive. Granted, at the time, I was completely dependent on the machinery. They couldn't comprehend the possibility that I was also keeping myself alive internally.

During these difficult two weeks, my mom had been sleeping on a cot, next to my hospital bed. I was moved into a room alongside the ICU, just outside of the main Emergency Room area. Every day, she would leave for only a few hours, take a shower at a flea-ridden cheap motel, grab a bite to eat, and then walk back to the hospital just down the street. Her sleep in the hospital was never easy and always interrupted. Twice during these first two weeks, exhausted and despondent, she seriously contemplated suicide by swallowing prescription painkillers with sleeping pills. Thankfully, she failed to see these attempts through to fruition.

On the sixteenth day after the crash, one of the nurses found my mom getting off the elevator, returning from her motel. The nurse's demeanor could only be described as both excitement and bewilderment, as she hurriedly led my mom back to my room. Just outside the door, they were met by the attending physician, who exclaimed, "I don't believe it, but he's responsive."

Just the day before, this same doctor was consoling her, encouraging her to temper her enthusiasm, and again strongly consider euthanization. He too was baffled. He was having trouble reconciling a conclusion that was counter to his programming. Defending his position for the past two weeks, he elucidated that in his experience, after years at this prestigious trauma facility, "plane crash survivors, even if they are able to regain consciousness, due to the severity of their head traumas, are most assuredly rendered in a vegetative state." His only offered explanation was divine intervention.

In his befuddlement, he handed her two pieces of paper containing barely legible chicken scratch, reading, "Am I dead?" and "Does it work?" My mom placed her coffee cup down on the nurse's station counter and followed the doctor to my bedside. Two other nurses, both audibly chuckling behind their surgical face masks, followed them in. They formed a semicircle around me.

My mother looked down at me and saw that I was awake. She caressed my hand gently. I blinked up at her, glossy eyed. She noticed that I was moving my hand in a circular motion. One of the giggling nurses, who understood my pantomime, placed a pencil in my hand and slipped a piece of paper under my fingers. After a moment of me scratching on the bedsheet my mother picked up the note that read, in barely legible, all capital scribbled letters, the one-word-question, "DAD?"

She looked at me, lovingly, and not having the heart to tell me the tragic news said, "Yes, he's fine. He's in the other room resting. He's not strong enough to get up right now. But you'll see him soon." With that, she grabbed my hand with hers and squeezed, as I drifted back into an anesthetized haze.

As elated as she was to see me awake, the doctor reverted back to his flawed conditioning, encouraging caution. Still in denial, he tempered his own enthusiasm and pointed out that I was far from "out of the woods." He issued an additional warning regarding, "not yet knowing the full extent of the brain trauma," and, reminded her of the "magnitude of my other injuries."

Despite his guarded counsel my mom was relieved that I did not appear to be imbecilic. This was her sign, affirming that she had made the correct decision.

The following afternoon, she was visited by Dr. Johnson, who confessed to also being mystified. Not just because I was finally responsive, and seemingly coherent, but amazingly, over just these last twenty-four hours, my body inexplicably began to heal. About an hour after I wrote those notes, my vitals dramatically deteriorated. And yet, only moments after that, I miraculously re-stabilized, and then astonishingly, began showing signs of improvement. Having no other medical explanation, he chalked it up to youth, strength, genetics, and luck. His denial and conditioning forced him to further caution her against being overzealous. He pointed out that in addition to my physical injuries, I was still contending with a massive infection.

The craziest thing which worked out to my benefit was his new strategy. Because I was cognitively responsive and inexplicably showing progress, he suggested a more aggressive, proactive approach, which included an invasive surgical reparative regiment, along with an intensive water therapy treatment to both cleanse my wounds and stimulate other bodily functions.

He then confided in my mother that if I were able to make a full recovery, I would be a case study for years to come. Almost as though automated, he repeated the phrase that my mother had now heard *ad nauseam*, "No one survives these types of airplane crashes, especially with the magnitude of his injuries."

My mother, for the first time, questioning her own preconditioning, had a fleeting thought, "It's no wonder that people do not survive these types of traumas because, apparently, no one believes that you can."

In my hospital bed, back in the present, my restful sleep was interrupted. My eyes shot open in abject terror. I was suffused in perspiration. I was on fire, yet I had chills. Instead of waking from a peaceful slumber, my subconscious had infused corrupted elements from my deep-rooted faulty conditioning and morphed my physical and emotional pain into a perpetual nightmare. Apparently, I was unsuccessful in erasing my darkest fears and anxieties. Where I required confidence, I still had skepticism. And while anesthetized, I was completely distracted and unable to concentrate. Drugged, and in pain, it was extremely difficult to focus on healing, and even more difficult to find consolation within my shelters.

I was instantly afforded a new epiphany. Once again, I had been grossly mistaken. It was impossible to delete my brainwashing. I was not a computer. Everything was here in the present. Everything included my faulty programming and all my mistakes, errors, and regrets. None of it could be erased. It was up to me to learn to accept them and live with them. My learning curve was going to be steep. My journey was going to be harder than anticipated.

Also, I had not considered the deleterious effects of the massive painkillers being pumped into me. Having never done this before, how could I? And, having only been fully conscious for a brief fraction of time, I wasn't even aware that I was being intoxicated. In retrospect, I'm told that all this was administered for my own good. So much outside programming. So much outside conditioning. So much was constantly being imposed on me. Perhaps it always was and always will be.

For my part, I could no longer see past the pain. I knew there was good stuff on the other side, but the pain was too much to bear. My new tools and all of this wonderful information I had just received...didn't appear to be enough. I questioned my purpose. I quickly conceded, having made a terrible mistake. I stared blankly at the ceiling and began to cry. Why did I choose life? Why was I being punished? What did I do that was so wrong? Why did all this happen to me? Why did I choose life?

Taking in the totality of my circumstances, as best that I understood them at the time, I was reconciling echoes of my own programming that I accepted will always be with me. I was also inundated with everyone else's predetermined anxieties and negativity. I not only had to deal with my own issues, but I was forced to confront theirs as well. I laid in bed, wide-eyed, overwhelmed by all this new information. Consciousness was a horror show. The battle between my preconditioning, everyone else's preconceptions, and my reprogramming was just beginning.

II

7

THE REGRET

Jolted awake. Sweating profusely. The past few hours had been an endless barrage of varied demonic forces, throughout numerous unrelated scenarios, filleting and boiling my flesh in acid or violently ripping the tissue from my bones. Reconciliation was impossible. My recently acquired mental supremacy was suddenly obstructed. Inaccessible. Intellectually, I knew I had these new tools but something was inhibiting them. And due to my loss of control, dreaming proved to be the worst of all paradigms.

※※※ ※※※

Unbeknownst to me, I was thrust into this new dynamic by Doctor Johnson, Chief of Surgery. He had made the clinical decision to shift from passively waiting for me to die, to aggressively working towards my recovery. This required several initiatives: concentrated reparative surgeries to assist the restart of my vital organs; massive infusion of antibiotics to fight my infections; thorough water therapy to address my muscle atrophy and cleanse my wounds; and a comprehensive anesthesia regiment, whereby I was administered powerful stimulants for twelve hours, simulating daytime, and substantial depressants for twelve hours, simulating nighttime. Additionally, because of the dangers associated with prolonged exposure to narcotics, as I physically improved, the dosages were incrementally reduced.

The twenty-four-hour artificial environment, as a whole, was frustrating, especially since I was cognitively unaware it was being administered. The forced drug-induced sleep intervals were maddening, trapping me in perpetual nightmares with no escape. Focus was nearly impossible, making it difficult to navigate safe harbors amidst the malaise. Furthermore, the pain was amplified by the weaning off pacifying medications, coinciding with the increased surgical procedures.

Additionally, the subordinate medical staff, misguided by their own faulty programming, was still convinced that I was never going to survive. According to them, I was already in a vegetative state, and thereby wasn't even mindful of my environment. They were unaware of the agony inflicted by their man-handling during wound dressing changes and water therapy. All of this was wreaking havoc on my subconscious.

Awake and motionless became my safest, least painful environment. It became apparent that the onus was mine to reconcile this new dynamic. No one was coming to save me. Capitalizing on brief moments of lucidity, successfully slowing time, I began further examining the present. It was thrilling to still have those moments, however fleeting, whereby I maintained psychological control.

I was in bed, lying on my back. Or more accurately, I was tightly secured to a bed, in a sterile hospital room, surrounded by medical equipment. There was a small color television attached to a short elbow-shaped swing-arm, suspended from the ceiling, directly across from me. A game show was on. There was no sound. Live action contestants, wearing silly costumes, were enthusiastically guessing price values for a variety of household products. The volume being off didn't add or detract from the visual stimulus. Underneath, against that same far wall, was a multitude of oversized nondescript medical devices.

A young attractive nurse with a dark complexion was dispassionately fluttering about the room, checking my vitals and performing ritualistic tasks mostly noting the functionality of the medical equipment. The slightest touch of my bed caused unbearable shockwaves. Seemingly, she didn't notice or care, possessing no apparent comprehension of my distress. Following every contact and tremor, I had to recompose myself, and resume my soothing meditation. Thankfully, she concluded her duties and exited the room, allowing me to lie still.

My head and neck were unrestrained, freely manipulatable, making it possible to take in the small room. Minimal movement facilitated small amounts of tolerable discomfort. The main door to the room was ajar. In the hallway just outside, medical personnel, adorned in light green scrubs, white uniforms, and lab coats ambled busily about. Nondescript individuals randomly hurried past, occasionally with a patient in a chair or on a roll-away bed.

To my left were several freestanding medical stances made of thin silver cylindrical metal bars bent and curved at the top adorned with hanging plastic liquid-filled sacks. Wires and tubes protruded from the sacks connecting to the nearby machinery as well as to my face, chest, arms, and hands. From my perspective it was impossible to discern associations or specific purposes. Excess plastic tubes and wires were bunched together, piled atop the blanket covering my chest and stomach. Just past the metal stand, several feet away, there was a tall wooden built-in closet.

On my right, a large picture window presented an overcast grey sky, obstructed by aged, commercial building rooftops. Underneath the window sat a full-length metal radiator. And seated adjacent to that, just below my bedrail, was my mother. My mother? Yes, it was my mom! She was peacefully asleep under a jacket in an uncomfortable looking padded wooden chair wedged between the radiator and my bed. Her legs were supported by a second chair, being exploited as a makeshift ottoman.

Utilizing my imaginary *Jedi* powers, I attempted telepathy, in the hopes of communicating "I was okay." I wished she would wake up so that we could possibly exchange some form of additional written communication. Selfish feelings of pity were replaced with compassion. If only it were possible to relay the unbounded comfort she provided, by simply being with me. I was eager to communicate my positive condition, my love for her, and my immense appreciation.

I tested my restraints and was frustrated by my tight confinement. My hands and fingers could move slightly, but my wrists were each securely fastened inside soft cuff-like shackles, firmly affixed to the protective guardrails. Shaking them only caused the bed to vibrate, delivering painful tremors throughout my body. Both escape and communication would have to wait.

Curiously, there was a bulky metal apparatus elevating and suspending my left leg. One long metal bar was attached to the headboard and footboard and jutted up about four feet high, extending over the length of my body. There were two additional metal support rods on each side of the bed, connecting to that one long bar. All four of those support posts were angled and met at the top, above my lower region. My left leg was bent at the knee, with my calf-section elevated, and attached to a long horizontal bar by two short vertical metal dowels, about twelve inches apart. The dowels disappeared inside the bandaged limb. My left leg below the knee hung in the air above the covers, bandaged and suspended firmly, immobilized by the two dowels. The suspension caused my left thigh to partially protrude, uncovered by the blanket. Internally, I could feel my left leg, foot, and toes, but movement was impossible.

At the end of the bed, my left foot, only partially covered in bandages, was also being supported by an additional strap, and my naked toes were fixed, pointing upward.

My right leg was under the covers, also immobilized and secured in some unseen way, and elevated slightly by what felt like several foam pillows.

My self-exploration was harshly interrupted, and time was thrust back into progression, by the arrival of a heavy-set dark-skinned female attendant carelessly crashing into my bed. She was wearing green scrubs and pushing a rectangular cloth bin, filled with stacks of folded white cloth. The nurse was followed by a boney, caramel-skinned, assistant. They stopped on opposite sides of the bed, not taking any notice of me, and began unraveling the bandages from my suspended left leg, discarding them into an empty smaller plastic receptacle, attached to the bin's side.

The initial collision with my bed caused searing pain, sending my body into spasms. Their reckless abandon only exacerbated my agony. I struggled against my bonds. To no avail. Release was impossible. Why were they both being so rough? Why didn't my mother wake up and put a stop to this? These were outside forces I needed to contend with. Like the nightmares, there was nowhere to hide. Relief was unattainable. My heart wanted to leap out of my chest. Every fiber of my being was once again cast aflame.

While struggling, I curiously observed that the heavy-set nurse appeared angry and annoyed at me. That was odd. The perpetrator of the torture, the aggressor, was upset with me? I lashed out and tried to scream, and yet made no sound. The pain was excruciating! Twisting. Squirming. My limited movements only added to my torment. My mouth and jaw were frozen, immobilized. Inexplicably, my throat could not produce audible noise. I was unable to cry for help.

These two nurses were both aware that I was awake. They had to be able to see my eyes. Every few minutes they would look directly at me. I tried to communicate with them, using my prior, successful 'pantomime for writing' with each of my hands, making small finger swirls under the covers. If only I could have convinced them to slow down. To be more careful. However, neither of them paid any attention to my hand gestures. I could barely move. Hardly breathe. In agony. Helpless!

Although my efforts were restricted, apparently my wriggling was enough to seriously anger the beast, that I aptly nicknamed "Ogre." Our eyes met. And then she addressed me, in a thick Jamaican accent, "*All des' chaka chaka trashin' mun! Dun know ef yer ev'n en dere. Dun know ef ye cun 'ear me. But, ef ya cun-not be still, tiz gonna 'urt cha, mun, much worse.*"

"The nerve of this brute," I thought. She was insisting that I gracefully accept this torture. And she was angry with me.

In life you must face ensuing battles as presented and they are rarely struggles of your choosing. You fight the fight you are in with the army that you have. In order to survive the present circumstances, I needed to contend with these violent, uncontrollable outside elements. Coexistence was essential. Acceptance was equally essential. Having nowhere else to go, I closed my eyes, relaxed, and retreated internally. I unclenched my fists. I steadied my breathing. Felt my heart rate. Slowed my pulse. Concentrated on the sound of my blood flow. It was working. I was simultaneously aware that externally my wounds were being painfully attended too, while internally I was being pacified by my circulatory and respiratory functions.

I was safe inside which allowed my body to remain passive. Outside, my stillness appeared to assist with their dressing-change procedure. I had calmed the beasts. Or so I thought. I was hit by a sudden tremor! The unwrapping of the final bandage! My eyes popped open, violently ripping me from my inner sanctum.

Nothing could have prepared me for the excruciation associated with the cold air contacting my severed nerve endings and exposed raw flesh. With my eyes open, this was my first surveillance of the brutality of my wounds. For the briefest moment, the insufferable torment was overshadowed by my fascination with my visual observations. I was mesmerized by what I saw. My captivation inadvertently paused time, providing ample opportunity for thorough inspection.

A huge chunk of my leg, between my knee and ankle, was gone. It looked as though a butcher had sloppily carved it out. It was fascinating! The meat from my now-exposed calf muscle hung down, attached by stretched dermis membranes on each side. I could see the puss-ridden, bloody muscle and tissue, inside the remaining section of my lower leg. My smaller fibula bone was exposed and intact. However, my tibia was completely replaced by a solid dark silver metal bar connected by the two dowels which were affixed to the long overhead horizontal apparatus. My bare naked leg just hung there, elevated. An enormous portion of my lower extremity was missing. It was surreal.

Most intriguing of all, was the inadvertent time manipulation, caused by the shock of my inspection. I was mesmerized. I was subconsciously moving time at an incremental speed. My heightened awareness opened the possibility that

I could influence the progressive flow of time, even amongst outside elements. Not just internally. If I could do it by accident, I could learn to do it deliberately. I reasoned that my preconditioning regarding universal laws, and self-doubt, had hampered my progress and abilities.

While Ogre, and her sidekick, "Ghoul" boorishly finished rebandaging my left leg, I was able to maintain relative time suspension by focusing on my mom. She was surprisingly fast asleep through all this. I imagined she was overcome with exhaustion. Who knew how many sleepless nights she endured? Time and space had lost all meaning since the accident, and my undefined period of internment. Trying to communicate with her telepathically again, I attempted entry into her dreams. I desperately hoped that she was okay. If only she would have woken up, we could have corresponded again, communicating that I was lucid and alert. And together, we could have stopped those nurses from torturing me.

My attention was recaptured by the she-devils, as they began abruptly working on my right leg. Concentration was again broken, reigniting my agony. Haphazardly, they lifted my other mangled limb, jostled it about and began unwrapping it, tossing the soiled bandages into the plastic waste receptacle. Similar to my left leg, the pain was exasperating. I exerted useless energy struggling against my bonds. All attempts to audibly cry out were met with utter failure.

Ogre looked over at me, shaking her head in disgust. I did my best to calm down, as she resumed her work. Despite the pain, I resisted the temptation to find solitude internally, because the shock associated with being continually ripped out of introspection was becoming unbearable. I either had to master reclusivity or contend with external forces. Putting my pain and preconditioned skepticism aside momentarily, I resolved to work on the latter.

They both continued unraveling the bandages, revolution after revolution, tossing the used rotted cloth into the trash. This time I watched as the very last bandage was exhausted, bracing myself for the exposure of my wounds to the cold biting air. The scream inside my head could have shattered glass. They were enjoying my suffering.

Witnessing my open wound again slowed time. However, I appeared to assist in the progressive augmentation on this occasion, which meant that relative time manipulation could be intentional and not merely coincidental. I was empowered. Heightened or extreme interest somehow provided almost mystical assistance.

This time, it was facilitated by the image of my right leg, marred, open, and exposed. Yet compared to my left, it was in much better shape. A small piece of my lower calf had been torn away as well as a hunk of flesh from the back of my thigh. Additionally, the lower half of the entire extremity, including the foot, was interspersed with silver-dollar-sized third-degree oil burns. However, unlike my left, the bones in my right leg appeared intact.

In slow motion, Ogre and Ghoul worked in tandem, unwrapping my wounds, cleaning the blood and puss. They then opened endless packages of gauze bandages and began redressing my injuries. I then realized the importance of mastery of all environments in the present. Especially if I were to survive future dressing changes at the hands of these two monstrosities. The pain was insufferable.

When my right leg was finished, Ogre slid her thick, sweat soaked forelimbs underneath my body, lifting slightly, cradling me like a baby. The maneuver was met with another round of unexpected shockwaves. While I was elevated, Ghoul removed my bedsheets and replaced them with fresh ones. I would have been more grateful if not for the massive and torturous pain.

And just like that, they were gone. The stillness was intoxicating. Peaceful! I looked over at my mother, still asleep. I closed my eyes. I had wondered why no one, including her, was trying to verbally interact with me further. I could not reconcile the absence of communication. Why was no one speaking to me? Why were those two so rough? Why wasn't my own mother helping?

During that period of my recovery, everyone on the medical staff was convinced that my few prior communications were a fluke. Each time they re-examined me, I was unresponsive, due to the dramatic anesthetization. Apparently, my brief periods of lucidity never coincided with their examinations. This only hardened their resolve, reaffirming their initial conjecture, based on statistics and experience, that my injuries, resulting from blunt trauma, meant permanent, untreatable brain damage. In other words, their brainwashing prohibited them from trusting their own eyes. Furthermore, they convinced my mother that even if I physically recovered, she should be prepared for me to have unending, full-time, assisted medical care.

※※※※ ※※※※

I was adversely affected by the totality of outside influences. Doubt returned. Despair grew. I was overcome with regret and self-pity. My grief was exacerbated by my inability to communicate, coupled with the residue from that traumatic dressing change. Exhausted, yet unable to sleep. I felt an ongoing rush of stimulation, keeping me awake, but not fully conscious. My mind was obviously still working, yet the lucidity had faded. Shocking images of my marred body resonated. I was again disoriented, muddled, yet logic and reason still applied. The smallest modicum of concentration required tremendous effort, like steering a ship through dense fog. Ironically, I was grateful not to be asleep, trapped in torrential nightmares. However, I was not exactly awake either.

I closed my eyes. In my drunken stupor conjuring enough strength, I was able to focus on my respiration. Internally, I was becoming specifically aware of my oxygen inhalation. The present appeared to always contain aspects of my breathing, circulation, and cardiovascular rhythm. Relaxed and calm, I felt my lungs, heart, and blood flow. My pulse was irregular. Rapid, and then skipping a beat. After several minutes of serious application, as if by magic, it slowed and regained its typical hypnotic, steady, pace. Subsequently, I focused on my nervous system. The present also appeared to always contain aspects of brain functionality. Utilizing all three, following my spinal cord, veins, and arteries, I reached out, surveying my torso, limbs, and extremities. It wasn't easy, but I was making progress.

My fingers, arms, and elbows were free to make tactile contact with the soft cloth bedsheets. Despite the miasma, I had remarkably bridged the connection between my internal and external environments. My mind was working overtime to explore options. I needed a plan. I needed hope.

And then it dawned on me, if my wrists were freed during my period of consciousness, I could somehow acquire my mother's attention. That would be enough. I could wake her up and we could communicate. I would convey to her the horrors of my captivity and the sadistic manhandling. She would be sympathetic. These nurses would be jailed or at the very least fired. She would save me. I needed to be ready!

I tested the strength of my bonds. Wrenching both sides, I noticed my left wrist cuff was loosening. I desperately hoped it was not a figment of intoxicated imagination. Or even just wishful projection. By rocking my forearm up and down, like a lever, it appeared to be working. With each crank, the meaty part of my hand slipped further inside the cottony bracelet. With every twist, the cuff slackened. I could almost fit my whole hand through. It was working.

Then, someone entered the room. I kept my eyes closed, and remained still, fearing it was Ogre or Ghoul. If either of those evil minions observed my loosened restraints, I was certain they would thwart my efforts. I concentrated on my respiration and circulation, remaining perfectly motionless, for what felt like an eternity. I knew they were looking at me. Inspecting me. All was lost. But no! To my relief, whoever it was departed, as ominously as they had entered. I was alone again.

In my solitude, I diligently resumed working on my bonds. Before attaining freedom, to my dismay, I was overcome by exhaustion. Everything faded to black, and I was once again plunged into the darkness of another inescapable hellish post-apocalyptic vision. On this occasion, the entire planet was incinerated by a global thermal nuclear holocaust with people melting all around me. As if my daytime reality wasn't horrific enough, I was a medicated prisoner trapped in a stream of nightmares feeling the anguish of every scenario.

Over the next six days, that became my infernal cycle. The artificial daytime was mostly hazy, while the artificial nighttime was merely one long excruciating trauma. Woefully, each period came with flashes of clarity and moments of colossal physical pain. And of course the medical staff never checked on me during my moments of lucidity. They only observed me as unresponsive. During the first few days, even my self-healing was limited due to the massive anesthesia. Additionally, I was never sober enough to successfully uncouple my restraints. Intoxication was my true enemy, as it inhibited sustained focus, concentration, and adequate exploration of the present.

Disoriented, the flashes of lucidity ran the gamut between simply being uncomfortable, achy, and unpleasant, to the truly bizarre. At times the satisfying sensation of being submerged in warm water was disrupted by careless, dispassionate orderlies and the harsh exits from the soothing liquid. Other times, I was violently awakened by reckless sycophants careening my body on a table through the hallways. Yet the scariest episodes were always at the mercy of Ogre and Ghoul, enduring the unnerving violent bandage dressing changes.

On numerous occasions, I saw flashes of Ogre and Ghoul devilishly laughing at me while I writhed in agony struggling through the dark slumber. During one such semi-conscious state, I distinctly overheard the masochist, Ghoul, exclaim that I should be more appreciative since this torture was "for my own good." The only thing grounding my sanity was hope and fixation on escape.

Dejectedly, each brief interlude, when I found myself awake, lucid, and conscious, my mother was nowhere to be found.

During one of the most peculiar evenings, still sedated and lethargic, I found my right arm unrestricted. Completely free! Just like that my wrist and hand were simply unattached to any bonds. It wasn't my doing. My arm's full range of motion was limited only by the connecting wires and tubes. Regardless, my right arm was essentially uninhibited.

This was my opening to escape and get to my mom. Through my semi-conscious state, while Ogre poured acid on my left leg, I seized the opportunity and unshackled my left arm. Both hands were liberated. After ripping out my tubes and wires, I battled the monster, smashing Ogre's enormous head with my fist. But that only antagonized the creature. She lunged at me restraining my arms. I dislodged one of the safety rails on the bed and was ready to finally slay that beast, when Ghoul arrived along with several razor-toothed, fire-breathing trolls. I was no match for the demons' collective strength. I blacked out from exhaustion and was once again embroiled in another nightmare.

When I awoke the next day, I found both my arms re-restrained, tighter than before, which only stiffened my determination to take advantage of my next opportunity. If only reconnection with my mother were possible, emancipation from the clutches of Ogre and Ghoul would follow. My mom would ensure justice prevailed. The evil duo would suffer, and ultimately be replaced by kinder, gentler, and more compassionate nurses. I would be released and vindicated.

After a few days, weaning off the pain medication was a double-edged sword. On the positive side, the less intoxicated I was, the more clarity, focus, and control I possessed to concentrate on healing. However, for the nurses, this caused complications, as I reacted more violently to the increased pain during dressing changes. Additionally, for me, that increased pain exponentially exacerbated my nightmares.

On one occasion, during a late-night dressing change, I somehow wrestled both arms free, violently yanking out all my life-saving wires and tubes, and even dislodging a bar from my bed's guardrail while grappling with the nurses and orderlies. The charge nurse received a black eye after I aggressively punched her square in the face. From that night onward, my restraints were tightly secured.

Intriguingly, during the brief periods of consciousness, I noticed encouraging changes to my mother's space in the room. Her two chairs were replaced by a roll-away bed. Subsequently, I saw additional personal items on the windowsill, including a paper coffee cup, romance novel, tissues, a newspaper, reading glasses, a sweater, and a crossword puzzle. These items had to belong to my mother, however, she was never there. Was I imagining all these things? Was the memory of my mom sleeping just an aberration? No! These things were real. She was real. She was here, with me. Just never during my brief periods of sobriety. She will return! She had to. And I would be ready!

My mother in fact had moved in with me. At first, she slept on a bulky wooden chair. However, this was soon replaced by a single rollaway bed. She would leave the room during the immensely painful dressing changes for myriad reasons. Mostly, because she couldn't bear watching. Imbecilic or not, I did appear to be in immense pain during these dressing changes. However, these procedures gave her an opportunity to get some fresh air, food, and even a shower at her nearby motel. Additionally, the rancid odor from my infected wounds, when exposed, made the room unsanitary as well as eye-wateringly intolerable. Lastly, believing I was in a vegetative state removed any motivation for her to wait around for further meaningful communication.

❖❖❖

During the latter part of the week, as my intervals of clarity increased, my focus augmented from escape to healing. I reconcentrated on my respiratory, circulatory, and nervous systems, controlling my breathing, regulating my heart rate, and connecting to my five senses. I resumed exploring wounded areas of my body, preliminarily focusing on larger sections, and then becoming more targeted. I visualized these damaged areas and internally massaged and caressed them. It was calming and pleasurable to nurture each minuscule element.

This is where things took an even more inexplicable turn. Fascinatingly, at the microscopic level, I instantly began to see images of cells transforming. Dark blemishes turned into healthy colors. At first, it was difficult to reconcile what I was witnessing. Also, I wasn't certain if I was imagining it, or if I was helping to guide and control it. Because of my engrained conditioning, I again interpreted it as a strange phenomenon, or even a hallucination. I was not immune to the brainwashing effects which inhibited awareness, even when witnessing things, extraordinary things, firsthand. The challenge was reprogramming, receiving that I had the ability to self-heal.

Experimenting, I would traverse parts of my body, targeting specific areas internally. Then, during subsequent periods of conscious lucidity, to my astonishment, I witnessed small sections of my external wounded skin healing. I saw it with my own eyes. Specific areas that I had focused on were magically getting better. It was amazing. Could my mind actually repair damaged molecules? And if so, would this same process work on my tissues and organs?

Thankfully, it appeared to be effective. I also noticed a correlation between the depth of my targeted meditative concentration and the efficiency and efficacy of the reparative process. The more intense the focus, the stiller I became, the slower I moved, and the more proficient the healing. This self-amelioration process inspired me with renewed hope.

My paramount lesson became one of focus and discipline. The more I focused, the faster I seemed to be healing. The more I concentrated, the more I was able to control my breathing, blood flow, and molecular restoration. The episodes of coherent understanding were increasing in frequency and duration every day. It all seemed to be coming together, building towards some climactic resolve. If only the hellish nightmares would cease, and my mom would return.

And then it dawned on me that in addition to my physical wounds, perhaps I possessed the power to heal my tortured soul. Why not? Pushing my regret and self-pity aside, emphasizing only my physicality appeared to be another mistake. After all, my overwhelming despair was also an aspect of the present. Instead of suppressing my emotional misery, I resolved to examine and mend it as well.

I made the conscious effort to work on both my physical and emotional wounds. And just like that, as though summoned, the massive wall of crucial pain instantly rematerialized. A collage of anguish surrounded me, raw, exposed, and vulnerable. Painful questions. Why did my dad take that flight? Why didn't he wait out the storm? What was the magnitude of my physical injuries? Why did I choose to suffer? Why did I choose to survive? Why did God allow this to happen? Why me?

I had to preliminarily address these questions and my regret. Despite my trepidation, uncovering my baggage and accepting it was curiously simplistic. Thorough examination would be significantly more challenging.

Sadly, I quickly became dumbfounded. Overwhelmed. Opening the present unleashed a virtual floodgate of psychological crap. Apparently, beyond the crucial pain, I possessed a lifetime of insecurities, mistakes, shame, and disappointments. Once again, I was raptured, wallowing in self-pity. How could I embrace the totality of my past? Isn't it easier just to bury stuff? How could I reconcile all my life's decisions that brought me to this place? To this horror? If I'm in control of my life then I somehow created this. I was stifled by mountainous despair.

Intuitively, it was unworkable to tackle everything at once. There was simply too much. The trauma was both too vast and too voluminous. I pulled back, examining the crucial pain in the forefront. The elements of anger towards my father, my injuries, and God. It too was massive. The pain associated with the rage was simply too great. I didn't believe I had the tools for this. Intellectually, I knew that my only way forward required microscopic dissection of my emotional trauma, the same that was utilized and effective in my physical healing. But how?

Then, it happened again. A massive energy surge. An adrenaline rush. Invigorating! It was the same one as before, yet infinitely more intense. And all my pain was gone. Feeling a distinct presence, I opened my eyes expecting to see someone. No one was there. Time was perfectly suspended. Dust particles froze in midair. And although I didn't see anyone, I knew I wasn't alone. Someone or something was with me. An immense consciousness. Infinite intelligence. And love. I searched the room. Empty. And yet I was accompanied. My level of comfort was almost indescribable. Like being wrapped in a massive soft blanket or cradled safely inside a giant warm hand.

No words were spoken, no whispers, no lecture delivered. Knowledge was simply revealed. There were three distinct messages: first, augment your thinking about regret and learn from mistakes; second, be the master of your own destiny, writing and crafting your own story; and third, you are exactly where you are supposed to be. That last one just hung in the air. The cumulative epiphany of this triumvirate was to find peace in the present. Each moment. Each "Gift."

Did I imagine that entire experience? Maybe. Sudden prophetic awareness of this magnitude seems unlikely, especially at such a young age. I have no earthly explanation. I merely received the insight and accepted it as genuine.

Reconciling the elements provided, I broke them down into generalities. I began by answering, "What is regret?" Essentially, regret is remembering an event or decision, with a feeling of loss or sorrow. It is a wallowing or mourning, wishing either that the experience had been avoided, or a different path chosen. Primarily, it was essential to acknowledge that the entirety of my existence, including all my missteps, existed here, in the present. One of my epiphanies was not to be restricted or limited by these errors, mistakes, or failures. Each individual disappointment was, and is, merely an opportunity to learn and grow. And considering the extent of my faulty programming it was clear that I had a lot to learn and plenty of room for growth.

As an aside, employing a growth mindset analogy, I recall teaching my daughter to catch a ball. Of course, she initially dropped it, repeatedly. However, instead of allowing her to regret each drop, we capitalized on the opportunities to discover and work towards perfecting a skill. Instead of focusing on the errors, we embraced the struggle as an opening to learn something and work through it. Each and every experience is an opportunity to catch a metaphorical ball and improve. Most importantly, remember that our collective ball-drops all exist in the present.

❧❧❧ ☙☙☙

Regarding the crafting of my own story, I have since taken that guidance both figuratively and literally, as is evidenced by this book. For decades there have been countless echoes prompting me to tell my life's story. Because of that one moment in the hospital, I was always confident that it would be drafted, recorded, and published at exactly the moment it was meant too.

While recovering, I needed to acknowledge that my entire story already existed in the present. The book, the self-authored biographic novel, was always there, at my fingertips. The paramount distinction between reality and metaphor was that my life was more akin to a draft than a published work. Paragraphs, pages, sections and even chapters could always be rewritten. Romance, adventure, comedy, love, financial success, drama, mystery, or anything imaginable could always be added, or removed. The luxury was that at any time I could flip through the pages or jump ahead several chapters. If I wasn't happy with the direction, or didn't like what I was reading, I could easily delete, edit, or alter it. Revisions were always possible. There were no co-authors. It was my book. My story.

❧❧❧ ☙☙☙

Your life is your own book! You can and should be the author. Write your own history. Embrace the detractors, while not allowing anyone to negatively impact your health, prosperity, and potential. No one should dictate what anyone else writes, or how they write it. And since the entire novel already exists here, in the present, if you do not like something in the future chapters, change it today!

My biggest challenge was digesting the concept of, "being exactly where I was meant to be." It is easy to accept one's station during times of accomplishment and success. For most people even rough times are tolerable – when things are bad but not catastrophic. We just deal with it. However, it is those catastrophic times that are difficult to rationalize and accept. For me, it was counter intuitive to acknowledge that I was meant to suffer, struggle and endure this level of agony. Imagine writing in your story , "I'd like to suffer through surviving a plane crash this year." It's heavy. As I questioned and resisted this notion, images of my daughters, from birth through adolescence, were presented like a cinematic montage. Their eyes, their faces, their souls. These were followed by my wife's warm embraces, as we witnessed an additional patchwork of our offspring graduating, marrying, and extending their own families. Our family. The amount of love, pleasure, and joy was immeasurable. My future prosperity, in the present, became my anchor.

My insight regarding regret was threefold. First, I realized that the struggles today shape the prosperity for the future, even if comprehension eludes me initially. Second, since I was exactly where I was supposed to be, if it were possible to change any past event, that alteration would detrimentally affect my present as well as future chapters. Lastly, I was comforted knowing that I had the power to continue minimizing my anguish by utilizing newfound tools, anchors, and safe harbors.

And with that, I began the methodical and meticulous process of emotional therapy. Lying in bed, meditating during stretches of clarity while diligently continuing work on my physical ailments, I was painstakingly dissecting my psychological concerns. Starting with the most crucial pain, I examined the trauma from the plane crash, including issues with my father and God. I embraced my anger. It was okay to be angry. Anger is not a primal emotion, but rather a reaction to being hurt.

Looking past the anger, I addressed the pain and disappointment. I faced the regret of getting on that dreadful plane, confronting my father's poor judgment. I experienced remorse for not convincing my dad to wait out the storm another day. I not only had to forgive him, but I also needed to absolve myself. The latter was far easier than the former. There was no scenario I could fathom whereby my father would have cancelled the flight. He perceived himself invincible. Forgiving him proved to be a more difficult challenge.

He was my dad. He was my hero. It turns out he wasn't invincible, and he wasn't infallible either. It was easier to be angry and blame him rather than to see him as human and flawed, with warts and all. Besides, he was writing his own story. He ended his life the way he lived, on his own terms. It's selfish of me to impose my expectations onto him. All I can do is accept and embrace his impact on my story. Not a single day goes by that I don't think about him. The colossal pain was actually behind the anger. Underneath it. Obscuring it. The colossal pain was my massive canyon of loss. The biggest scar I endured in the plane crash was the chasm created by his physical absence. I wasn't angry at him. My anger was a manifestation of the enormous loss. A loss that might never fully heal, but one that I would learn to live with. From my perspective taking that flight was a mistake. It turned out to be a fatal mistake for him. And it was the last chapter of his book. However, in my novel he will always be my hero and I forgive him. I miss him. And I will always love him.

In order to achieve that level of peace and forgiveness, while embracing the pain, I used visualizations of my future love and success that became dependent on this tragedy occurring. In other words, my grandchildren would never exist if not for this crucial pain. And when any issues or elements were too much to bear, I secured myself inside a safe harbor, either from my future, like cradling my newborn baby, or a memory from my recent past, like being submerged in soothing warm water. The process was slow, but efficacious. Piece by piece I replaced regret with amity, as I began to emotionally heal.

Throughout the present, I experienced myriad childhood regrets and disappointments. Times when I didn't stand up to a bully, or times when I fought and let my temper get the better of me. Times when I wasn't honest. Times when I lost, cheated, or stole. Times when I let fear and insecurity prevent actions. And other times when I allowed different fear and insecurity to cloud my judgment, prompting poor decisions. Then there were those regrets from times when I was merely lazy, reckless, or careless. I began addressing them individually, using the same process. They were all with me in the present. They could not be erased. Each one would always be a part of me. Gradually, I continued to heal.

I was making progress. The emotional work was helping. But the reality was that my recovery was going to be lengthy and arduous – longer than I had perceived. I had to learn to respect incremental progress, no matter how minuscule, to maintain my sanity and optimism. Does a great athlete ever stop training? No. Does an artist ever stop creating? Of course not. I had to look at myself as my own masterpiece. A work in progress. It might take a lifetime, but I couldn't lose hope. I found this moment comforting because every stage of my development, including this prolonged recovery, already existed. It was here. My future motivates me in the present. It was in that moment I resolved to find joy in the journey of healing.

※

Throughout my restoration process, over the past decades, I repeatedly encountered multitudes of frightened, conditioned individuals, still asleep, who have quipped, "This is easy for you to say, because you're successful." Adding, "of course you have no regrets anymore, your life is wonderful."

To this, my response is always, "yes, my life is wonderful. Actually, it is perfect. And so is yours. You just don't know it yet." My experience is that most people are not ready to receive this. Most people are unaware of their own immense value and significance. I further point out that every obstacle, or painful conflict, is an opportunity to overcome something. Embrace the challenges. Embrace the difficulties. Embrace the pains. Embrace the decisions. Do not regret them. There is nothing to regret. The past is a collective opportunity to learn and shape your future, while the forthcoming chapters are the motivation.

Detractors are also apt to quip, "Well, that's just hogwash!" Often adding a conditioned response like, "I can't do anything I want!"

To them I merely say, "You are only bound by your own self-created limitations, based mostly on your faulty programming, as well as other people's misperceptions." I further avoid responding to the banal trap, "I can't jump out the window and fly like a superhero!" To those folks I merely direct them to Chapter 9 and my discussion regarding truth. Furthermore, I humbly admit to my own personal struggles in overcoming my own faulty programming. I empathize with you. And I recognize the Herculean task. For example, I was taught that, "people do not survive plane crashes." Therefore, I should not be here. But here I am, sharing my experience and my enlightenment with you.

When I was told, "You'll never be able to walk again." I jumped forward to a time when I was running. "You'll never be able waterski." So, I jumped forward to a time when I was waterskiing, and then snow skiing, both of which activities humorously came with a lot of falling and bruising, along with a lot of happiness. And those are only a few of my physical accomplishments. Most of my achievements came after being warned of either their extreme difficulty, remote impracticability, or even their impossibility. You cannot live inside other people's fears and apprehensions.

Some of the harshest doubts, or cautions, came from people who warned me, for my own benefit, that "because of your deformities, scarring, disabilities, and physical limitations, romantically, you should be prepared to either settle or be alone. You will never have a 'normal' relationship or 'normal' family."

THE GIFT

Which of course prompted me to simply hug my, yet unborn, grandchildren. Reviewing future chapters of my own history, I embrace a man that never settled, experiencing a lifetime surrounded by love and purpose.

Utilizing visualizations from my future was not an act of clairvoyance or prophecy. I was merely accepting all my potential in the present. Remember, you are the one writing your own story and anything you can perceive, you can ultimately achieve.

By the beginning of the fourth week, Chief Surgeon Johnson was astonished that huge sections of my skin were healing, and that most of my organs inexplicably began to function. He could not reconcile my seemingly miraculous recuperation. Humbly, he refused to take credit for my inexplicable restoration. He deemed it a medical phenomenon. His preconditioning clouded his perception and the possibility that I was actively aiding in my own recovery. Regardless, my progress prompted him to order an even more aggressive weaning off the highly addictive and toxic painkillers.

My internal therapeutic meditation was abruptly interrupted by the sound of laundry bin wheels entering the room. I opened my eyes, revealing Ghoul, already at the foot of my bed getting things ready for another torture session. During this past week, the painful cycles all bled into one horrific brutalization. Since I was unaware of the drug-weaning process, I could not comprehend why these bandage-change-episodes became increasingly more painful. I knew my body was healing. Therefore, the amplified pain did not make any sense.

Regardless, while these monsters commenced their ritualistic assault, my best defense was to retreat inward. I steadied myself, concentrating on my breathing.

Relaxing. My focus and discipline had improved immensely. As Ogre entered the room, I was about to shut my eyes and begin my meditation, when my mother raced in and quickly crossed to the window. She had forgotten her sweater. My mother? Yes, my mother! She was there! I was awake, and she was there!

This was the opportunity I had been anticipating. The moment had to be seized.

I began pugnaciously struggling against my firm bonds. Apparently, I had also regained some strength. I relentlessly shook the bed, knocking over one of my medical stances and dislodging several of my intravenous fluid tubes. While this annoyed Ogre, it was clearly enough to get my mother's attention. I could not let up. I had to capitalize on this moment.

In her thick island accent Ogre consoled my mom, "*E dun't eb'n know bare e is, or dat yur ear mum. 'ed tramas are 'orrible enuf. 'Is wit-drawal is makin' it dat much hadda.*" Ghoul added, "You get your coffee mum, we'll tend to him."

Withdrawal symptoms? Withdrawal from what? And what did she mean by, "I didn't know where I was?" I knew where I was! I wasn't brain dead! Damn it! What was that sadistic monster talking about? I couldn't let my mother leave the room. Mustering all my might, I dislodged the left guardrail, inadvertently freeing my left hand. The recoil knocked Ogre back a few feet. Ghoul quickly grabbed and tried to restrain my wrist.

As we fought, my mom hesitated in the doorway. Our eyes met. She took a few steps back inside the room. "Don't let his thrashing temper tantrum fool you," Ghoul continued. "He's just reacting to the pain. You should wait outside. We can handle this. He's always much better afterwards."

Fearing she would go I increased the intensity of my struggle. My window of opportunity was closing. Overpowering Ghoul, pulling away, I found a piece of dislodged hard plastic from one my tubes. Thinking fast, as Ghoul grabbed me again, I began rhythmically tapping, against the remaining guardrail. The only melody I could think of was the tune, "*Shave and a Haircut.*" Silly, I know. But it was all I had in the moment. Tap, tap-tap, tap-tap, pause, tap-tap.

Everyone stopped. All three women in the room took notice. I repeated the measure tap, tap-tap, tap-tap...tap-tap. My mom came closer to the bed. With Ghoul's hand still attached to mine, I executed once more tap, tap-tap, tap-tap...tap-tap. Ghoul released my wrist. I pantomimed my swirls for 'wanting to write something.' My mother immediately understood. And unlike my earlier communication, I now had full freedom of movement of my neck and head. This further facilitated my reactions to 'yes or no' questions. My mom asked if I wanted to write something down. I nodded incessantly and affirmatively. "Yes!"

My mother hurried to the window and retrieved her folded, newspaper crossword puzzle, which contained a pen, clipped inside. Within the margins, I scribbled, "please right hand."

Understanding, and complying, my right hand was quickly unshackled. Instantly, communication became much easier. I described how much pain I was in. My mom's eyes filled with water. It was difficult to know if she was upset because of my pain, or happy because of my articulate communication. She just tenderly held and caressed my left hand. Both Ogre and Ghoul were awestruck. Ogre darted out exclaiming that she would return *"right 'way, wit da docta."*

I then wrote to my mom, "Why can't I talk?" My mom, still crying, didn't respond. Didn't she understand my question? I wanted to discuss the extent of my injuries, my recovery, and the inexplicable increases in pain. There was simply too much to write.

Just then, the attending physician entered with Ogre in tow. He looked at our written conversation in bewilderment. He then took out a penlight from his breast pocket. "Not another incessant flashlight," I thought.

He proceeded to shine the light closely into my eyes, asking me a series of pedantically absurd questions. "Do you know where you are?" I shook my head yes. "Do you know what happened to you?" Again, yes. "Do you know why you are here?" I looked at my mom and raised my eyebrows as if to indicate that that was the same question. After a beat, I looked back and shook my head, yes. Holding the newspaper with my scribble on it, he asked, "Are you able to write your answers on this piece of paper?" This time, I blankly stared at him as though he was a complete moron. I glanced at the newspaper and then back up at him. I just took a moment, blinking...in disbelief. How did this idiot get through medical school? Then I thought, how did he put his pants on this morning?

I simply reached over, grabbed the paper, and scribbled in the margin, "Fire away!" My mother, still crying, smiled and let out a single chortle. She was always my best audience.

Noticing that the newspaper had little available space, he handed me his medical script pad from one of his lower coat pockets. I then conjectured that he wasn't a complete idiot. And yet he followed up with another ridiculous inquiry, asking, "Do you know your name?" I paused at the inane nature of the question. There were so many more important things to discuss, like my injuries, my recovery, and the incessant increases in pain. This was quickly becoming almost as bad as the bandage torture. He asked again, "What's your name?"

Playing along, I wrote, "Laurence."

"Do you know what year it is?"

I wrote, "1984."

To which he exclaimed, "Amazing! I don't believe it. And can you tell me who is the President of the United States?" I scribbled Ronald Reagan. However, upon reflection, I'm certain I spelled Reagan incorrectly. He appeared so impressed by my response that I don't think he held my misspelling against me.

After the brief inquiry, he escorted my mom out to speak privately, leaving me alone at the mercy of Ogre and Ghoul. Ogre stared down at me. I was certainly going to pay for this whole episode of defiance. I was bracing for her vengeful wrath and retribution. If only I could call out for help, my mother would certainly return and save me. Ogre ominously approached the bed. Her expression and hesitation confused me. Why didn't she just attack? Her eyes were bloodshot, red, and filled with water. Her dark-skinned complexion was otherwise flush. She reached out, embracing my right hand, tenderly caressing the wounds on my wrist and arm, and simply whispered, "oh child."

There was no retribution. No reprisal. No revenge. For the first time, I had noticed a name tag on her chest pocket. It read, "Vanessa, RN." As we stared at each other, I too became overcome with emotion. Instantly, I saw her in a whole new light. As if a veil had been lifted. I scribbled on a new sheet of paper, "Hi, Nurse Vanessa." She smiled through her tears, as I added, "Sorry I've been so much trouble."

I then looked over at Ghoul, who's mouth was still agape, dumbfounded by the past few minutes. I then inscribed, "Hi, Nurse Kelly." To which her expression changed from disbelief to a tender smile. I motioned them both to wait, holding up the paper for them both to read, adding, "Sorry I've been such a terrible patient." Nurse Kelly came over and patted my other hand affectionately.

Nurse Vanessa, gently sobbing, simply shook her head and repeated softly, "Oh child."

I promised to remain as still as possible during dressing changes and asked if they could keep my hands free. Vanessa agreed, assuring me that they would continually check with me, minimizing the pain, as best they could. She did stress that the restraints were still needed during the overnight dressing changes, for my own safety. She explained that because of my withdrawal symptoms, on numerous occasions, I had dislodged my wires and tubes.

Which prompted my scribbled inquiry, "Withdrawal from what?"

She explained that I had become addicted to Demerol, and that they were in the final stages of weaning me off, transitioning to morphine. In response to my obvious confusion Nurse Kelly chimed in, explaining, "No one expected you to make it this far. The doctor will explain the withdrawal process to you better." Nurse Vanessa just shook her head, and repeated, "oh child."

Apparently, as the drug dosage was decreased, not only did the pain increase from my bodily injuries, but it was compounded by both an incredibly unpleasant chemical, physical, and psychological withdrawal.

Mom returned from the hallway without the doctor. While I wanted to continue our conversation, I felt myself fading fast. I mustered just enough strength to jot down, "how's dad?"

She paused silently with her hand over her mouth. The horrifying answer was on her face. It was in her eyes. This time she didn't lie. She took my hand in her hands. Through a cracked voice she explained that my father had passed away in the crash. He didn't survive. She apologized profusely for not telling me sooner. She said it was for my own good. The doctor had cautioned her, before our prior brief written communication, not to tell me anything that might negatively interfere with my recovery. She quickly added, "He didn't suffer. He broke his neck and died on impact."

I looked over at Nurse Vanessa, we made eye contact briefly. She then looked down, shaking her head, crying and continuing to do busy work. I looked back into my mom's watery eyes. I too wanted to commiserate with them. But I didn't cry. I had this strange urge to be strong. Although, crying seemed so much more appropriate.

Nurse Vanessa ushered my mom out, reminding her, that due to my infection it was healthier if she wasn't present during dressing changes. We all agreed and understood. My mom said she'd be back soon and would be there when I woke up again. I drew a heart. My mom exited. I tapped on the railing to get Vanessa's attention. Again, we made eye contact.

We now had an understanding. I accepted that these dressing changes were still going to be brutal. But they were no longer going to be torture. I would get through them. Nurse Vanessa and I had this. I scribbled on the note paper. "Thx Nurse V!" And gave her a "thumbs up." I closed my eyes, concentrating on my respiration and circulation. As I began my internal healing mediation, I heard Nurse Vanessa faintly mutter to herself, "Oh child!"

※※※※

When I closed my eyes that time my healing was abruptly interrupted. Inconsistencies and incongruities caused me to short circuit and question everything. Lies about my dad, observations about the serious nature of my condition and...my programming. The most haunting were my injuries which appeared extensive, possibly permanent and irreparable, irrespective of my prosperous future visualizations, which my programming prompted me to question their veracity. Lies, so many lies. My faulty wiring kicked in and I doubted all my abilities, all my insights and all my potential. My pulse increased rapidly. My body unnervingly tingled. My immediate present consisted of an arduous recovery of unknown intensity and duration. So much for finding joy in recovery. My programming and the outside influences were wearing me down. In order for me to get through this period there was a massive chunk of encoding that I needed to rewrite. I looked around frantically for any of my tools but all I could see was my brainwashing. All I could hear were the echos of negativity from outside. I was encircled by fear. My safe harbors were nowhere to be found. Fear that I was being lied to about my injures. Fear that I wasn't strong enough to deal with the magnitude of this situation. Fear that I wasn't good enough to deserve such a wonderful future. I searched for answers as to how to deal with the debilitating fear. I searched for any insights. I searched my programming. I searched the present. I couldn't find any answers. All I could see was the fear.

My breathing became erratic. Focus was difficult. I wrestled with my defective encoding. Were all my insights just delusions? Were all my visions just fantasy? Focus was fleeting. I couldn't rewrite the past. Even if there was a prosperous future, which I now questioned...but even if there was one on the other side...I did not possess the ability to skip any chapters or jump ahead. I had to live through this. There was no way to rewrite the plane crash. It already happened. No regrets. I was exactly where I was supposed to be. And where I was supposed to be was excruciatingly miserable and depressing. Why would anyone have to endure such suffering? My temperature rose...and yet I began shivering with chills. I was petrified. That chapter was horrifyingly filled with laborious struggle and pain. There was no way to jump over this. There was no way to write my way around it. Survival meant I had to live through it. Panic set it. Dizzy. Sweating. Trembling. Filled with doubt, I questioned everything! Focus was gone.

And then...I froze. Time was still progressing. I didn't stop its forward momentum. It was me that was motionless. Immobilized, in shock. My physical and emotional trauma was so much worse than I had imagined. My pages ahead were so much worse than I had conceived. Hadn't I undergone enough? I was overcome with fear. Stifling fear! If I could't move freely within my thoughts I couldn't heal. I was stuck here, in the present. I was terrified of it. My chest heaved. I couldn't breathe...

Instinctually, I knew that the only way forward was to face that fear. My life depended on it. I had to break free...but how?

———◆O◆———

8

THE FEAR

"**B**ang!" The answer came like a startling gunshot, rather than a typical whisper. I didn't have a gun, I simply screamed internally. That microsecond of clarity was all I needed. Once jostled free, I augmented time and pivoted to a safe harbor. Everything was there in the present. I had the tools to liberate myself after all. I merely needed a little help to show me how.

My fifth week of internment had begun with a mixture of pain, torture, and despair. While I was terrified with paralyzing fear, I knew there was little chance of getting to the future if I couldn't get through the present. Thankfully, as if responding to my desperation I was provided another infusion of divine insight. Like a paralyzed "deer in the headlights" I just needed an internal jolt to shake myself free. And because of my predisposition, and doubt, I still couldn't fathom where the insight was coming from. Regardless, I was immensely grateful.

Utilizing my newly practiced skills, I separated myself from the fear. Focusing, I calmly transported myself two hours into the past, back to the therapy treatment room, where I was submerged in soothing, warm water. The cleansing liquid pulsated around my body and my wounds. Regulating my breathing and heart rate, I was safe once again. The rhythmic water jets delivered a mollifying sensation. Their tactile comfort amazingly assisted my concentration and focus, providing a calm, serene shelter.

The pain, conflict and doubt had paralyzed me. The imparted wisdom and internal scream had liberated me. I accepted the present. I now had to figure out how to deal with the fear.

※※※— —※※※

While I was tranquilly floating in the past, in a metallic whirlpool tub, I was cognitively aware that my physical body was two hours in the future, across the hospital, three floors above me, lying in bed. I was simultaneously in both places. In my room, I was aware of my mother sleeping on a cot next to me. I could hear her softly snoring. From the sanctity of the therapy tank, I took out the metaphorical box. As it approached, lifting the lid, I caught a glimpse of the fear. It was massive. My dad. My injuries. Inconsistencies. My childhood. And massive pain! My heart pounded and my panic level rose exponentially. Before paralysis overtook me, I slammed the lid closed, and pushed the box away again. My heart was beating against my chest. I concentrated on the tepid water. The cascading steady rhythm calmed me. I wasn't quite ready yet. Almost. I just needed a little confidence boost! Some added reassurance.

Returning to my room, I opened my eyes. I was hoping to draw comfort from my mom. There she was, asleep, propped up on the uncomfortable-looking portable bed next to me. At first glance she appeared to be the epitome of contentment, angelically sleeping, at peace. However, upon closer inspection the illusion faded. She was flush, pale, and gaunt, wearing her tension and anxiety on her face. Witnessing her son cling to life was too much. She was shattered. Broken. Her clothing was crumpled, as though worn for days. My poor mom. Not fully reclined, she was merely slumped over, leaning against two small pillows and the window, blanketed only by a light sweater covering her chest and shoulders. Chilled air was consistently blowing from the cheap ceiling vent, causing a lock of hair to flutter atop her forehead. Her right leg was extended, while the other dangled off the side of the undersized bed. The whole enterprise looked horribly uninviting. I reasonably conjectured that what little sleep my mother experienced was achieved inadvertently by passing out on occasion from exhaustion. My poor mom.

While my mother slept, I relaxed, closed my eyes, and returned to the water therapy room to try again. The combination of the maternal consolation coupled with the pacification from the water therapy provided enough strength to continue. I proceeded slowly, cautiously. I took all the fear out of the box at once, assessing the vast scope of my potential challenge. At the forefront, were those glaring inconsistencies between what my mother and Chief Surgeon Johnson were telling me, versus my actual perception, in the present. I couldn't reconcile why people like Dr. Johnson, who couldn't fathom my recovery suddenly became idealistic. When questioned, they dismissed my wounds as minor, temporary conditions while deflecting any discussions concerning scope and permanence. What the heck? My sixth sense highlighted these obvious, illogical incongruities based on all material observations, as well as the ongoing severity of the pain.

Their guarded programming ensured them that my recovery depended upon a positive outlook. Therefore, they refused to divulge the true extent of my injuries. They were certain that a complete, honest disclosure would devastatingly depress my morale and stymie my recuperation. In other words, they kept things from me "for my own good." I spent every waking moment during that fifth week trying to extrapolate as much information as possible. How could I deal with the totality of my circumstances if I had no idea what they were. The problem was that my lucidity and communication were still limited, and I needed information and discovery from the outside world. That information was not easily obtained.

✹✹✹

I desperately wanted to continue my investigation of the present. However, interacting with the medical staff was a slog, scribbling at a sloth's pace on small pads and scrap paper. The speed of my thoughts vastly outpaced my ability to jot them down. I found myself continually motioning my mom, doctors, and nurses to pause for my responsive participation. I must've written the words, "wait", "repeat that," "stop," or "please go slower" countless times. Medical personnel were always seemingly in a rush and the briefest conversation required multiple pages. I was burning through tree-fiber at a rapid pace. My bed and floor became littered with balls of thin white pulp.

Then my mother made a serendipitous discovery at a nearby store. While buying scores of spiral notebooks, she happened upon *Magic Slate* drawing pads, which were cardboard tablets with plastic cover sheets you could write on with a plastic stick and "erase" by peeling them off again and again. They were fast, effective, and efficient at facilitating quick thoughts. Over the next few weeks, while the spiral notebooks were wonderful for lengthier responses, those simple childhood toys turned out to be a most brilliant form of communication. My mom was both consoling and resourceful!

✹✹✹

An added bonus obtained by this small cardboard and plastic communication device was being able to quickly articulate pain at varying levels from bearable, to uncomfortable, and even excruciating. It was also with the repetitive use of this device that I was finally able to communicate to the medical

THE GIFT 151

staff and visitors that even the slightest touch or movement of my bed delivered shockwaves of searing pain.

⋘⋙

For the remainder of that fifth week, I used my improved communication and moments of tolerable pain to meticulously explore the present. I was on a fact-finding mission. I attempted spontaneous discussions with each and every member of the medical staff in order to reconcile these inconsistencies. Apparently, many of them were not privy to Dr. Johnson's 'deception of positivity.' Additionally, the parade of doctors, residents, and interns that rotated in and out of the intensive care unit brought their own baggage. I had to be careful, ascertaining whether their pessimism and caution were justified, or if they were merely projecting their own preconditioning and ingrained fears.

For example, the reason I couldn't verbally communicate was because my mouth was wired shut. Doctor Johnson explained that this was a minor, temporary condition. However, a resident who had witnessed my initial surgery, graphically described the condition of my face as dismal. He explained that, apparently, my mandible, or jawbone, as a result of smashing against the dashboard of the plane, had been shattered into so many pieces that its amelioration required a mesh metal wiring affixed to my maxilla, or upper jaw. The intact remnants of my natural teeth were fractured like barbwire fencing. While it was plausible that these ailments would heel amiably, as Doctor Johnson suggested, the resident frightfully conjectured that I would most likely require extensive orthodontic surgery and a host of cosmetic repairs.

Another example involved my overall appearance. I still had significant bandaging on my face, and my mother went to great pains obstructing access to my own reflection. How bad were my facial scars? Aesthetically, was I going to be a monster? It felt as though my mother and the chief surgeon weren't being completely honest. I surmised that my reparative medical procedures might be substantial, lengthy, and painful. Or worse, ineffective.

※※※ ※※※

On another occasion, Doctor Johnson dismissed a stiff, protruding bulge underneath my chest bandages as a temporary and routine suture. However, during rounds in the chief surgeon's absence, a random, eager intern inadvertently pulled back the bandages, revealing a hideous metal fixture. He explained that since the accident, I had already undergone several dozen grueling surgeries. He was privy to many of them and was amazed that I was still alive. His amazement was unnerving. He further elucidated my ongoing necessity for future surgical procedures and that it was too traumatic, continually cutting and sewing back my chest and mid-section every few days. Therefore, for medical convenience, and my own good, they affixed a common, unappealing, metal zipper to the upper portion of my chest cavity running down just above my belly button. My torso had become a literal "garment."

The same intern explained the need for an additional, awkward, plastic apparatus fastened to my neck. His visit was ripe with joyful tidings. Apparently, a temporary tracheotomy hole, with a valve and plug, was installed. It was a small one-quarter-inch oval valve with a removable rubber cylinder, or plug, used to facilitate artificial respiration, or oxygen, and anesthesia during future surgeries. All of this was anything but temporary and minor. Logically, the zipper and trach valve pointed to the inevitability of many forthcoming invasive procedures. Also, should I ever make a full recovery, these devices were most likely going to result in considerable permanent scarring. If things were as positive as Doctor Johnson alleged, they would not have turned me into human apparel with an accessible air hole.

※※※ ※※※

Interestingly, I was now audible. Even though my mouth was wired, I was able to communicate through limited sounds when the air-valve in my neck was "plugged." I could make affirmative or negative grunts, as well as stuttered laughter, or more commonly, groans of misery. However, I was mostly consigned to writing.

The majority of my additional revelations that week occurred during medical rounds and bedside evaluations. Doctors, residents, and interns often discussed my condition in the third person, as if I wasn't there. None of them would fully commit to my complete recovery. Their training, and individual fear, had them convinced of my long-term injuries such as brain trauma, heart stress, major organ trauma, internal scarring, and an invariably shortened lifespan. The colossal amount of pain I was continuously enduring affirmed their observations and conclusions.

I was still reliant on the machinery. One doctor observed that both my kidneys and my liver were still not fully functional. Unfortunately, these organs were still in shock. He further pointed out that, ultimately, their restoration would be required for me to stop feeding intravenously and nasogastrically in order to begin consuming solid foods once again. While Chief Johnson brushed this off as a temporary setback, it was clearly not an automatic inevitability.

On another occasion, one of the seasoned trauma physicians, during rounds, pointed out to his medical contingent of interns, that, because of my, "one prior collapsed lung and one rib-punctured lung," that I would have, "a greatly decreased long-term respiratory capacity, equivalent to that of a senior citizen." He concluded that even though I no longer required a ventilator, that my decreased breathing capability would most assuredly curtail my physical prowess and my life. Everybody was amazed that I was still alive. They were all waiting for me to drop dead any minute.

Additionally, during my twice daily bandage dressing changes there was the incessant reminder by the nurses that my severe infection was not abating. Johnson continued to reassure me that the massive antibiotics would eventually wipe out the contamination. However, many of the medical staff vocalized their counter opinion that, in the interim, the infection was "rapidly killing me." My investigation wasn't unearthing very encouraging news, to say the least.

Furthermore, there were the repeated, idiotic, and banal cognitive questions related to my cerebral trauma. These were maddening. No matter how often the doctors interacted with me, because of their predilection and preconditioning, they all, including Doctor Johnson, were certain that I had suffered permanent brain damage, despite my daily lucidity and improved clarity. Their training instructed them to believe statistics over their own observations. They believed that my mental impairment must be delayed, repressed, or latent. Therefore, they all asked the same foolish questions, *ad nauseam*. My name. The date. Current location. Circumstances for my being in the hospital. The country. And the President.

A drop of water is pleasant. A million drops of water on your forehead is torture. Torture!

I reasoned that there must be a pamphlet in medical school entitled "idiotic questions to ask brain-injured patients to test coherence." I also vowed to find and destroy that pamphlet one day. With a heavy sarcastic sigh, I still have yet to follow through on that one. But one day...

After only the very first day, the questioning was mind-numbingly monotonous and demeaning. My brain function was normal. Recognizing all those inconsistencies regarding my condition, I didn't want to waste time with insipid questions. I eagerly and anxiously aspired to engage the senior doctors in more substantive conversations regarding my overall health and condition. Didn't they realize that we could all be working together? Nevertheless, my attempts were ignored as they proceeded robotically with the same banal interrogations, followed by repeated amazement at my remarkable coherence. Then they would check a few boxes on their medical charts and hurriedly move on. It was infuriating!

As the rotations circled back to the same familiar faces, for my own amusement, I began scribbling sarcastic and nonsensical answers. My mother would often have to chase them down the hallway explaining that I did not have dementia, and that I did not sincerely believe I was Marie Antoinette, Joan of Arc or the Empire State Building. Upon their return, I had a preprinted quip handy, explaining that my jokes were never funny when they needed to be explained. None of them ever laughed or even smiled. I reasoned that most trauma physicians either lost their sense of humor over the years, or never had one to begin with. Interestingly, while my snarky responses angered most of the seasoned medical staff, by the beginning of the sixth week, the senseless daily questioning thankfully ceased. At least that torture had come to a conclusion.

As I began my sixth week in the hospital, compiling all the evidence regarding the palpable contradictions, I was amazed at how much this awareness of the present was having a positive effect on reducing the tension related to my fear. One might find that positivity counterintuitive, not recognizing the power of the truth. By then, I was remaining awake and coherent for lengthier durations, facilitating more substantive conversations as well as offering sharper focus for my remedial meditation. I was also better able to comprehend the mammoth pain I was experiencing as they continued weaning me off the powerful narcotics, which only amplified my anxiety and desire to amp-up my physical self-healing. Medically, whatever they were doing in the hospital was not enough. I needed to help heal my own body. I needed to get over the stifling fear, and expeditiously!

By that time, I was becoming proficient in transporting myself back and forth to the water therapy room, enjoying the submersible pacification, while simultaneously drawing strength and reassurance from my mother resting next to me. Carefully reopening the metaphorical box, I observed the enormous patchwork and diverse gradients of fear. Something unclear relating to my dad was inseparably attached, in my periphery, to something else relating to my injuries. I managed to separate and push aside the inexplicable fear associated with my dad in order to give primary consideration to the seemingly infinite mounds of childhood fears. They contained all my youthful trepidations enmeshed with recent ones, mostly based on my faulty conditioning. Those fears were calling me. The idiom, "There was no time like the present," could not have been more apropos.

Concentrating on the immense collection of childhood fear prompted yet another spontaneous infusion of celestial acumen. This time, regarding the distinction between irrational and rational fear. I still didn't comprehend the source, the how, or the why, I was merely grateful for the knowledge. Certain irrational juvenile fears are easier to identify like dreading the darkness or a monster under your bed. These are easier to recognize and dismiss in adulthood. However, as we mature, deep-rooted psychological traumas often manifest themselves into irrational fears, phobias, and paranoias. Or worse yet, they can materialize from mass hysteria brought on by geopolitical or sociological forces designed to condition and control people through fear. Over the past century, governments, technology companies, special interest groups, and corporate propaganda machines have mastered the skill of praying on people's irrational fears. Unfortunately, it has confused and muddled the difference for many people. Apparently, I too was a victim of my own faulty programming.

※※※※

My adolescence was riddled with mostly irrational fears of failure and inadequacy — being smart enough for a test, handsome enough for a date, or skilled enough to meet a physical challenge, etc. I spread them all out in front of me. From a distance, they were massive and overwhelming. Upon closer inspection, individually, they all appeared quite pedestrian. Despite the mountain of collective garbage I had accumulated, as I methodically proceeded with my examination, it was unexpectedly easier to work through them than I had otherwise imagined. Thus, I began a microscopic dissection exploring, absorbing, and accepting all my baggage one issue at a time. And I began to feel better.

Through my survival and recovery came the realization that my fear of rejection and inadequacy were both an illusion. On the one hand rejection often resulted in only minor suffering, hurt, embarrassment, and humiliation and never resulted in serious bodily harm or death. On the other hand regarding inadequacy, surviving the plane crash gave me awareness that I was infinitely more powerful and talented than I had previously perceived. If I could survive a trauma of that magnitude, surely I could overcome the pettiness from my past. And I began to grow.

My penultimate epiphany regarding irrational fear was accepting that every disappointment was an opportunity to experience, learn, grow, and potentially do better next time. I further recognized that it would be impossible to go back and erase any of my past childhood fear. They would always be a part of me.

However, by embracing the past I began to draw strength from it, motivating my present recovery so that I could prove to myself that I would hopefully not be inhibited again in the future. And I began to heal.

As I methodically waded through my childhood trepidations, both rational and irrational, I became fearful regarding the ultimate scope of my success. How could I be certain that I would not be inhibited similarly in the future? To which my inner voice promptly echoed, "use your tools." Concentrating, scouring the present, flipping only a few short chapters ahead, I transitioned out of the hospital, and into the future.

I was having trouble breathing. The air was thin. Shockingly, I was falling from the sky, plummeting to earth. I was not in an aircraft, I was just falling. I was a few years older, in my early twenties, falling, weightless, from about twelve thousand feet, toward the ground. I was skydiving. It wasn't clear if I were in the military, on a mission, or merely enjoying a recreational activity. Regardless, I was evidently challenging myself with a one-minute freefall. It was awesome!

I glanced at the altimeter on my chest. Six thousand feet. I was terrified. It was a rational fear though. And yet I was not stifled. Five thousand feet. The view was awesome. My adrenaline raced, I was afraid, and it was exhilarating. I could see for miles and miles in every direction. Four thousand feet. My heart pounded. Three Thousand five hundred feet. I was completely weightless. Three thousand feet. As I pulled the ripcord and the chute opened, I had my answer. I was shown that very soon, not only will my body recover physically, enough to engage in this type of activity, but that I was also going to recover emotionally, enough to confront a most dramatic rational fear, and not be stifled by it.

That fascinating future experience was regarding a rational fear. It prompted me to dig deeper and challenge the compendium of my irrational puerile reservations of failure, inadequacy, and rejection. The fear of injury or death paled in amount, size, and scope, by comparison, to fears of failure, inadequacy, and rejection. Looking at my mountain of garbage...I was never tall enough. I was never aesthetically pleasing enough. I was never intelligent enough. I was never talented enough. I was never good enough. I was never worthy. And I recognized that both my physical and emotional traumas from the plane crash only exacerbated those negative, pessimistic, unhealthy apprehensions. Especially with my newfound revelations that I now possessed myriad permanent physical injuries. If I was inadequate before, then I was truly a disaster now.

Focusing, I flipped forward many, many chapters. I had to know. The visualization in the present was fascinating. It was decades later. I was an older man, of an indeterminant age. I have no idea how old. But it was me...I was just older. I was seated at a long table, smartly dressed, next to a few close friends and family members. However, standing in front of me, across the table, was an angry young man, adjacent to an even angrier young woman, both in about their early twenties. Behind them, stretching several dozen yards, was a row of people patiently waiting to speak with me. Apparently, I was at a book signing and speaking engagement for a work I had written about the plane crash, survival, and my revelations about "The Gift."

My heart raced. There I was, being chastised for putting myself out there. Being told that I was a horrible person. That I was proselytizing and selling a book of lies. That I was a false profit and that my compelling fantasies were dangerous. Thus, I was a failure. That was so much worse than skydiving. With every harsh word of criticism, I felt the sting of rejection. I was aware that many other people, who hadn't even availed themselves of the material, were critical of it based solely on my religious and political views, and they associated me collectively with other activists — most of whom I had no affiliation with whatsoever. The quality and merit of the literary piece was irrelevant. Again, most of them hadn't even read it. Sadly, I reasoned that I was so much older at this event because it had taken me decades to overcome this irrational fear and share my experience with the world. Comfortingly, I was relieved that regardless as to how long it took, I did eventually get the courage to publish my story and mustered the strength to risk failure and face all criticisms.

Most importantly, I was provided a glimpse at the finished work itself, along with my wife, children, extended family, and friends. In the aftermath of the book's publication, I was afforded a huge sense of accomplishment, dispelling and dismissing my irrational fear of inadequacy. After all, I didn't write the book for my critics or for extrinsic rewards of any kind. I simply wrote it, chronicling my traumatic experience, explaining how I overcame it, sharing my astonishing revelations and truly hoping to inspire others.

In the years since, I learned that most worthwhile endeavors come with some initial failure or rejection. Successful people welcome the opportunity to grow whether it be through challengers, critics, or even envious adversaries. Challengers and critics should be confronted and objectively evaluated, regardless as to their motivations. The important thing is recognizing wholesome positivity for yourself so that you can make the best objective evaluation when dealing with outside influences. Healthy people rejoice in the success, not failure, of others. If someone does not experience joy from another's successes, that places their character into question. And certainly their criticisms. Be inspired by others. Be happy for their success. Their win is not your loss. If they could do it, so can you. Perhaps even better!

Throughout this lengthy healing process I utilized my newly developed tools, repeatedly augmenting time and jumping to future chapters to experience occasions when my irrational fear was ultimately overcome — like the visualization of completing my book. Michelangelo famously quipped when asked about creating a sculpture that he merely had to "chip away the stone that didn't look like David." He perceptively understood that everything was already in the present, including his finished masterpiece.

⁂

This all came with the knowledge that I could accomplish almost anything if I put my mind to it. Nearly anything you can conceive you can ultimately achieve. You are only bound by your preconditioned limitations. And whatever you do, do not be hindered by negative outside influences. And with that, one by one my childhood irrational fears and apprehensions began to fade. They didn't disappear, and I knew they would always be with me. However, they were all manageable and navigable. I could call upon any of them and learn from them at any desired moment.

⁂

I was finally ready to tackle the massive fear relating to my father. The crucial pain I had been dreading. I proceeded with caution. Upon closer inspection, it appeared to be related to some enormous guilt I was harboring. I reasoned that it was connected to my lackluster response to the news of his death. A few weeks prior, I egotistically rationalized that he wouldn't want me lying in bed floundering in self-pity. He wouldn't want me feeling sorry for myself. He'd want me to be strong, tough, and resilient. Therefore, it was incumbent upon me to focus on my own healing and mourn him later. On display, I could clearly see that guilt from several weeks ago. Was that all this was, the need to face that guilt? How did that relate to my injuries?

Whatever it was, the overall fear was still too massive to examine here. Using my newfound tools, I resolved to jump ahead again, to a moment when I was already mourning my father's passing. Experiencing that conception would hopefully assuage the guilt and resolve this mystery. Concentrating, scrolling through upcoming chapters, I searched for a period when those feelings manifested into peaceful harmony. And with that, images and sensations of atonement were presented.

Concentrating, I was eager to see where my mind would take me. Cognitively, I was still deep inside my body, lying in bed, while simultaneously experiencing comfort, floating several days earlier in a water tank. And then, I was gently transported away — out of the water tank in the past and into the near future. It was bright and sunny. I was standing, leaning on crutches, in an open field, adorned in a blue button-down shirt, and a white loose-fitting linen suit, draped over my thin frame. No, it wasn't an open field. It was a cluttered outdoor space. A grassy knoll, perhaps. And I was surrounded by loved ones. While faces and features were indiscernible, a little like a dream, I was clearly among immediate and extended family. I felt it. I felt their essence.

Elements and details that were unclear, were filled in by strong emotions. For example, familiarity. I had been to that very spot many times. We had buried my great uncle and my grandmother there. I was in a cemetery. My dad and I had visited that place several times each year to pay respects to various family members. I thought I was in the future. Was this a memory? Was I reliving a prior funeral? I looked around. No, I was not in the past. I was in the future.

I intuitively sensed that it was approximately one year later. Still a victim of my faulty wiring, doubting my newfound abilities, I questioned my vision's authenticity. Thinking it was merely an elaborate drug-induced delusion, or a dream, I looked down half expecting to read my name on the fresh headstone, about a yard from my right foot. But it wasn't my name. It was my father's name etched into the polished, silver rock.

Yet instead of guilt or relief, I felt anger, rage. This was a new sensation, feeling intense negative emotions in an augmented reality. I wasn't mourning my father. I was angry. At him! Angry that he took the plane up in a storm. Angry that he risked both our lives. Furious that his business appointment was so important that it couldn't wait. Incensed that he had died! Even though I had forgiven him my anger was manifesting from this newly discovered massive fear.

I was confused. This couldn't be a memory of my dad's funeral. There was no way I was there. Logically, that burial would have already taken place while I was still unconscious in the hospital, a year earlier. Putting it together, I reasoned that it must have been his unveiling. In the Jewish faith the family returns to a committal site one year after death to ceremoniously unveil a person's headstone. The chief purpose of an "unveiling" is to mark the final resting place of the deceased, to remember and honor the life, and to serve as a focal point for people's memories throughout the ensuing years.

Regardless as to the ritual observance of the event, I was angry. I had not yet embraced the totality of the hurt. I questioned whether or not I had sincerely forgiven him. Irrespective, I was not feeling guilty. I was feeling rage! I was prepared to let it all out, directing my wrath at that single focal point in the ground, and to the decomposed corpse buried underneath. I reasoned that somehow, experiencing that indignation was a cathartic step to facing my mountainous fear.

Shockingly my fury was interrupted when a bear-like, dirt covered, masculine hand, reached up and out from under the packed earth, inches from the headstone, and grabbed my leg, knocking me off balance, pulling me downward. Family members rushed over to help. I fell hard, struggling to kick myself free. Horrifyingly, a second hand and forearm, wearing my father's gold watch, emerged from the grave, lunging at me, pawing at my shirt and stomach, grasping at my midsection, pulling me under. It was happening too fast for anyone to assist. The pain in my abdomen increased as I was being sucked underground. I struggled to break free! Before being completely submerged, pulled beneath the soil, I was violently yanked back to my hospital bed, writhing in pain.

My eyes were wide open. Awake! What the hell just happened? "Survival!" My heart was racing. I was alert. Adrenaline on overload. The familiar whisper provided a new message, "Or transcend!" My chest was pounding. "Survival!" The pain was unimaginable. There was no doubt, I was back in the hospital. In my hysteria I could not reconcile that recent nightmare. Was it a premonition?

Hallucination? Everything was spinning. Then the room filled with white smoke. Fog. Haze. Loud alarms sounded and several monitors buzzed and whirred vehemently. The whisper reverberated, "Or transcend!" Despite my initial panic, my heart settled. A calm washed over me. My pulse had slowed. It wasn't me doing it. I was dying. Two ethereal doors appeared suspended in my periphery. I was again being offered a choice.

The room was already crowded with men and women in scrubs and lab coats. My mother was watching from the corner. Physicians and nurses were reaching over me in every direction. "Survival or transcend!" The cacophony of sounds dimmed to a low white noise. Then silence. The medics' lips were still moving...but without sound. My chest zipper was quickly unfastened. I could see my internal organs and exposed chest cavity. I felt their hands all over, and even inside, parts of my upper body.

As I gently began to lose consciousness my contemplation was to choose survival or transcend! This was another opportunity. I was provided the answers and the choice. The fear was real, and it was massive. However, it wasn't an irrational fear of dying. It was the fear associated with survival. It was a rational fear of living! I could stay and face that fear or move on...peacefully. Looking at the pages and chapters ahead I chose to face the massive fear. I chose to stay.

When I awoke briefly that evening, the on-call physician explained that I had an internal hemorrhage, or bleeding, as a result of a stomach-suture rupturing. Apparently, my hypothesis and weeklong investigation proved correct. My condition was extremely fragile. Much worse than I was told. It was unclear what had caused the rupture. And the doctors could not explain how I mystifyingly resumed consciousness so quickly. What was clear to me, regardless as to my choice to "stay," was that my time was running out. I had to complete my emotional exploration and tackle this stifling fear so that I could resume my physical self-healing, or ultimately, I would not survive.

When I closed my eyes, the intensity of my focus, and concentration, prompted an almost immediate answer. It all materialized in pristine clarity. It was not an irrational fear of failure, inadequacy, or rejection. It was not an irrational fear of the truth surrounding my injures. It was not even a rational fear of death. I was reawakening, reprogramming, and learning how to overcome those. Instead, the massive stifling fear, the crucial pain, was revealed to be insecurity and loneliness, directly related to my father. It was nothing that I had expected.

Growing up, I always experienced incalculable safety. Admittedly, this may have been a false sense of security. However, I believed my father would always save me, regardless of the circumstances. It is heartbreaking that far too many children do not grow up with similar feelings of safety. My father was truly a blessing. In the dark my dad was always the light that would chase all the monsters away.

While I found safety in my mother's arms, it was always my father's immutable, stalwart presence that provided the illusion of absolute safety. He was the resolute force that stood between me and any real danger. Lost at sea, he would find and rescue me. Trouble with sports or even bullies, he would teach me to play, fight, never quit, never give up, and ultimately how to win. Even if he wasn't physically there, he was always a phone call or a brief cry for help away.

Don't get me wrong, my mother was also a strong force, however, whenever an issue of material security arose, her mantra was always, "wait until your father gets home." Heck, he protected her too. He protected our family. He protected me. Always had, and always would. Leveling off the plane and avoiding a nose-dive crash would be the last time he would save me. There would be no future rescue. No future safety. He couldn't be there. He died. I was on my own. It wasn't enough to forgive him. It wasn't enough to mourn him. The crucial pain, the massive fear, was accepting that survival meant facing life, and all of its challenges, along with the totality of my permanent injuries without my hero, without my protector, without my dad.

I spent the subsequent two weeks slowly embracing my revelations. Scanning all my future accomplishments without my dad. As far ahead as I could envision, I never quite got over that loss. However, the massive fear abated and morphed into both sadness that he wasn't physically with me, along with an immense warmth of his memory and essence that would *always* remain with me. Confident that fear, rational or irrational, would no longer be a stifling impediment, uninhibited, unabated, I immediately resumed my physical self-healing.

As a quick aside, during these weeks of remedial introspective contemplation, my only fond memories of that horrific hospital confinement were all credited to my mother. She was my only positive outlet beyond my meditative internal therapies. When I was awake, we would spend the better part of the day either watching television and sharing knowing glances at its banal stupidity or pass the time playing cards. I was truly blessed by my mother's company, as she provided necessary maternal comfort, helping to ease my physical and emotional distress. The modicum of joy I experienced during that period all derived from her company.

It had been seven and half weeks since that fateful crash. Regardless as to how much emotional healing I did, physically, things were so much worse than I could have imagined. There was no way for me to ultimately heal without grasping the totality of my situation. Accepting the present required truth and honesty. I was still not presented with an entirely accurate picture. I was at an impasse. It was impossible for me to ameliorate without knowing everything. The medical staff and I were not working in tandem. This travesty was about to finally come to a head.

My mother and I had just completed a marathon game of Gin Rummy and she excused herself to go back to her motel for a light dinner, shower, and a quick rest. Refreshed, we'd pick up again early in the morning. After Nurse Vanessa finished her shift, I retreated inward with the television on, broadcasting some random syndicated rerun, which created white noise in the background.

I was alone in the dark room, meditating, focusing on internally repairing my liver and kidneys, when I felt all of my energy drop. I opened my eyes and witnessed a red stream of liquid shooting out from my bed across the room. That was another surreal moment. And it wasn't a past or future transient experience. Nor was it a nightmare or an illusion. I clicked a button on my bedside remote turning the ambient room light on. I was covered in blood. The room was being painted with it.

A steady stream of blood was gushing horizontally through and out of the stitching around the lower portion of my left leg, still suspended by a metal bar above my bed. Apparently, an artery had burst and was hemorrhaging through the bandages. I cried out, but the trach-plug was not inserted, so no voice or sound was created.

I felt light-headed. Instinctually I knew I only had moments of consciousness remaining. I reached for the call button to alert the charge nurse, but it was on a hook, too far away. I struggled, violently shaking the bed, in hopes of making noise. But I was too weak. It was too late. Nurse Vanessa had left for the night. The late-night staff was scarce. There was surprisingly no pain. No sound. Nothing. I was fading fast.

I shook the bed again forcefully. One last burst with my remaining energy. And this time, surprisingly, the call button fell from the hook landing next to my right hand. I pressed the button repeatedly with my thumb. But no one came. I watched the stream of blood from my leg lessen like someone turning down a water hose. The only minute noise I could muster was created by banging the hard plastic call-button-box against the guard rail. Clang-clang-clang. I was barely cognizant. I was bleeding out. Clang-clang-clang. I was about to die. Clang-clang. Weaker and weaker. I was fading. Everything was getting foggy.

It was happening again, but this time there was only one door. The decision was being made for me. By outside forces. There was no internal whisper. No choice. I glanced over to my left and saw my father, wearing the same blue short-sleeve button down shirt from the airplane. His big giant paw reached over me and covered my hand. I stopped clanging the call button against the railing. I relished his embrace. I acquiesced. In this frozen moment we were together. Everything was okay. Everything was going to be okay. Everything was always okay.

Holding on, I vowed to savor that last moment. I was going to enjoy it! I accepted the possibility that everything in my perceived future was merely my potential. My last realization was that the present can only be accepted through absolute truth. I was never going to fully heal without it. Perhaps that wasn't necessary any longer. Perhaps knowing and accepting that was enough. Perhaps I had ultimately experienced and learned everything required here on earth. The last thing I remember as I lost consciousness was a feeling of peace, without any fear. The present was wonderful! I passed out cold. I was ready for whatever was coming next.

9

THE TRUTH

Flash! Snap-snap! "Can you hear me?" A female voice alarmingly barked. Fingers were clicking and snapping. I was no longer unconscious, yet I wasn't fully awake. My eyes were pried open. Nothing was visually discernible beyond a blinding flashing light. "We're losing him!" The same voice commanded to a crowded room, seemingly filled with people. Click-click. Flash! Flash-flash! "Come on stay with me." Snap-snap! When the light was removed, I could see the movement of a young female surgeon obstructed only by the snapping of her slender, calloused fingers less than an inch from my face. I was so weak.

For a moment I had a memory blast of being woken up by the floating head doctors. It was remarkably similar, apart from the doctor being male instead of female. Had I dreamt this whole past month? Was all this just an elaborate fantasy? No, this was different. This was new. I was so weak. And this time, I was dying.

I was floating. It was so different from my drug induced incorporeal experiences. I was barely conscious, wafting peacefully toward that door hovering just above me. It opened slowly as I approached. "Code blue, stat! He's crashing." The terrestrial voice was muddled through the haze. For the first time I could see beyond the door. Love and light emanated from the other side, just beyond the threshold. It was bright, but not blinding. Soothing, like a warm spring morning. I was at peace. Drifting. And then suddenly, I was violently yanked back.

I wasn't fully returned though. It was as if I was caught between co-existences. The periphery of everything visual was cloudy and soft, like a dream sequence in a classic movie. Flash! Snap-Snap. Aside from the continuous snapping, the only muffled sounds were commands, orchestrated by that fearless female medical warrior struggling to save me. "Head down damn it! Keep his feet elevated. We're moving him." Snap-snap. Snap! While she was calm and in control, the serious nature of her taut face expressed the dire nature of my predicament.

"Why wouldn't they just let me go?" I pondered. "Why was she so serious?" For all their inability to conceive that I could survive, they sure were doing everything they could to save me. I found the whole thing amusing. Endearing, but not necessary. "Why all the fuss?" I was okay. Content. At peace.

When the penlight was removed again, I observed the most remarkable spectacle. Surprisingly, they were only four people in the room huddled around my bed. I'd have sworn there were upwards of fifteen-to-twenty people. But alas, there were only four. Three of them were wearing light green medical scrubs, masks, tight caps and gloves. One was on my left, steadying my elevated and mangled leg, keeping my body still. I couldn't comprehend why someone was needed to secure me, since I barely had the energy to move.

On the left side, even closer to my head, was a male attendant examining the equipment, along with the wires and tubes protruding from my body. Most notably was Nurse Vanessa, standing on my right, at the foot of the bed, dressed in jeans and an oversized Hawaiian shirt. Seeing her out of uniform for the first time only added to that marvelous spectacle.

I then witnessed something surreal. Nurse Vanessa was actually reaching inside the fleshy exposed bottom of my left calf. I presumed that had to be a hallucination. The lower portion of my left leg was still attached and suspended by the metal bar about two feet above the bed. And that same limb was being held in place, steadied from the opposite side by one of the other attendants. Nurse Vanessa's hand was locked inside my leg. Actually inside! From my perspective, I couldn't see past her wrist, as her hand disappeared buried deep within my open wound.

The majority of my bandages were still intact, wrapped around the remainder of my left leg. And there was Nurse Vanessa in her civilian street clothes, kinky hair flopping about her face, covered in blood with her fist clasped tightly inside my exposed limb. If that were real, she was a rockstar! She was fixated on her grip. Forearm muscles bulging! Logically, I should have been reeling in pain. And yet, I felt nothing. The female surgeon reached over, inserting a large silver metal clamp, replacing Nurse Vanessa's hand. Backing away, Nurse Vanessa turned her head for a fraction of a second making eye contact with me. And just like that, I knew that entire experience was real.

Everything went black...and then the brilliant light returned. Instantly, I found myself perched in the doorway looking back down at the four medics working on my unconscious body.

Flash! Snap-snap! "Okay, on three!" I was violently jerked back again by irritating flickering lights, as the female doctor's slender-calloused-hand continually snapped in front of my face. Something was forcing my eyelids open. Each time I was jarred awake my energy diminished. My earthly life was fading.

Amazingly I felt my essence awash in contentment, tranquilly slipping away. No pain. No fear. Completely surrounded by love. "Why wouldn't they just let me go?"

Snap-snap. "One, two, three. Lift!" Two additional muscular male orderlies were now in the room. They lifted me from the left side carefully moving the entire metal apparatus above me, securing my suspended and mangled leg. Nurse Vanessa and the female super-doctor helped from the right side. In my stupor, as prepared as I was to transcend, I was mesmerized and captivated by the hospital staff's proficiency. It's entirely possible that the only reason I didn't die right there was because I was truly enjoying the show. I watched from the doorway above, as they shifted me from the bed to the gurney by using my sheet as a hammock-like conveyance. In my dysphoria I was dumbfounded as to why nothing hurt. For months, the slightest movement had caused searing agony. And yet, I was now completely at ease. As they moved my body away, I felt myself drawn across the threshold and out to the other side. Warm. Inviting. Peaceful. Love. Closer and closer. Love!

And once again, I was pulled back. Flash, flash-flash. More light! But this time it wasn't the doctor's pen, but rather a blur of fluorescent ceiling lights, as they raced me down the hallway, at a sprinters' pace. In unison this team of heroes were all running in sync, including Nurse Vanessa who stayed with us. Their cohesion was remarkable. However, my energy was depleted. Hovering suspended, just above me, the convivial doorway remained open accompanying us down the corridor. Its peaceful emanation was invigorating. I was ready to drift away. Through to the other side. Ready for whatever awaited me. "Why wouldn't they let me go?"

Just then, a rush of adrenaline jolted me awake! My body was infused with a powerful stimulant and oxidizing compound. All my senses were overloaded. It was akin to inhaling deeply, immediately following temporary apnea or asphyxia coupled with an adrenal boost of espresso. I was instantly cognizant of everything! Noises returned at an amplified volume. Acutely aware of my surroundings I could see and hear everything. The haze was gone. Sadly, with clarity the pain also returned with a vengeance! Through my wired jaw I groaned in agony. Only moments earlier I was at peace. Now I was once again suffering. "Why couldn't they just let me die?"

Despite my writhing in agony, they traversed the passageways at a quickened pace, hurrying as fast as they could. The chief surgeon looked down at me with a changed expression. Instead of her determined game-face, she conveyed an expression of deep sympathy. Her face was upside down from my vantage point, directly above mine. Her breath smelled of stale coffee. "I'm so sorry but I can't give you any painkillers right now. We have to test to see if there's a blockage. The next twenty minutes are crucial. Bear with us the best you can. You're doing great!" She patted me sympathetically on the right shoulder, adding, "Hang in there!" And with that, she looked down the hallway focusing on her mission, game-face back on. The pain was unbearable and the chemical mixture of oxidized stimulants assured my sharp sensory perception. In other words, I acutely felt it!

Observing this doctor and seeing how she approached life, specifically my life, inspired me to reconsider my yearning to transcend. In my stimulated condition

I was instantly aware of what was beyond the doorway and what remained here on Earth. Before being amped up I didn't quite make it all the way across, but I had experienced enough. Part of me did cross the threshold and touch the other side, providing me a rare privilege of experiencing multiple planes of existence. I now knew for certain there was something else awaiting me. I knew it was glorious and that it would always be there, so there was no urgency to get there. That provided me ample comfort to remain with this angelic surgeon here on Earth a little while longer.

An oversized wooden door electronically swung open as we rushed into a spacious room filled with high-tech machinery. My gurney stopped in front of an array of electronic equipment. A tall slender male doctor joined the group. He was concealed, head-to-toe, in sterile light blue polyester scrubs and latex. Only his eyes were visible. Sadly, my painful throbbing refused to abate. If not for my distress, I otherwise would have found this experience fascinating.

Because the pain was so terrible I desperately tried to pivot away. I focused on the hot tub and the serenity of the water. But the stimulants were too powerful. The drugs would not afford me the opportunity to break free. They anchored me, captive to the pain. Another insightful epiphany: "drugs" and "artificial chemicals" have a direct adverse effect on the present, inhibiting my newfound tools. I would have to remember that.

With nowhere else to go I made the most of this intriguing theater. Taking it all in. The tall attending medical technician, resembling an animated blue beanpole with eyes, was conferring with my female surgeon about me in the third person. I'm not certain you ever get used to everyone speaking as if you're not there. Still unable to verbalize or audibly clear my throat, I loudly tapped my hand against the cot's guardrail to get their attention.

Addressing me directly Doctor Beanpole began, "this scan is essential to tell us if there's a blockage. What we do is insert a purple dye into your bloodstream here" pointing to several elongated rectangular monochrome screens, which displayed my entire body in silhouette. He then proceeded to inject a purple liquid into a tube attached to my arm, while an orderly fidgeted with equipment behind him. The Beanpole continued, "as you can see, the colorful dye travels through your body and we follow it making certain that it can flow freely, unobstructed."

I watched in amazement as the little purple dot on the rectangular screens traveled like a digital ball in a video game up, around, across and throughout my body. The liquid was warm, passing through the respective areas. However, the sting was excruciatingly painful at times, which only compounded my already agonizing torture. This whole experience was awful! In response to my wailing, Beanpole explained, "Unfortunately, it can be a little painful."

I blankly looked at him wide-eyed, silently expressing, "Ya think?" If that moment were in a sit-com someone would have handed him a "Captain Obvious" award as confetti dropped from the ceiling.

The inane Blue Stalk continued, "Most of the time we do this test while the patient is sleeping or at least anesthetized." Someone must have plugged my trach-valve in, because my cries became amplified as the purple dot traveled to the lower part of my body. "It'll all be over soon. You're doing great!" I suppose he did his best to reassure me, as though I had any choice. "Unfortunately, we need you awake, and we can't give you any painkillers until we're done because we don't want them to adversely affect the movement of the dye."

Thankfully, the familiar female surgeon returned, with her sympathetic smile. She was right-side up this time, facing me. It was comforting to see her. Examining the screens while she spoke, "You gave us quite a scare young man." Then, looking directly at me she added, "Don't you do that again." While one of the male nurses injected something colorless into the tube affixed to my arm, she explained, "He's giving you something to help take the edge off. Rest. You're going to be okay. Close your eyes and count back from a hundred." She patted me affectionately.

I felt the warm, pacifying flow of the newly introduced liquid up my arm and shoulder. Silently I counted backwards, "One hundred." I was melancholy. As I began to fade, the floating door, above me, closed and then dematerialized. "Ninety-nine." The door was gone. After months of pain, this past week had been the worst yet. Brutally torturous. I was ready to die. "Nighty-eight." And yet outside forces, again, brought me back. But this time was different, I had touched the other side. The choice was mine to stay. I hoped this was a turning point with the severest pain behind me. "Nighty-seven." I had been through enough. Since I was resolved to live, I was determined to heal. "Nighty-six." Peacefully drifting off into a dark drug-induced slumber, I reflected on the future.

I woke up on a lounge chair, on a beautiful white sandy beach. The light-blue crystal ocean glistened several yards away. The place was familiar. But it wasn't a specific memory. It was more like an amalgam of memories from a few nondescript beaches from treasured childhood family vacations. I was acquainted with that shallow clear blue ocean. I could have walked a half-mile from shore and still been up to my waist. It was beautiful.

I dug in, scooping handfuls of sand, letting the grains fall gently through my fingers. However, they became hot. Scorching! I recoiled at their touch. I looked down, my hands had second degree burns. The beach, empty moments ago, became filled with people. They were pouring out from the tree line behind the sand. They were all running away from something. As they reached the blistering shore their feet and legs melted. Some of them burst into flames. A few made it to the water, steam emanating from their bodies. This wasn't a memory. This wasn't a time augmentation. This was a nightmare.

Glancing back, above the tree line, I could see a nuclear mushroom cloud. A gray plume of smoke with radioactive thick dark rings rising high above the treetops. Thousands of people were now surrounding me, many of them smoldering, burning and liquefying in the sand. My own lounge chair was melting. My left leg, completely submerged in the sand, burned as if consumed by lava. I knew it was a nightmare. Another manifestation of my pain. And yet, because of the narcotics there was no escape.

The horrific nightmares were expressions of my chemical withdrawal. And as the weaning process ramped up they exponentially worsened. This was just something I had to pass through. It didn't matter how much I focused. It was no use. Concentration was futile. The drugs being pumped into me created an artificially induced prison of terror. There were no shelters. No safe harbors. Nowhere to hide. I was incarcerated deep within my own intoxicated mind, forced to endure one outlandish aberration after another. This involuntary weaning brought unbearable physical pain to the surface, combined with shaking, heavy sweats and severe dehydration.

The week prior, my doctors had successfully weaned me off the powerful opioid, Meperidine Hydrochloride, using Morphine, a slightly less addictive opioid. However, the physical and psychological pain increased tremendously as they began weaning me onto Methadone. The optimistic expectation, depending upon my reaction, was to drop me down to Codeine by the following week.

The ambient Intensive Care Unit surroundings only amplified my intoxicated nightmarish state. The violent television news, disturbing commercials, endless hospital hallway noises and cries of pain from other patient-inmates, all enhanced my horrific delusions. Not to mention, during my medicinal meditations, or on those rare occasions of peaceful slumber, I was routinely interrupted by the hospital's scheduled protocols, rousing me every six hours, checking my vital signs.

The whole experience was annoying, distressing and maddening. I repeatedly reminded myself, tongue-in-cheek, that it was my choice to stay.

Intriguingly, all the drug induced dreams were similarly themed. They were painfully graphic and grotesque, taking place either moments before, during, or after a post-apocalyptic nuclear holocaust. Images and ideas engrained into my programming. In one way or another, they involved visible mushroom clouds, acid waterfalls, blazing forests, cauldrons of oceanic fire, and flotillas of corpses being incinerated. I would transition from one disaster to another, endlessly. These echoes were clearly a byproduct of the fear mongering and brainwashing from my childhood. In the nineteen eighties the threat of global nuclear annihilation permeated every aspect of American culture, news and entertainment. And sadly, those vivid nightmares all remain in the present.

My overnight torment only reinforced my conclusions and solidified my resolve. I was not being told the truth by my doctor or my mother. I was not being provided a complete picture. There was no way to reconcile the extreme and increasing pain if my condition was improving. Intuitively, I knew there was no way to effectively self-heal without knowing the scope and totality of my ailments. My only chance for survival and recovery was to be afforded the absolute truth. And I vowed to demand it from Doctor Johnson!

Outside forces and influences presented ubiquitous impediments from within the hospital. On the one hand, as proficient as my self-healing ability was I still required assistance from the medical community. The problem was the faulty programming, preconceived notions, of the entire medical staff.

Firstly, all of them, including the chief surgeon, believed that any negative news would shatter my morale and hinder my recovery. Therefore, the gravity of my dire condition was being withheld from me, for my own good. Secondly, and more importantly, almost everyone believed that I was not going to fully recuperate. From the first paramedics who rescued me, to the interns on call, the majority of the medical staff were convinced my death was imminent or at least permanent brain damage was a surety. That was their truth. Their honest reality regarding my prognosis was negative and pessimistic. They did not believe my self-healing claims, and yet they were all continually mystified by my improvements and baffled that I was still alive. Their brainwashing obfuscated the truth, so much so that they couldn't believe their own eyes.

How could they possibly expect me to survive if they were certain my death was imminent? While many tried to mask or withhold their apprehension, their cynicism was palpable. If someone believes they'll fail, they often do. It's even worse when that pessimism is projected onto others. It becomes a self-fulfilling prophecy, often by both parties. If only they could have seen past their programming. The reality was that my injuries were significant, and life-threatening, however, there was also a strong possibility that I could make a full recovery. Their collective patronizing and false positivity only added to my frustration.

On a random morning of clarity, as the predawn stimulants took effect, focusing intensely on my dilemma I received new guidance, "Truth!" Each day at this time I was busy managing my restoration as best I could despite not having the whole picture. By then, I fully accepted the grace of that whisper. Relaxing my breathing and heart rate, I concentrated on both my overall condition and the incoming message. It was as if my meditative questions were continually being answered. Intriguingly, I began ingesting insight regarding "truth," in general. I narrowly focused my attention on that one concept. Providentially, basic fundamental knowledge was revealed. It was insultingly infantile. I recall feelings of idiocy and foolishness at its simplicity and straightforwardness. As if it had always been there. Right in front of me. The obvious universal absolute is that "truth" is objective. "Truth" is not subjective. It can't be. The "truth" isn't an opinion. It just is. I digested and accepted the powerful, yet elementary, insight. In its simplicity, it was heavy.

Truth, in and of itself, is absolute, or a finite, definitive fact. It does not evolve or change. It is not an opinion. It is the same for everyone and everything. The truth is not affected by ignorance. Therefore, misperceptions are merely anchored by ignorance or naivety. Similarly, theories and philosophies are subjective beliefs, desires, and opinions.

But isn't our knowledge of all things always evolving? Yes, of course it is. Knowledge is also individual, personal, and subjective. It develops, changes and grows. For example, do extraterrestrial, interstellar or inter-dimensional beings exist? I don't know. My firsthand knowledge is subjective, and presently limited. However, my belief, or skepticism regarding their existence in no way effects the truth of the matter. They either exist or they do not, regardless of my knowledge or belief. This was huge. Truth is objective!

Another alarming insight I received regarding truth was that I was at a crossroads, physically. If I did not obtain the objective truth regarding my condition, I would not survive. It was imperative that I confront Doctor Johnson as soon as possible and get the information from him.

Hearing my mother enter the room, I reopened my eyes, relieved to see her loving smile. "You poor thing," was all my mom could think to say. Pale and flush, she had small bags beneath her bloodshot eyes. Under her arm, she held an oversized, adorable, plush stuffed white monkey. She asked me, "How are you doing?"

I briefly scribbled on one of the plastic sketchpads about the recurring nightmares and that it was preferable to be awake. I drew a crude representation of a nuclear mushroom cloud, explaining that, "the weaning process was taking its toll on me."

She sympathetically expounded, "I had been here all night watching you sleep, observing you." She paused. "You tossed and turned, crying out in pain all night long. It's impossible for me to sleep. And I'm not allowed to wake you up." Referencing the doll, she said, "Here, I bought you this from the gift shop." She placed the monkey on my pillow next to me. "They told me that you could finally sleep with a toy. I thought he might bring you comfort."

I scribbled, "Thanks." With a smiley face, adding, "I'm so sorry." And, "I hope you at least got 'some' sleep." I looked at the monkey. I wrote, "Don't you think I'm a little old for stuffed animals?" She smiled. I looked at the monkey again. He was adorable...and so fluffy. I then hugged him tightly and quickly wrote, "I love him! I'll call him Doc."

My mom clarified, "I don't think my nightmares are as bad as yours, however, mine are all pretty horrific too." Apparently, she wasn't getting any sound sleep either. I offered her Doc, but she simply pushed him back towards me, saying, "No, he'll watch over you when I can't be here." She then gently stroked the monkey's puffy head. "I'll take him from you if I need him." We tenderly and tightly held hands, soothing each other. We were in this together. "The doctors called after you hemorrhaged," she explained. "I rushed right back over. I didn't even have a chance to shower. When I got here you were already stable and passed out. I've been wandering the halls with this monkey all morning waiting for you to wake up."

Confused, I wrote on the plastic pad, "hemorrhaged?" Although I'm certain I misspelled it.

"Yes," she continued. "Don't you remember? Last night, the artery in your left leg burst. You lost a tremendous amount of blood. We are so lucky your father chose to fall out of the sky next to this hospital. Almost anywhere else in the country and you probably would've bled to death." She paused again, catching her breath. "Yeah, you almost died again last night. That's two times in one week! Thank goodness for this place. The crash team here is one of the best in the world."

"I remember blood shooting out of my leg," I wrote. "Thought it was all a dream." I captioned a stick figure caricature of a leg gushing liquid, "so that's what happens when an artery bursts?" She half-smiled. It was disappointing not being able to execute that line orally. Written deadpan deliveries were never quite effective. Regardless, being my best audience, she gently offered an uncomfortable courtesy guffaw. And I appreciated it.

Just then, the man of the hour, Doctor Johnson, entered the room to check on me. This was my opportunity to give him both barrels. I was prepared to let him have it. A week and a half of reconnaissance, compiling data and reconciling inconsistencies. He had been lying to me. Holding things back. My condition was way more fragile than he had attested. I had almost died twice in the past seven days from hemorrhaging. I was resolved to survive. The afterlife could wait. But only if I could have the facts. Damn it! Even if he didn't believe in my self healing, I knew that its success depended on the truth. I had my pen and paper ready to demand it. And I would not allow him to exit the room until I was satisfied.

He looked at my mom, "Oh good, you're here, and he's finally up." Turning to me he inquired, "How are you feeling?" I nodded and began writing. He rhetorically continued, "Rough night?" I nodded again and continued writing. Not waiting for me, he added, "I'll bet."

Before I could finish my first sentence, he jumped in, asserting, "I have already spoken to your mother while you were sleeping." Without missing a beat, getting right to the point, and uninterested in my side of the conversation, he affirmed, "Your condition is much worse than we have led you to believe. It is about time you knew everything."

I was stunned. I didn't even have the chance to give him one barrel. Mid-sentence, I dropped the pad and plastic red pen onto my chest. On the one hand, this was exactly the information I was about to demand. This *son of a bitch* stole my thunder. Took the wind right out of my sails by giving me what I wanted. On the other hand, now that my desired result was forthcoming, I was dreading the news. "Be careful what you wish for."

He jumped right in. "While we need to address your overall condition, it's the infection that's most disconcerting. It's not abating as we had hoped. Frankly, it's killing you. Now we could try and fight to save the knee, but the artery in your lower leg is almost completely gone. Ineffective. There are invasive bypass procedures, but at this point it isn't worth it." He paused briefly. "Son, the leg has to come off. You're out of time, with limited options."

Wow, that was direct, I thought! So much for objective truth. I meekly asked, "today?"

He quickly replied, "no, not today, but soon. The artery that burst in your calf earlier this morning is still weak and exposed. It's only a matter of time before it gives out completely. It's no longer a question of if, but rather when. And we'd always like to be proactive and avoid another rupture." He looked and my mom and then back at me. "Your skin grafting has been unsuccessful largely due to the infection eating away at everything. Also, your foot is not getting adequate circulation and while we've localized the infection, if we don't amputate soon the infection will spread to your entire body and eventually kill you."

※

As a quick aside, a skin graft is a procedure performed with a medical cheese slicer, whereby a thin epidermis layer is taken from healthy parts of the body and used as a bio-bandage, covering other raw exposed sections in hopes of healing open wounds. Over the past two months in order to salvage both legs, they were using skin grafts from my upper right thigh, lower back and buttocks. In general, grafting is routine, commonly accepted and typically vastly effective, except in cases of severe infection like mine.

※

Johnson continued his explanation, "For the most part your grafts have been successful, helping heal your hands, arms and lower right leg. However, the problem with your left leg is that the infection is eating away the healthy grafts before they have a chance to take hold. For example, during your first week here,

Doctor Cohen successfully used a microscopic graft from your thigh to repair your perforated eardrum."

Knowing how impatient he was, unwilling to wait for lengthy diatribes, I simply wrote a one word question, "options?"

He had another unemotional, blunt response at the ready. "If it were me, I'd take the leg off just above the knee. As soon as humanly possible. However, there's a chance we could make the cut a few inches below and try to save the knee." Not waiting for my retort, he clarified, "Frankly, your knee is a mess. You're most likely going to need years and years of painful reconstruction surgery, an artificial knee, and then who knows, you may eventually need a resection after all. Meaning the knee may ultimately need to be amputated anyway. But..." He then hesitated, which I knew couldn't be good. Especially coming from this new guy, Doctor Blunt-Bad-News.

Also, being that I had just experienced the longest oration since meeting him I knew he was serious. Hanging on his incomplete thought, I wrote, "But?"

He cleared his throat and continued, "Well, your mother expressed an interest in getting a second opinion at Schneider's in New York. Which I don't think is a terrible idea. I know the chief there and he's fantastic."

I re-underlined several times, the same one-word question, "But?"

"Because of your hemorrhage this morning, and your overall weakened condition, I don't think it's safe for you to travel yet. Frankly, you've lost a tremendous amount of blood. I think it's best if we give it at least another week and then reassess."

He turned to go. I held up my right index finger motioning for him to wait. Then, pointing to my pad, indicating that I wasn't finished. He reluctantly exhaled, being the busy man that he was. But I was successful in getting him to remain. While I was writing he said in an aggravated, impatient tone, "You have another question?" Before I could finish, I shook my head affirmatively several times.

My mother read over my shoulder as I scribed as fast as I could. I held up the pad which read, "Give it to me straight. The whole truth!" He folded his arms, thinking. I cleared the plastic toy, and quickly added, "Everything! All of it!" Followed by an underlined, "Please!" He seemed confused, having just provided his complete opinion regarding my leg. To clarify I wrote, "Not just the leg. Everything else."

He returned closer to the bed, and began, "Well son," looking sternly down at me, as if I had done something wrong. "I'm not going to mince words, it's not good." He expounded, "As we just discussed the leg has to come off. The only question is whether or not we try to save the knee. But assuming you make the trip, you can get that answer in New York."

I inserted a quick thought, "This pain cannot be normal." Adding a huge solitary question mark, filling the entire page.

He scrunched his face, thinking before responding, "The truth is that the majority of pain you are still experiencing is emanating from your leg. The body has billions of nerve cells. You have thousands that have been lacerated, opened and exposed to the elements. That's why you've probably noticed an increase in pain during the dressing changes. Right?" I nodded affirmatively. "It's bad enough having those nerve endings bandaged, but when they hit open air, it must be horrible. I can only imagine."

Looking over my chart, he continued, "Regarding the rest of your condition. I wish I had better news. Your kidneys and liver are still not functioning properly. And your strength will only improve if we could get you off these machines and eating solid foods again." He looked me over, preparing to meticulously cover everything. I think it was cathartic for him to get it all off his chest. I reasoned that the truth was liberating.

He didn't hold back! "You've lost vision in your right eye, and although we believe the damage is permanent, there is an experimental surgical procedure that Doctor Gold will discuss with you tomorrow. Regarding your hearing, although Doctor Cohen was able to repair your left eardrum, you've probably suffered significant permanent hearing loss in that ear. Grafted ear drums are never as effective as natural ones, and they're much more susceptible to future infections. Shall I continue?" He asked while carefully looking me over and flipping through pages of my chart.

I nodded and quickly scribbled, "Please."

"Well, you're going to have substantial visible scarring throughout your entire body. Fortunately, there has been tremendous progress in the world of plastics. They have come a long way since I started practicing. You'll have to decide what you can live with and what you'd like to try to repair. The same thing goes for the advancements in prosthetics. They too have come a long way." Pausing to think, he added, "I also imagine at some point you'll want to deal with the emotional trauma associated with the entire ordeal. We have trauma counselors here at the hospital. Now that you're awake and alert more during the day, I put in a request and someone should be by any day now. But that's a long process. Eventually, when you get home, you'll probably want to sit down and talk to somebody in your own area. You'll be pleasantly surprised that with a considerable effort you can still live a full, normal, and productive life."

I took in all the information. One word prompted a response. I questioned what he deemed, "Normal?"

Sliding back into preconditioning, he chose not to respond directly. I had hoped that we were now past the bullshit. His silence and lack of retort spoke volumes. Exhaling, and speaking from his authentic, albeit preconditioned, truth, he proclaimed, "It's a miracle you're still alive." He then concluded with a macabre caution, also based on his years of training and experience, "The reality is that your body has undergone a massive shock and a lifetime of physical stress in a matter of months. People who have survived similar traumas typically experience chronic pain as they get older, and most have regrettably shortened lifespans. It doesn't mean that it will be that way in your case. But you should be prepared."

I hurriedly scribbled, "I understand." And "Thank you for your honesty!" I could tell he was ready to leave ten minutes ago. I scribbled as fast as I could asking him to "Please, thank the doctors last night for saving my life."

He paused and proudly offered a rare smile, "It's what we're here for."

I wrote quickly, "Please thank Nurse V. for staying late."

"Why don't you tell her yourself. I don't know her schedule, but I'm certain she'll be happier hearing it directly from you."

I replied, "Ok. But please thank that very pretty doctor for me. I may not see her again."

He warmly replied, "Okay, I promise to relay your gratitude to everyone and especially to Dr. Laske when I run into her." He added, "You and your mom discuss everything, and I'll check back on you later today." Turning to exit, he paused glancing at my chart, adding, "I almost forgot. There is a bit of good news. Your wires come off in a couple of days. Happy Thanksgiving! At least that's something to be thankful for." He made a circular motion around his mouth with his pen. I gave him a 'thumbs up' gesture with my right hand and raised a similar 'thumbs up' from my new stuffed white monkey.

Looking at the doll, his smile evaporated immediately, unmoved by my stuffed animal. It's possible that his mind just turned to other more serious things. Or maybe he just hated stuffed animals...or white monkeys. Regardless, he dropped my chart back into a plastic sleeve mounted to the front of the door, turned, and left.

My mom and I spent the next several hours discussing the hard truth. I was both anxious and relieved. It was about time I received an accurate depiction of the entire present, allowing for me to accept and process my path forward.

⋙ ⋘

Examining that objective truth was heavier and more difficult than I anticipated. At age sixteen, my left leg was going to be amputated. I had recently lost my father, and vision in my right eye. I was permanently disabled and permanently disfigured. I was also preparing for a lifetime of varied pain and discomfort. While diminished hearing was going to be inconvenient it paled in comparison to my dramatically shortened lifespan. That was all going to happen. It wasn't subjective. No matter how hard I wished these things to be otherwise, I was unable to alter reality.

I asked to see my reflection. My mom brought me a small handheld mirror from the closet. I was instantly taken by the patch over my right eye. Up until

Doctor Johnson's revelation a few hours earlier, it never dawned on me that I had only been seeing out of my left eye. I then examined the bulky trach-valve in my neck. My face was gaunt, flush and pale. My hair was frayed. My teeth metallic. I was a monster. Who was ever going to love this face? I began to cry. Which prompted my mother to cry with me.

I gave her back the mirror, hugged the stuffed monkey and recomposed myself. I was not going to lay there wallowing in self pity. Survival was my choice. I closed my eyes, aware of the truth and the totality of my condition. I now had the essential tools necessary to resume my regiment of self-healing, both emotionally and physically. I focused on my circulation and respiration, immediately going to work, concentrating on restoring my liver and kidneys, while simultaneously flushing out the infection and detoxifying my entire body. I had the whole picture now. For the first time since the crash I was armed with the whole truth. Despite my own preconditioned pessimism and limitations, I now knew better. Reprogramming was going to take time. I reflected for a moment on how much healthier I might have been had they told me the truth from the beginning. And then I was reminded that I can't go backwards. I cannot alter the past. No regrets! I am exactly where I am supposed to be. Outwardly I would need to project strength and confidence. Reprogramming was going to take time. Let it take time. I was going to rise above my superficial appearance. I was going to survive. I was where I was supposed to be, and I was going to be okay.

The next day, my mother and I agreed that getting a second opinion in New York was the best course of action. As soon as I was healthy enough to travel we would relocate to Schneider's Children's Hospital, in New Hyde Park, New York, about eighteen miles outside of Manhattan and just about twenty miles from my Long Island childhood home, in Melville. Everything would be easier for my mother being closer to home. And Schneider's boasted one of the best pediatric orthopedic facilities in the country. Dr. Rosenthal, their world renowned chief orthopedic surgeon, would ultimately make the decision regarding my amputation.

My mother interjected, "I know Doctor Johnson is adamant about taking off your leg. And he's certain that nothing can be done, but I'm still hoping that maybe there's something that this doctor in New York can do." I then told her that in all my future visualizations I did have two legs. However, I'm fairly certain she thought my prognostications were merely delusional hopes and dreams.

Our only remaining conundrum was related to the return trip. We could either drive by ambulance or fly by private medical carrier jet. Driving the entire distance, just under one-thousand miles would take approximately three days. Or we could take a short, ten-minute drive to the Jacksonville Municipal Airport and charter a two-hour medevac flight. Both options were quickly approved by our insurance company. The choice was ours.

Doctor Johnson and the resident psychologist cautioned my mother about the trauma associated with even discussing air travel with me. My mother, assuming my debilitating emotional traumatization, didn't risk asking me. Therefore, plans and arrangements were being made for the lengthy ambulance trek, with nightly stops at local hospitals along the coast in early December. No one consulted me. For my own good.

※

That afternoon, while my mother was busy coordinating our trip home, the wires locking my jaw in place were surgically removed. It was such a relief being able to verbally communicate once again. While the vast majority of my articulations involved complaining about my ongoing excruciating pain, it was also brilliant being able to just blather on about nothing. Writing had been such a chore. I then reflected on my appreciation for the whole experience, closed my eyes and resumed my self-healing.

※※※

Over the next few days, when I wasn't dealing with post-apocalyptic drug induced nightmares, I was fully committed to my overall healing. Being aware of and accepting the totality of the present, I utilized my ability to slow time, pacify myself in water therapies, and sooth myself with future visions of love and prosperity. I also continued to heal my body and spirit through cautious and meticulous focus and concentration. The entire medical staff was stupefied that my liver and kidneys mysteriously began functioning again. Regardless as to the how or why, the good news was that solid foods were immediately reincorporated into my diet. They were also dumbfounded that both of my recently injured lungs seemed to be performing at full capacity. Their programming concluded that it was all a miraculous coincidence.

While my vital signs were stable and improved, the most amazing aspect of my recovery was that the infection in my leg was almost gone. And although not completely eradicated, the negative overall effects were dramatically reduced. Doctor Johnson, outright rejecting my intentional healing contributions, once again attributed my remarkable recuperation to both a Higher Power and my being an otherwise healthy, nonsmoking adolescent with excellent genes. Everyone was so quick to dismiss the power of the mind to heal.

※※※

The very next day, while my mom was out getting some food, I was visited by the hospital's resident psychologist: a bespectacled female therapist in her early thirties. Holding a clipboard and a pen, she came over to the bed, about to lean on the railing in order to connect and get a little closer to me. Using my stuffed monkey's hands I quickly held up a preprinted sign, "Please do not touch the bed! The slightest touch hurts him very much!"

She caught herself, stopped, and balled her open hand into a fist, holding her pen tightly, pulling it back making sure not to touch the bed. Looking me over, she said, "Yeah, I'll bet you're in a lot of pain."

I thought to myself, "Oh boy, this is going to be a rough conversation."

"My name is Dolores, I'm just here to see how you're doing. Is it okay if we talk for a bit?"

"Sure. It's nice to meet you." To myself I thought, her name will be easy to remember, as it rhymes with a female body part. I kept that thought to myself. I was only sixteen and still had an extremely silly, off-color sense of humor. I then babbled, "I just got my wires off. Talking is my new thing. What do you want to talk about?"

"Do you know your name?"

I was right. This was going to be a doozy. I replied, "Sure do." That was proceeded with a few moments of silence. Then I politely responded, "Laurence, it's some day in mid-November, Jacksonville Memorial, plane crash, USA, and Ronald Reagan. What else would you like to talk about, Dolores?"

"Okay, I get it. You're tired of the stupid questions. Overall, how are you feeling?"

"Like I was in a plane crash. You?" Again, silence. She just looked at me. I thought that was pretty funny. Maybe I'm a little rusty and my delivery was off, I thought. "Dolores, I'm just kidding with you." After a beat I added, "I feel great. You want to go for a race around the nurse's station?" Still nothing. She was going to be a tough crowd. But I wasn't going to give up. "Seriously, you go, I'll give you a head start." She scribbled a few notes. "I'm really fast. Go!" I motioned with my hands and arms as if I just ran like a track star, at lightning speed. Then I settled them quickly back at my side, as if I had just returned. "Okay, you weren't ready. You want to go again?" Crickets. She was a really tough crowd indeed. I pretended to wipe my brow and pant heavy from running. "No, you're right, we should stay here and chat. That's much better."

Pretending to catch my breath while speaking I continued, "Okay, okay, you're the hospital shrink. Let's jump to the part where you tell me I'm going to have a normal life and move on."

"Is that what you want me to tell you?

"That's what Doctor Johnson told me. Are you sure you don't want to race again?"

"You like to deflect with humor, that's good. Do you mind if I sit?" She pulled up a wooden chair from the corner and sat down next to me. "Well, he's right you know. There's no reason why you can't make a full recovery and enjoy a normal life."

She opened the door, I figured I could vent a little, "Okay, you want me to be serious. Well, the truth is that nothing about my life is going to be normal. I'm going to have a ton of pain, discomfort, disfigurement, physical therapy, disability, restrictions and struggle. Oh, and my life will probably be cut short because of all the physical trauma my body's just been through." She did not respond, and instead just scribbled a few notes onto the yellow legal pad attached to her clipboard. While she was writing, I added, "Don't worry, though. Aside from all of that stuff I just said, I will have a wonderful life. It just may not fit your definition of normal." I proceeded to list many of the wonderful things I was going to accomplish, which included several different careers as well as cultivating a loving family.

She patronizingly commented, "It's wonderful you believe you will accomplish all of that. Several different careers, that's impressive. Eventually, you might want to narrow that down a bit. But you're young. You have plenty of time. Regardless, I wish all the patients here were as positive as you. Can I ask, how can you be so certain things will be so wonderful?"

I tried to explain, "I'm not being idealistic. I can see it. It's all here in the present. I cannot give you exact dates and details, but it's all here. Some of the things I will definitely do and some I may never get to, but they are all here in the present." To which she nodded, clueless as to what I was talking about. I could tell by her reaction. According to her preconditioning, my positive affirmations were healthy, but they were merely hopes and dreams. Childish fantasies. She couldn't actually comprehend the notion of visualizing and creating one's own future.

She snidely added, "Well, Superman, it looks like you've got it all figured out. You should be out of here in no time. I'm here several days a week if you'd like to talk further." She smiled and handed me a business card.

While she got up, ready to leave, my guiding whisper boomed a one word question, "Why?" The echo was loud and included a much more in-depth meaning than the one word, which I somehow intuitively understood. It prompted me to say, "Delores, before you go, can I ask you a question?"

"Sure."

And I just blurted out, "Why?" She stared at me silently for a moment not understanding the question. Then words and thoughts just came to me. I couldn't turn it off. "Why didn't I die in the plane crash? Why was I spared? Why did my father die, and not me? Why me?" And then I just simply repeated, "Why?"

Without pausing she said, "Why do you think?"

I replied, "I'm sincerely asking you."

This reengaged her back into the conversation. She appeared very interested again, as if she were breaking through, connecting with a new patient. She sat back down and said, "Well, um, I don't have an answer. You're very lucky I suppose."

"Dolores, That can't be it. Lucky people do not get into plane crashes in the first place. Lucky people land their planes safely on the ground." It felt good taking that one out for a spin the very first time. I began by explaining, "There's only one objective truth." And then the strangest thing happened. The nature of the conversation instantly changed. It was no longer clinician-patient. I hadn't even scratched the surface yet and she was listening, intrigued, almost captivated. From there on, the words, knowledge and insight continued to flow. I was merely a conduit. The insight was emanating from somewhere else and streaming through me. My mind was open like a cosmic receiver and my mouth was a local transmitter. These weren't my words. I was merely saying them aloud. While I was communicating with her, I was really educating myself.

I continued, "Why was my dad taken and I spared? Coincidence or divine intervention? It would be extremely egotistical to claim divine intervention. That I was chosen by a deity for some higher purpose. How gauche of me to even consider it." I got to the point, "What is the objective truth?"

"Are you asking if I believe in God?"

"No, I'm saying it's irrelevant what you believe. Or even what I believe. There is no need to debate the existence of God. Whether God is a 'male,' a 'female,' a 'light,' 'love,' 'energy,' 'the universe,' or, whether God exists at all." I quickly explained, "Ignorance of a fact in no way negates the objective truth."

She leaned back in her chair. She was intrigued, curious, no longer writing. Just listening. However, I could sense her skepticism. I added, "My faith in God is immutable and personal. And I would otherwise capitulate that my faith is also subjective. At its very nature faith is subjective. However, my miraculous survival, along with the insights throughout my recovery and my ability to self-heal all indicate an objective truth and the existence of God."

"So, you're crediting your survival and insights to a Higher Power?" She rhetorically asked. "You do see the contradiction? Right? You admit that faith and belief are subjective by nature."

"Yes, faith in and of itself is subjective. It's a belief. It has to be subjective. It's like an opinion. It's personal. However, God exists irrespective of my faith or belief in him. He objectively exists or he doesn't. What I'm saying is that his existence simply has nothing to do with my belief. It's like your existence. You exist whether I believe you're here or not. Your existence is an objective truth."

Before she could chime in, I added, "And, these insights that I have been flooded with were not self-generated."

"How do you know that?"

"This stuff is way above my pay grade," I laughed. "And frankly, I'm not that bright."

"Do you believe God is speaking to you right now?"

"As a matter of fact, yes. But he's doing so through both you and I, with this conversation. Which means he's speaking through you too." It was true. Things had never been clearer. The entire conversation was yet another surreal experience. I seemed to be having a lot of them lately. And this was exciting, because for the first time I experienced the insight and received wisdom through an interaction with an outside force. My entire body tingled.

"So, objectively, what answer is God telling you in response to the overall 'why' question?"

I paused, focusing and listened, and heard nothing. "I don't know. It doesn't seem to work that way." I waited again, listening, looking around the room as though something might appear or some thought might materialize. Nothing happened. "But maybe that is the answer, that we're not meant to know the answer. Only the question. The grand scheme. God's plan. A higher purpose. You know, I've been overwhelmed for years with a strong desire to have kids. And one of the first thoughts I had, my motivation to live when I woke up over a month ago, was procreation. Perhaps I am here to do something special. Or perhaps I've just been spared at this time so I can have a family and my kids, or grandkids, or great grandkids, will eventually fulfill that higher purpose. Who knows?"

My mother returned with a cup of coffee. "So did you guys have a nice chat?"

I said, "It was okay. Nothing special. I was just giving Dolores pointers on how to race around the building while you're in traction." My mom looked confused, but being my best audience she smiled and chuckled quietly. It was always nice to see my mom.

The therapist jotted a few final notes, got up, took a deep breath, and said, "That was the most interesting conversation I've ever had with a patient. I hope you feel better soon. Dial that extension if you'd like to chat further." I waved goodbye using the plush, stuffed monkey's paw, and made it look like Doc was reading the card. On her way out she commented to my mom, "You have quite a son there, Mrs. Kaldor."

"Thanks! I know," was all my mom added. And Dolores exited, leaving us alone to watch a little mindless television and play cards.

Over the next couple of days, I spent as much time as possible focusing on my self-healing, both emotionally as well as physically. Every day the medical staff commented on how shocked they were regarding my recuperative progress and spirits. Doctor Johnson expressed his amazement that all my bodily functions including digestion and excretion were finally functioning normally. As an aside, without being too vulgar, I recall how thrilled everyone was the first time I successfully completed a bowel movement. I'm not certain anyone in my life has ever celebrated that before or ever will again. In an attempt to add levity, covering for my embarrassment I interjected an off-color joke attributing my metabolic success to the hospital's lousy Thanksgiving leftovers. I think my mother was the only one who appreciated my sophomoric sense of humor. It was great to have her around.

My extraordinary physical improvement coincided with the final days of the weaning process, whereby I was no longer chemically addicted to any powerful narcotics. Sobriety dramatically enhanced my focus and concentration.

During the morning of the second-to-last day of my ninth week in Jacksonville Memorial, my mother was busy on the phone making final arrangements for our relocation trip up north. It was a Thursday and if things went well with the drive we'd be in New York by the end of the weekend. My internment in that Florida hospital was finally coming to an end. I was shuffling the cards waiting for my mom to hang up so we could finish the game. We had been playing all morning in between her calls.

I was pretending to have Doc deal the cards when there was a gentle knock on our door. It was Dolores. I knew her name would be easy to remember. She poked her head in and began, "Hi Laurence, Hi Mrs. Kaldor, I heard you were cleared to leave the day after tomorrow. I just wanted to check on you before you left, say goodbye and wish you well."

My mom rose to greet her, with her hand covering the bottom part of the telephone receiver, and said, "Thanks. I'm on hold. That was very nice of you to stop by." She then put the phone receiver back up to her ear.

I chimed in, "Hi Dolores." I waved Doc's paw.

She smiled and waved at the stuffed animal, "Hello Monkey." She folded her arms, hugging her clipboard, stopping a few inches from my bed. "I remember, don't touch the bed."

"So did you think about our conversation?" I asked.

"Yes. It was very interesting."

I chided, "Not convinced, huh?"

My mom hung up the phone. "I'll finish making these calls later. I'll give you two a minute to chat." She then collected the cards and excused herself. "You were winning that one anyway. We'll play a new game later."

Dolores asked, "Does it matter if I'm convinced?"

"Not really."

My mother politely moved towards the door, "I'll go get some coffee and be right back. Would you like a cup?"

Dolores kindly responded, "No thanks, I'm okay, really. I have other patients to see. I was just stopping by for a minute to see how Laurence was feeling, catch you both before you left, and say goodbye. I'll walk with you."

I was amazed that her presence triggered a massive infusion of insight again. As long as I remained open, I couldn't turn it off. I was again bombarded with thoughts that were not my own. I was compelled to curiously goad her, "Do you at least accept that every moment is a gift? That every moment is precious?" There was something about that woman that prompted those thoughts. Perhaps she's the conduit. Or perhaps because she is receptive, she is the perfect sounding board for me to teach myself. Regardless, it was fascinating.

She stopped in the doorway, and turned back, "Yes. But..." As she was carefully thinking, she fully turned facing me and returned a few steps into the room.

My mom let herself out, "I'll leave you guys alone. I'll be right back." And she was gone.

Dolores glanced at her wristwatch and then refolded her arms, "Okay, I have a few minutes, go ahead. What's your point?"

I jumped right in, "Every moment is precious, right?"

She nodded affirmatively, "Uh huh."

I continued, "We all exist. We are all alive. We all receive innumerable gifts during our lifetime. "The Gifts" are these precious moments, all the moments or micro moments of our lives. Right?" She nodded again.

Like a lightning bolt, all the missing pieces came together regarding, "The Gift." My body was tingling again. As I spoke with her, I was overcome by how elementary, clear, and simple it all was. Almost too obvious. Again, I felt infantile for not getting it sooner. After receiving the present and thoroughly exploring it, all that remained was to appreciate it. Step Three was merely appreciation.

I explained to her that the key is to, "Live each gift as if it's your last and be grateful for where it came from!" I then rhetorically asked, "Who or what gave us these gifts? Where do these gifts come from? They objectively came from somewhere or were generated by something. And that answer must be an objective truth."

She cleverly replied, "Maybe they just exist."

I sarcastically questioned, "You mean they came from nowhere? Everything just appeared out of nothing for no reason at all?"

She had a textbook answer ready. "Sure enough, it could all just be existential, with no purpose. We come from nothing and we ultimately transcend to nothing. I'm not saying that is what I believe. I'm merely suggesting that it's possible. Many famous scholars and philosophers have postulated just such a theory."

I quickly responded, "Ah, so there may or may not be a purpose. But there is an answer. Logically, one of those things must be true. Remember, ignorance does not negate the objective truth."

"Sure. Sure, I'll give you that."

I continued, "And the same thing goes for when you die. The moment after you receive your last and final gift. Either existentially nothing happens or you transcend to some afterlife. Correct?"

She was taking it in, still hesitant, cautiously choosing her words, responding slowly, "I suppose so."

"Objectively, something will happen. Nothing is still something. Either life will just stop, or your energy and soul will perpetually continue. And, regardless as to what you believe here on Earth, when you die, you will instantly find out. Correct?"

She was okay with that. "Sounds right."

I too was eager to hear where I was going with this diatribe. "So, upon death, ignorance will be replaced with answers and the objective truth will be revealed. For everyone. Because everyone will die, eventually. Truth does not require faith for it to be the truth. Therefore, ultimately it doesn't matter what your faith, religion, or philosophical subjective opinion is regarding what the truth is. The truth will be revealed to all of us the moment after we die. When we perish and our life ends, we will all know for certain what the objective truth is."

She was now mystified. It may have been my imagination, but the entire room seemed brighter, as if rays of sunlight filled the space. I was being preachy and longwindedly proselytizing. I also knew that for me this digression was paramount because genuine appreciation of "The Gift" could only be achieved through acceptance that truth is objective.

I added, "We all receive our own gifts every moment of our existence because we are all special. Each and every one of us. Even you." I wished I hadn't made that joke. It was essential for me to hear, receive, and absorb everything I was saying. I quickly tried to keep things serious. "All kidding aside, the present is "The Gift" we receive and keep receiving all our lives. We are all chosen to receive these gifts. We all matter. Our gift is our life, given to us, repeatedly, in the form of this very moment, or the present."

Dolores only responded, "That sure was profound."

"Wasn't it?" I humbly agreed. I too was impressed. Then I added, "My subjective faith is that we all exist in the hand of God, always. But that's merely my subjective interpretation of God." I paused, putting the monkey's hands together as if he was praying. "What we do with the present or presents we receive are entirely up to us, individually. I'm not the same guy who fell from the sky a couple of months ago. I will never take a single gift for granted, and never let a moment or a present go unappreciated."

My mom returned holding two cups of coffee and a few condiments, and asked, "so what are you guys talking about?"

I jumped in with a silly, "Nothing much."

My mom handed Dolores a coffee along with a second cup, that was tucked under her pinky, containing a few packets of sugar, artificial sweetener and two small plastic containers of cream. "Here, I didn't know how you took your coffee."

Dolores took the coffee and condiments from my mom. Lost in thought and speaking a little disconnectedly, she stuttered, "thank-thank, thank you. That was very thoughtful." She was a little flush as if she had seen a ghost. "I sincerely hope you both have a safe trip." And she drifted out of the room, lost in thought.

My mom repeated in a whisper, "What did you guys talk about?"

I just smiled and handed her the cards. "Nothing terribly important. I'll tell you about it while we play. It's your turn to deal." Mom sat on her cot next to my bed, dealt the cards, and we started a new game of Gin.

At some point during the game I asked, "Why are we driving up to New York?"

She looked at me concerned, as though I had actually suffered brain damage. For the past forty-eight hours she was handling those arrangements almost non-stop. "Lau, you know, we decided to go to New York to get a second opinion and hopefully save that leg."

"Of course, I know that." I laughed at the confusion. "What I'm asking is why are we driving? Isn't it going to take like two or three days?"

"Yes, but the only other option is to fly."

I quipped, "And? Wouldn't that get us there in like only two hours?"

"Everyone, including Doctor Johnson and Dolores, felt it would be far too traumatic for you to fly again, especially so soon."

"But Mom, you know how much pain I'm in. The idea of bouncing around in an ambulance for days sounds dreadful and unbearable. If we could make this trip in a couple of hours..."

"Honey, I'm shocked. It didn't even dawn on me to ask you. I'm so sorry. Are you sure? You're not scared? Flying would be so much faster and easier."

"Mom, it's a no brainer. Let's fly home!"

Excitedly, she replied, "Wow! I'll call now. I have the number right here." Immediately, my mom picked up the phone and scheduled our departure. After the briefest conversation with the charter service, she said, "That was easier that I thought. We leave for New York Monday morning!"

With that, as if we were living in a dark television situation comedy, on cue, the second after my mother hung up the phone, the weather report on television was alerting us of an impending storm expected to hit the southeastern United States' coast this weekend. You can't make this stuff up. If this were a movie script no one would believe it. Talk about facing your fears. Irrespective of my bravado, I was anxious to say the least. I wasn't certain if I was tempting fate, being strong, or challenging God. Regardless, I was resolved to go. In only a few short days I was going to be back up in an airplane...potentially flying through another storm.

10

THE JOURNEY

The inconsistent gusts jolted the plane up and down and rolled it from side to side. Boom! Crackle, flash-flash! The thunder and lightning were unsettling, while rain hypnotically danced along the small circular windows. I watched intently as long liquid veins steadily streamed down the glass cabin portals. Memory flashes of the rough flight with my dad...Rat, tat-tat-tat-tat!...along with images of tree branches smacking into and cracking the front windshield echoed in my mind. Thwack! Thwack-thwack! Every turbulent tremor delivered painful shockwaves, riveting throughout my body. The extra doses of medical sedation were hardly effective. Having just completed chemical withdrawal, my pain medication was severely limited so as to avoid dependency relapse. In addition to my physical agony, the irony of being transported in a small aircraft during another tropical storm was not lost on me.

Amidst the bleak exterior panorama, I was fixated by the aircraft's red and green flashing wing-lights, highlighting the dark sky and gloomy clouds above and below us. As the plane was tossed about, I was amazed by the jet engines' powerful thrust, as compared to my dad's significantly inferior propeller-driven craft. I was also impressed with my portable bed. The transport gurney was surprisingly versatile and compact. The base was collapsible so it could fit comfortably and securely, mounted to the cabin floor along with the overhanging traction apparatus and necessary travel medical equipment.

Inside, a few yards in front of me, I could see the backs of the pilot and copilot in the open cockpit, as they calmly maneuvered through the raucous sky. Just behind the cockpit, two paramedical technicians were in jumper-style seats, facing me. Eli, a retired Air Force lieutenant, the larger of the two muscular men, was intently reading a magazine. His seat mate, Ryan, a retired Air Force colonel, stared blankly out the window next to his seat. Every few minutes or so, Ryan would look over at me and scan my travel bed, tubes, wires, and check my vital signs. My mother was seated directly across from me on a love seat along the cabin wall. She comfortingly held my hand intermittently throughout the flight. I propped Doc up so he could peek out the window. I know I was sixteen, but I have to admit it was comforting having him along for the trip.

The cabin was small enough that I could chat with everyone on board. Because of the congested ambient noise, the pilot and medical techs used their headsets, microphones, and cabin speakers to communicate. The pilot spoke to me without turning his head. "Hey there sport, how you doing back there?" It was difficult for me to verbalize an answer because of the pain caused by the turbulence. Through clenched teeth, I returned a smile and a thumbs up. He then continued, "You're a brave young man for taking this trip. Especially after all you've been through. If it were me, I'd be terrified to fly again."

Eli, shook his head knowingly, never looking up from his magazine, and commented, "Mmm-hmm, terrified."

I wanted to impress these gentlemen. I managed to laugh through the pain. Recalling my visualization of skydiving, mustering the strength to speak, I replied, "Terrified to fly? No sir, Captain, I love flying! I'm still hoping to join the Air Force once I'm fully recovered." This conversation prompted smiles, head nods, and silent glances from and between everyone on board, except Eli, who was lost in his rifle magazine.

The pilot slapped his copilot on the arm, "Can you believe that?" The young copilot turned and gave me a thumbs up over his shoulder. The pilot looked back at me and announced, "Son of a bitch. You're alright kid! You know that? Awesome!"

Eli, still engrossed in his magazine, added, "Mmm-hmm, awesome."

My mother announced to everyone, "Thank you all so much. You know, we were supposed to leave tomorrow. We truly appreciate you getting him out on such short notice."

Ryan replied, "It's our pleasure ma'am. I'm just glad the weather cooperated. This tropical depression just kicked up. We were fortunate to catch a lull and punch right through it. I served with all three of these guys in Nam. They were just little boys when they went in. But they were men when they came out. I assure you, you're in excellent hands."

Eli interjected, "Mmm-hmm, excellent!" never once looking up.

As the plane continued to bounce around, the pilot added, "We're almost past the rough patch. You just hang in there, okay? In a few minutes, it'll smoothen out. It's pretty clear the rest of the way. We'll have you on the ground in the Big Apple in no time."

The turbulence felt like driving on an unpaved road with a maniac at the wheel. Despite the brave face I was putting on, it was excruciating. I looked down at my bandaged leg, still in traction, and then out the window. Focusing, I relaxed my breathing and circulation. Concentrating on reducing the throbbing pain emanating from my severed nerve endings, I reflected on our hasty exit from the hospital earlier that day. I was impressed with the ease with which I utilized my recently acquired ability, navigating within the present. Staring out the window at the dark clouds, visualizing that morning, I recalled our harried exodus.

Our original plan was to leisurely travel at any time over the weekend. Unfortunately, we were delayed because of an impending storm, approaching from the Caribbean. Relying on the radar forecast, we scheduled our departure for Monday, giving the nasty weather system enough time to pass. Our plans were unexpectedly altered early Sunday morning when Nurse Vanessa found an alarming development during my routine bandage dressing change. Doctor

Johnson burst into my hospital room followed by my mom. Apparently, the situation warranted pulling the Chief Surgeon out of bed, on his day off.

"I got here as soon as I could. Okay let's take a look." Surveying my foot with his penlight, he muttered, "Yeah, uh huh. Uh, huh." His serious demeanor was unflinching, more so than usual. To Nurse Kelley he said, "We're going to need the portable cart with a number five and a number six. Before you go, hand me that handheld mirror," referring to a small mirror on a nearby shelf. Holding it up to my foot, he explained the exigent circumstances. "Son, let me show you." It was yet another surreal hospital experience. In the reflection I could see that my entire foot was red and several of my toes had turned purple. "See, these have already become gangrenous." With his pen, he pointed to the decaying, blackening, crusty tips of my two smallest toes.

My mom's right hand was covering her gaping mouth, unable to comment. I wasn't certain if she was going to gasp, vomit, or pass out. Nurse Kelley had already exited in a hurry, routinely knowing what the doctor needed her to get. Doctor Johnson continued, "The artery just isn't doing its job any longer. Your foot isn't receiving adequate circulation." His predictions were now materializing. I know I had been extremely critical regarding the negative impact of his preconditioning. However, there clearly was something to be said for his years of practical experience.

I asked, "What are those black bands?" Referring to two small elastic strips wrapped around the base of my toes.

"The nurses already put on a tourniquet, which will slow the spread, but there is no way to stop it." Doctor Johnson explained.

My mom asked, "So what does that mean?"

Without hesitation, Doctor Johnson bluntly said, "The toes have to come off now." After a brief pause, he added, "But we should be taking the whole foot." Nurse Kelley returned with a pushcart adorned with sterile, surgical tools, gauze, and neat stacks of cloth.

I asked, "What about the second opinion in New York?"

Doctor Johnson had walked into my room's small private lavatory to wash his hands. Through the open door he asserted, "You're out of time kid. And I hate doing this piecemeal." He stepped out, arms raised, hands firm, so that Nurse Kelley could put rubber gloves on him. Addressing my mother, he said, "Why don't you go outside and make that call?" Looking at me he suggested, "Turn your head, son. You don't want to watch this." He methodically grabbed his tools and began working. I couldn't look away. It was horrific and fascinating. I was captivated. "It shouldn't hurt at all. I've already injected the area just in case. But the tissue is already dead, it should feel like trimming your fingernails or cutting your hair. Only a little pressure. Do you feel this?" Then he poked my toes with a pointy silver implement.

I shook my head, responding, "No." I covered my stuffed monkey's face with his paws. He definitely didn't need to see this. I, however, was fixated on the doctor's hands, holding a long and thin pair of medical scissors that looked like forceps. The sensation of tight pressure on my foot was followed by a slight grinding sound. Snip-plunk, snip-plunk. And just like that, he cleanly removed both of my two smallest toes, placing the dead crusty nuggets onto a small silver tray on the mobile cart. There was almost no blood. No pain. Nurse Kelley stitched up the area quickly. Then, Nurse Vanessa sprayed something brownish purple onto my foot and expertly rebandaged it.

My mother returned almost immediately and said, "I just spoke with the charter company. There's a break in the weather, and they can get us out in about an hour. I don't want to look. How is he?"

Taking off his gloves, pleased with his work, Doctor Johnson spoke directly to my mom, "He's fine right now. This isn't the way to do it. I should have taken the whole foot." To both nurses he said, "Make sure the paramedics know that they have to monitor his circulation closely." He came over to my side of the bed. "Have a safe trip young man. I hope you get better soon."

My mother softly and tenderly said, "Thank you Doctor Johnson."

I added, "Thank you Doc." After a brief pause, I followed with, "for everything."

Not being one for long goodbyes, he just smiled, raised one of his hands, and said "Goodbye kid." And exited.

I thought about how nice it would be to come back years later and show my appreciation. Again, in spite of all my criticism, he had been the instrumental medical authority, working tirelessly in this trauma facility to save my life. Even saying that I am eternally grateful hardly feels sufficient to express the scope of my gratitude.

Grabbing a quick coffee, my mother had caught Doctor Johnson in the hallway before he left, allowing her the opportunity to thank him one last time. He reiterated his amazement that I had miraculously survived and his admiration for my resilience to live. He told her that he had already begun drafting a paper and outlining a lecture series chronicling my recovery, and how eager he was to follow my progress. They wished each other well, and my mom hurried back to get everything ready for our trip.

Upon returning, my mom quickly straightened up her small section of my hospital room, which didn't take very long. As for me, being the patient, other than my stuffed monkey and a few small trinkets and greeting cards, I had nothing to pack. All my medicines, fluids, portable machines, tubes, wires, and bandages were all prepared for us by the medical staff.

Lisa, one of my mother's closest friends from Long Island, had flown into town the night before specifically to help us get ready for our trip and take some pressure off my mom. This allowed my mom to stay with me, while Lisa coordinated with everyone outside the medical facility regarding our departure. Aware of our last-minute change of plans, she rushed over to the hospital, dropping off a small travel bag containing my mom's things from the motel. Reassuringly, she promised to settle the motel room charges. They only allowed

Lisa to visit for a few minutes, as the Intensive Care Unit room was fairly small and compact.

Lisa came over to greet me, keeping her distance, being forewarned not to touch my bed, and could only repeat, "Mmm, mm-mmm. You poor thing," and "Oh, dear God," over and over.

I greeted her politely, "Hi, Mrs. Goldberg."

To which she responded, "Mmm, mm-mmm. You poor thing." I just smiled and nodded my head silently, figuring we had already concluded the extent of our very meaningful conversation.

My mother was on the phone and reported to us, "There's been a break in the weather. We have been cleared to go." While she was talking, a slender, muscular medical technician, wearing a dark blue jumper-style uniform with orange suspenders entered the doorway. Not realizing he was standing behind her, she continued, "The guys should be here any minute to come and get us."

The technician gently knocked on the wall, and said, "Hi ma'am, I'm Ryan, we're here to take y'all to New York."

My mother, looking at the telephone receiver, still in her hand, then back at Ryan, and then again at the receiver, and once again at Ryan, "That was fast," adding, "I'm still on hold with your company."

Ryan interjected, "I think it's safe to hang up now, ma'am." She hung up. He continued, "We were already here, waiting. They must have cleared your flight before you called."

"That's great. We just need the discharge papers," she responded.

Ryan motioned for her to stay in the room. "Not to worry ma'am. My partner is taking care of that now. We should have y'all out in a few minutes." Then he walked away, back towards the nurse's station.

Lisa kissed my mom's cheek and gave her a warm embrace, "Have a safe flight home. This whole thing is a nightmare." Looking at me she said, "You poor thing. Oh, dear God! I can't believe you're okay flying. If I'd been through all this, you could never get me back on an airplane. Take care of yourselves. I'll see you both in New York." As she walked away, she assured my mom, "Don't worry, I'll handle everything. You just get home safe." After one last embrace and a tender kiss on my mom's cheek, she rushed off.

As they got ready to wheel me out, I pleaded, "Mom, we cannot leave without saying goodbye to Nurse Vanessa and Nurse Kelley."

"I know honey, I think they are still finishing their morning rounds. I've already told the staff. By now, the whole floor knows you're leaving. Hopefully the nurses will be here soon." She walked just outside the doorway scanning the hall in each direction.

Convinced I was about to be taken away in a hurry, I began writing a note of gratitude. However, I was uncertain what to write. All I had was, "Dear Nurse Vanessa, Thanks for everything." How pathetic. While I pondered my message, I was distracted, watching the two paramedics outside my room flirting with a couple of young nurses. There was so much more I wanted to express.

About a minute later, the two paramedics came back with two male orderlies. They wheeled a travel bed into my room, parallel to my hospital bed. While the foursome transferred me from bed to bed, I was moaning from the pain. Ryan said, "Sorry about that. Once we move you, that's it. This bed will take you all the way to New York."

"That's efficient," I thought. I was impressed by how well-organized, bulky, and sturdy the travel bed was. It had pockets and bags hanging on it and over a dozen hooks along the side rail. Its base was hydraulic and collapsible, allowing it to be lowered to the floor or adjusted to the height of my bed. It also had a similar overhanging metallic traction support for my leg. Within minutes Doc and I were neatly transferred. However, the new gurney wasn't as soft and padded as the hospital bed, to which I had grown accustomed. My off-the-cuff observational comments regarding its rigidity and stiffness prompted the orderlies to sneak me a few extra pillows for my right leg, back, neck, and head. Those folks were awesome. My mom whispered to me, "Nothing's free here. I'm sure the hospital will charge us for those." And we nodded, exchanging knowing smirks.

I asked one of the orderlies, "Do you have any idea where Nurse Vanessa and Nurse Kelley are? I really want to say goodbye."

He responded, "I'll see if I can track them down for you."

Watching the local television weather report was reminiscent of being with my dad in that airport motel room. Just like before, I ominously found myself waiting for the weather. Ryan and Eli wheeled me out into the hallway and parked my travel bed along the wall just outside my room. A random unfamiliar nurse came over to Ryan, "Here are his discharge papers." Ryan stuffed them neatly into a plastic sealable pouch hanging from the bed.

"Excuse me," I said to the nurse. "Any chance you know where Nurse Vanessa and Nurse Kelley are?"

She politely replied, "I don't, but I'll check for you." And she scurried off down the hallway. Everyone in the hospital was always so busy.

My mom came over with a few small travel bags, laying them on the floor next to my bed. "Okay, we're ready to go. How can I help? Is there anything else we're waiting on?"

Ryan replied, "We have your discharge papers, ma'am. We're only waiting on the updated transfer orders from New York. They sent us the ones for Monday. They have to fix them. It shouldn't be long now though. They should be faxed to the desk any minute, I reckon." He walked over, across the hall to the nurse's station, joining Eli, who was flirting with a different trio of nurses.

It was a relatively quiet Sunday morning. A few familiar hospital staff faces casually sauntered by, stopping for a few seconds, conveying similar farewell sentiments of kindness and warm wishes. "Goodbye," Good luck," "We'll all miss you here," and, "I hope you have a speedy recovery," were repeated as the diligent staff went about their business. For my part, while their heartfelt remarks were comforting, it was pleasing having the opportunity to thank a few of them personally for taking such good care of me. I wished it was Monday, when the place was heavily staffed, and filled with additional familiar faces so I could thank more of them.

And just then, Nurse Kelley rushed over, out of breath and smiling. "Oh my, I'm glad I made it before you left," still panting.

I was beaming. "Nurse Kelley, I'm so glad to see you. I thought I was going to miss you. I just wanted a chance to say thank you, to your face. And say goodbye!"

"It was our pleasure." She said to both my mom and I, observing the gurney, and all our stuff, "Bloody hell, it looks like you're ready to go."

My mom gave her a sincere hug and said, "Thanks for everything, Nurse Kelley."

I asked, "Do you have any idea where Nurse Vanessa is?"

"I think she's stuck with a patient up on six. As soon as I finish over here, I'll try to track her down for you. We're a little short staffed today. Oh, it'll break her heart if she doesn't get a proper goodbye." She leaned closer as if she was telling me a secret, "You know, since you woke up and starting scribbling, Vanessa has referred to you as 'the miracle child.' You're all she talks about. You've really inspired her. We see so much suffering and death in this place. For what it's worth, you've inspired all of us."

To my mom she added, "We're going to miss you two around here. We all thought you guys were leaving tomorrow. We had planned a small going away celebration. Vanessa put the whole thing together." Motioning over to the nurses' station, "Once we found out your plans changed, we all scrambled at the last minute. The gift shop wasn't re-stocked yet. It's not much, but there's a few things over there for you. Hopefully you guys can stop by on your way out." She looked over at me. I reached out, grabbing her forearm, pulling her close, tightly clasping her hand. Although the movement did cause tremors of pain the tenderness and connection was worth the momentary discomfort. We squeezed our palms together. She uttered, "Oh my, you're going to make me cry. I have to finish up this side of the floor. I'll try to come back and see you one more time if I can. I hate goodbyes." She affectionately caressed my hand, ever so gently, careful to avoid jostling the bed. She knew. She was wonderful. And then that angel darted off down the hall.

My mom, sipping her coffee, was met by the two paramedics. "We have all your paperwork, we're good to go. Let me help you with your bags, ma'am, "

Ryan offered, hanging the two small shoulder bags on a hook attached to my bed.

My mom grabbed the handle atop her small travel suitcase. "Don't worry, I've got this one," eagerly picking it up.

Ryan looked at his watch, "Ma'am, it's time to go."

Finally, I saw Nurse Vanessa exiting the elevator. She pivoted in slow motion, turning the corner and moving towards us. She rotated her head, looking up. We made eye contact, both smiling at each other. Then, she was suddenly stopped by a commotion behind her, as another set of elevator doors opened revealing several patients, requiring immediate medical attention. Two were walking, and one was in a wheelchair. They were being led by one nurse and a pair of orderlies. Nurse Vanessa turned quickly to help usher the patients into the Intensive Care Unit. I heard a resident tell a nurse as they hurried past, "There was a fire at a nearby factory, next to the military base. More are coming. The ER is filling up fast." The charge nurse barked, "page all on-call staff, stat!"

Ryan and Eli gently moved my bed out of the way as people rushed about. Patients continued to be chaperoned off the elevators and neatly put into medical stations. Ryan said to my mom, "When it rains here, it pours."

Within minutes the entire floor was inundated with doctors, nurses, orderlies, and patients. The entire Intensive Care Unit exploded into controlled chaos. It was evident why this place was rated one of the best. Bloodied and partially bandaged victims were being wheeled in with open wounds, visible broken bones, and severe burns. All the beds and stations were active. I was reminded how crowded and frenzied this place gets. Only moments ago, it was a fairly sedate Sunday morning. I then reflected on my own injuries and how I must have appeared upon arrival several months ago. This place was a machine.

Seizing an opportunity of calmness near the elevators, Ryan motioned my mom, "Okay ma'am, I think this is a good time. Let's do it. Here we go!" The ex-combat officers pushed me across the hall, towards the elevators, and over to the nurses' station. On the counter there were a few balloons, two small floral bouquets, and a stuffed cat wearing a doctor's white lab coat. Leaning against one of the vases was an oversized greeting card, adorned with signatures and well wishes. There was a sign made of large colorful paper capital letters hanging on the counter that read, "GET WELL SOON!" As we got closer I couldn't believe my eyes. Next to the stuffed cat-doctor I saw an oversized bag of strawberry Twizzlers. There was a handwritten note attached that read, "For Laurence, With all my heart, Nurse V." The entire display was overshadowed by the pandemonium of the moment.

My mother leaned over to the lone nurse behind the counter, who was busy typing and working the phones, "My friend will come by later this afternoon and collect anything we might have forgotten." The nurse nodded, half-smiling politely, and then went back to work. My mom added, in a loud whisper, "I know you're busy. I just wanted to thank you for everything."

The nurse said, "Please hold," then covered the receiver, smiled sincerely, and said to my mom, "It's been our pleasure. Here." And she handed my mom the stuffed cat-doctor and the bag of Twizzlers, then returned to the phone and her typing.

My mother crammed the little toy and the candy into one of the bags hanging on my bed and said to Ryan, "Ok, let's go!"

Ryan and Eli wheeled me toward the elevators. Just then, from across the crowded Intensive Care Unit, through a sea of light green medical scrubs and white lab coats, I caught a glimpse of nurse Vanessa's distinctive profile. She was tending to three different severe burn patients all at once. Two were lying on adjacent beds and one was in a wheelchair. As the elevator doors opened, I pleaded with Ryan, "Please wait just one more minute. Can we take the next one?" He thankfully complied, allowing the doors to close.

I slowed time, settled my breathing and heart rate. Looking across the room I concentrated on Nurse Vanessa, sending her thoughts and feelings of immense love and appreciation. I'm not certain if it was telepathy, but she paused and looked directly at me, staring at me. It was only a moment, a single beat, but it felt like an eternity. Her warmth was intoxicating, even from across the room. We both knew there was no way she could walk away from her patients. We were going to have to settle for this moment as our goodbye.

She interlocked her fingers, clasping her hands tightly together, closed her eyes, bowed her head, and prayed. She opened her eyes, looked at me and I mouthed the words, "thank you," and then extended my arms wide apart and mouthed, "for everything." She smiled, shaking her head, I knew she was chuckling even though I couldn't hear it.

The elevator doors reopened. While her hands were busy wrapping a bandage around a patient's charred head wound, our eyes locked again and she mouthed the words, "oh child." Ryan inched me forward, and then stopped, waiting for two doctors to exit the elevator. I gave Nurse Vanessa a thumbs up. She smiled, stopped wrapping the bandage for a split-second, and returned a thumbs up. Her cheek winced, and she wiped a small amount of water from her eyes, blinked, then caught her breath, and went back to work on her various patients.

Ryan wheeled me forward. Time resumed its normal pace. As we were moving, I savored that moment, knowing it was probably the last time I would see Nurse Vanessa, or anyone else from that hospital, for the rest of my life. Thankfully they will always be with me, especially her. I owe her so much. My last memory before the elevator doors closed was of her taking care of those multiple patients, barking orders, and navigating the triage line. In this auspicious trauma hospital, she was the conductor masterfully guiding the machine. She was amazing. And she was my friend. And just like that, no one seemed to notice that I had been wheeled out.

※》》》 ««««※

A slight bump of the elevator coincided with a small pocket of turbulence, returning my attention back to the medical service plane's cabin, and our flight home, staring out the window into the now clear and sunny blue sky. The captain, good to his word, provided us a mostly calm and smooth flight home. My mother, seeing that I was coherent, repeated a common sentiment, "this was so much easier than driving," adding, "I cannot believe you were okay with flying home. You're incredible!"

I responded, "I wanted to," which was the truth. I reflected on all the preconditioned fear that I was surrounded by. Almost everyone was convinced that I would be too traumatized to fly, and they projected their fear and disbelief onto me. However, moving forward, I was resolved to not be inhibited by fear.

Even though I was only in the infantile stages of my reawakening, it was a fascinating juncture to experience. I was better able to recognize the projections, impositions, and fears from outside forces. They were overwhelming at times, and even relentless, compelling me to conform, validate, and give in to their inhibitions. Regardless as to my recent awareness and growing ability to navigate their negativity, I admit it was often a challenge. Back then, I simply could not fathom that this particular lifelong tribulation would be repeatedly inflicted in perpetuity. In other words, I became aware that I would always have to deal with and overcome other people's fear.

Our landing and the subsequent ambulance ride to the hospital was relatively uneventful. Seeing my warm breath materialize in the cold air during the transfer was a stark reminder we were no longer in Florida. New York gets quite chilly in December. The short ride on the Long Island Expressway was picturesque and serene. The evergreens, sprinkled throughout the landscape, added a gentle contrast to the brittle autumn's otherwise leafless flora. It was a reminder that winter was only a couple of weeks away and, contrary to the frigid temperature, it triggered a nostalgic warmth of sixteen years of wonderful memories. I grew up here. There was comfort to the familiarity. To coming home. I reflected on my dad. He was here too. Everything was in the present.

Long Island Jewish Medical Center (LIJ), in New Hyde Park, New York, was quite a contrast to Jacksonville, Florida. Unlike the tropical Florida hospital, LIJ sat on a plush forty-eight-acre wooded campus only about eighteen miles outside Manhattan. While the main institution opened in 1954, the Schneider's Children's Hospital facility was much newer, opening only a year earlier in 1983. The hospital was state-of-the-art, fresh, clean, and much more luxurious than the Florida trauma hospital. Also, unlike Jacksonville's claustrophobic Intensive Care Unit, in New York, in the orthopedic wing, I was provided a large, bright, private room, with an oversized three-panel window, offering views of endless picturesque treetops and blue sky.

When they wheeled me off the elevator, I was taken by the vivid, colorful decor afforded a children's hospital. The hallway was tastefully decorated with balloons and a variety of oversized plush toys. As we turned into my new room I was awestruck by the flamboyant ornamentation. It resembled a wonderland. Every inch was adorned with flowers, cards, letters, photographs, and stuffed animals. Apparently, my arrival was anticipated and expected by my New York family and friends, who had been closely monitoring my progress. Unbeknownst to me, my mother had been updating the folks back home, almost daily, since the accident. Even the medical equipment was decorated, revealing only the switches, buttons, and information panels. The nurses who greeted us explained that there was so much more. This stuff was merely all they could safely fit inside the room. There was a vast overflow of my gifts decorating the hallways, nurses' station, and other sections of my floor.

Ryan and Eli transferred me quickly to the new bed. It was soft and spacious, infinitely more comfortable than the travel gurney, and more elaborate than the bed in Florida. My mother graciously said, "Thanks guys for making it such an easy trip."

Ryan kindly responded, "It's our pleasure, ma'am. I've never seen a hospital room this decked out. You're in good hands here. I hope you heal up real soon."

Eli just nodded, and said, "Mmm-hmm. Real soon!"

As they headed out the door, pulling the travel gurney I said to Ryan, "Thanks man." To which he smiled and gave me a thumbs up with his free hand. I reciprocated with a smile and a thumbs up. Then I added, "Thanks Eli, I've really enjoyed our long chats together."

He stopped, grimaced, as if he was annoyed, clenching his right fist. Then he broke into a half-smirk, winked, offered me a military salute waving his hand off his forehead, saying, "The Air Force would be lucky to have you, son. Take care of yourself, and your mom. Kid, you're alright." I quickly replied, "Mmm-hmm. Alright!" I saluted him back and we shared a smile. And just like that, they were gone.

Several family members and a few of my closest friends were already waiting in the lobby. They had learned of our premature arrival from my mother. However, visitors had to wait until after my intake examinations were completed. A young physician, in his early thirties, neatly dressed in a collared button-down shirt, tie, and white lab coat entered and immediately went for my eyes with his penlight. "Hi young man, I'm Doctor Wexler, the on-call today." He spoke while examining and looking me over. "Open." Flashing his light inside my mouth. And then my ears. "Let's take a look here." He walked around the bed and roughly undid the bandage covering my foot.

While it was strange seeing two of my toes missing, the excruciating pain from the jostling was more distracting. I winched, "Please do not touch the bed. The slightest movement is extremely painful." I made a mental note that my monkey needed a new sign for everybody entering my room.

He continued, "Okay. Sorry. I'll try to be more careful." He poked my foot in several places with the back of his pen and asked, "can you feel this?" Each time I replied yes, and that it hurt immensely. Then I asked if he could please stop poking me. He eventually stopped and rebandaged my foot with the same dressing and insensitive demeanor. The pain was agonizing. He then looked at my chart. "Oh my God. A plane crash? Is that right? You're lucky to be alive young man."

I looked over at my mom, thinking, "this guy cannot be for real." Unable to contain myself, I quipped, "Truly lucky people safely land their planes."

He paused. Stumped. After thinking about it, he replied, "You know, you're right. I never thought of that."

Being still, regaining my composure and catching my breath, I added, "Glad I could help."

After flipping through several pages of my thick medical history chart, he asked, "Hmm, can you tell me your name?"

I took a deep breath and just said, "Really?" He looked up from the chart, confused. "Isn't my name at the top of each and every page of the chart you're holding?" He continued to look at me, perplexed. I added, "Upper right corner. Of every page."

He looked at my mom, who was smirking. She shrugged, extending an expression as if to say, "don't look at me." Despite being a little uncomfortable by my rude sarcasm, she was still my best audience. The doctor asked her rhetorically, "So, no detectable brain damage, huh?"

"It's still too soon to tell," my mom quickly replied. I childishly stuck my tongue out at my mom and then retracted it. To which she reciprocated and stuck her tongue out at me. We both then repeated the gesture to each other. Then, we both retracted our tongues, stopped playing, and looked at the doctor innocently, as he looked up from my thick bound chart papers.

After closing and re-hanging my chart onto a hook at the foot of my bed he muttered, "Remarkable."

I chimed in, "Thanks." And then asked, "I thought I was going to see Doctor Rosenthal, no?"

"He knows you're here. He had an emergency procedure this morning, and asked me to check on you to see if things could wait until tomorrow."

"And?"

"Your foot looks okay. I'm just waiting for the nurses so I can get a look under the dressing here. But I'd say everything will keep until tomorrow."

My mom inquired, with an air of desperation, "Do you think they can save the leg?"

"That's not up to me. Chief Rosenthal is the expert. If anyone can do anything, it's him. He's the best there is."

My mom asked, "Can he have visitors now?"

"Well of course, he's the Chief of Medicine, he can have visitors anytime." There was a momentary uncomfortable silence in the room which Doctor Wexler broke, "Ha, ha-ha, ha. I'm just funning you. I like to make jokes too."

"There's a bunch of people waiting," my mom added.

"So I've heard. This young man has a lot of fans. They have been decorating this room since Friday." He paused, thinking. "Normally we wouldn't allow visitors during intake. However, we'll make an exception. But he needs his rest. So, today I think we should limit it to only thirty minutes. Tomorrow, if he's up for it, people can most likely come back during regular visiting hours. The Chief will make that call after he sees him, but I'm assuming it'll be okay."

※

While it was wonderful to be in a brighter, upbeat living space and receiving such an unexpected warm welcome, I was still experiencing an excruciating amount of pain. Additionally, I was utterly exhausted from the trip. Not to mention that only a few hours earlier, two of my toes were amputated. Following another insufferable bandage dressing change and a more thorough examination by Doctor Wexler, I retreated inward for a few minutes of intense meditation. After regaining my composure, I opened my eyes, exhibiting a convivial posture, reminding my mom to kindly ask all the visitors to avoid touching me or the bed. All things considered I was ready and eager to receive a small retinue of guests. I longed for a reconnection with my family and friends.

※

I was sedated, groggy, and barely coherent as family members and some of my closest friends paraded in. I was not very interactive. Most of the visitors spent the time consoling my mother, who was thrilled to have the company. Everyone did their best to hide their horror and shock at my frail, weakened, and mangled condition. This was the first time they had seen me since the accident. None of them were adequately prepared. I'm not certain there was any way around their initial shock. I had to take that in. I was forced to absorb the totality of their grief-stricken reactions. Some of them nervously concealed their repulsion with plastered fake uncomfortable smiles, well wishes, and loving platitudes. Don't get me wrong, I am certain that every single person who came to visit me had the best intentions. However, from my perspective the truth was self-evident. They felt pain, sympathy, and pity for me, and experienced fear and horror for themselves.

After about forty-five minutes, the nursing staff ended visitations so that I could rest. While I was grateful that they were there, I was thrilled to be alone. Their reactions to me were heartbreaking and exhausting. While I meditated and rested, my mother took everyone down to the cafeteria and commiserated for hours.

Their responses to my condition were normal and should have been anticipated, had I been properly educated. I was learning firsthand that when faced with a trauma or tragedy a primary response is to personalize it, first fearing that the same thing could happen to you, and then secondarily becoming thankful that it didn't. This normal reaction translates to, "better you than me." It may seem selfish however I've discovered that it is quite natural. The only two exceptions I'm aware of, generally, exist for parents and loving spouses who would eagerly exchange places with their injured children or significant others, respectfully.

Regardless, on that very first day, I was not prepared. I wasn't strong enough to deal with all their pain. Still a victim of my own preconditioning, I was learning to contend with those outside forces and exterior stimuli. I closed my eyes and withdrew, visualizing the soothing water therapy room. While continuing to heal myself, I simultaneously concentrated on embracing empathy for the tremendous aching my loved ones were feeling. I resolved to be better equipped when they came back the next day.

<hr />

The world-renowned chief orthopedic surgeon, Doctor William H. Rosenthal, sauntered into my room at seven o'clock in the morning. I had already been awake for over two hours because the nurses came in at four forty-five a.m. to check my vitals and bring me an early breakfast. I was able to efficiently use that time to meditate on better dealing with my anticipated visitors. But for now, my immediate attention was fixated on the man of the hour. The doctor, wearing light green scrubs under a brilliant white laboratory coat, was a middle-aged, tall, handsome gentleman who conveyed an air of seriousness, knowledge, and authority. As he walked into the room, he scowled at the clutter of decorations. Addressing both my mother and I, his smile was serious and brief, "Good morning." He was all business.

I echoed his seriousness without any sarcasm, "Good morning, doctor."

My mom contributed, "Good morning, doctor."

Looking at my leg he asked, "How are we feeling today?" Before waiting for an answer, he walked around the bed to my right side, reached over and began abruptly removing the bandages. "Let's take a look, shall we," he muttered to himself.

I winced, "I'm okay. Still in a lot of pain though." Then I groaned as he continued unraveling the gauze. This only prompted him to remove the bandages faster and more abruptly, causing more pain. Giving him the benefit of the doubt, I imagined that he sped up in order to get done quicker. He didn't strike me as a masochist. Regardless, it hurt like hell.

"Hmm, I'll bet that smarts." Two other female nurses were now in the room helping him discard the wrapping. A young male intern silently stood nearby, observing.

As I watched the doctor nearly complete the undressing, I braced myself for that familiar excruciation when the air connects with the open nerve endings. I opted to remain here, in the present, with the pain, and not retreat to my water therapy haven. Despite the agony, I wanted to be cognizant for his examination, reactions, and conclusions. I wasn't going to miss his assessment. When he unraveled that final gauze, my expectation did not disappoint. I rolled my eyes up, clenched the sheets with my fists, and audibly cried out in agony. The doctor appeared unfazed, almost immune to my grief and performed a thorough examination of my exposed, puss-ridden, bloody flesh with complete disregard for my exclamations. With a flashlight he scrutinized my still swollen, purple knee and seemingly every angle of my thigh and exposed calf. He paid very little attention to my foot.

Surprisingly, his entire examination lasted only a couple of minutes. Due to the immense throbbing it felt much longer. He looked at the nurses and commanded, "Wrap him back up," to which both of them promptly shuffled into position and began cleaning and re-wrapping my leg in sterile bandages. As soon as those first nerve endings were covered I exhaled a massive sigh of relief. The people there respected that man and obeyed his instructions. The pain, while still present, was dramatically reduced the moment the wounds were resealed.

While the nurses worked, he took out a pen and scribbled a few notes onto my chart, then handed it back to the intern, without saying a word. My mother asked, "So Doctor, what's the plan? Is there any chance of saving the leg?"

Without hesitation, or emotion, he replied, "No. The leg has to come off, and right away. We'll schedule it for tomorrow morning. First thing." And he turned to leave.

My mother quickly maneuvered to the door around him and got up in his face, impeding his exit, apprehensively asking, "I thought...Isn't there anything? We were hoping...maybe just his foot, and..."

He looked down at her and then back at me. My mother again shuffled around the room to catch his gaze. His facial expressions transitioned, exposing his restrained response. He began with annoyance, as he wasn't used to being questioned. My mother took one step backwards towards the window, but then straightened up and held her ground. I'd swear she grew two or three inches. Then he grimaced, glancing at his watch, relenting and softening slightly, observing my mother's frustration. He displayed a dispassionate professional seriousness, "Look, from what I can see, this leg probably should have come off weeks ago. It's riddled with infection and his arteries are all but gone. I spoke with Doctor Johnson about your case, and he expressed to me your concerns. I've known Reggie for years. You were in excellent hands down there." Turning to me he added, "You were lucky to have him as your doctor. You know, you're lucky to be alive."

I knew better than to interject my sarcastic response regarding luck and plane crashes. Besides, he never paused to give me a chance anyway. He merely continued, "The only question is whether or not we can save the knee, and frankly, it doesn't look good. I'll make that call when I'm in surgery tomorrow." Seeing my mother's stunned and teary reaction, he paused, softening the tenor of his voice, and offered the first modicum of compassion, "I wish I had better news. I truly do."

As my mom began openly crying, she squeezed my hand tightly. Doctor Rosenthal turned to me, and said, "Try to rest today and not move around so much. We don't want another hemorrhage. You may not believe it, but you'll feel a lot better after the surgery." He looked at his wristwatch again, then abruptly turned, put his pen back into his breast pocket and walked out, followed closely by the intern.

※

Moments after the doctor left, while the nurses were still finishing up my dressing, a male nurse entered. He was young, late twenties, extremely well built, with a square jaw and high cheekbones, wearing a neatly pressed white uniform. He was clean-shaven with short jet black hair, neatly slicked back. Introducing himself he began, "Greetings and felicitations, I'm your nurse.

The agency sent me." His demeanor was professional and respectful, and he conveyed confidence along with a youthful, charismatic, boyish charm.

I asked, "greetings and what?" Everyone ignored me.

My mom extended her open hand, "Hi, Nurse Antonio. We're so happy you're here. We didn't expect you so early." She turned to me, "Lau, Antonio is a private nurse. He'll help take care of you."

"Hi, Nurse Antonio." As he came closer to shake my hand, I motioned for him to stay away. "Please, do not touch the bed. The slightest movement hurts so much."

He stopped himself, raising both open hands, pulling himself back. "Ah yes, pain has an element of blank. You got it. You're the boss. And please, it's just Tony."

"Okay Tony. And thanks. It's nice to meet you." I then furrowed my brow and asked, "Pain has an element of what?"

He smiled, knowingly and cleared his throat, "Pain has an element of blank young man." Then he extended his arm in a grand gesture, opened his hand, fluttered it theatrically and continued referencing my body, "It cannot recollect when it begun, or if there were a time when it was not."

I looked at my mom who merely shrugged, wide-eyed.

Antonio quickly chimed in, "That's Emily Dickinson's interpretation of pain. It's one of my favorites."

I again looked at my mom for reassurance. She replied to Antonio, "That was beautiful. I love poetry. I just don't really know any."

I interjected, laughing, "I don't know any either."

Antonio let out a friendly chortle, grabbed an overstuffed notebook from his duffle bag and put it on the shelf next to a giant stuffed panda under the television. "This is my personal collection of my favorites. I'll teach you. I find them such an eloquent escape and a most pleasant form of expression. Especially in a place like this. You'll see. You'll love it." His affinity for literature was in stark contrast to his appearance. He more resembled a burly kick boxer than a poet.

Antonio coyly inserted, "I don't know if you're aware, but you guys have a few visitors." He motioned for my mom to look out the window. Just below they could see a mass of people, mostly teenagers, intermixed with a few adults stretching along the sidewalk and into the open parking area. "That's nothing, the lobby was full when I came in. And look at this." He walked my mom out and pointed her down the hallway. She could see crowds mixed with many familiar young faces pressed against the glass entrance just opposite the Nurses' Station. "The Chief said visitors were okay today." Introspectively, glancing out the window, he jovially added, "It is not given to every man to take a bath of multitude. Enjoying a crowd is an art."

I looked endearingly at Antonio, "Mom, I have no idea what he is talking about. But I can tell he's going to be a lot of fun to have around."

Antonio expounded, "That's just Baudelaire's impression of how to navigate a crowd." He looked at me and then to my mom for a reaction.

I shook my head, "I've never even heard of him."

My mom conceded, "Of course I've heard of him, I just can't quote him."

"It's okay, we'll have plenty of time to explore Charles Baudelaire later. The point is that visitors are okay today, so long as you rest and don't get overwhelmed. And it will be up to you to find safe haven amongst the crowd. But if you need me, just say the word." He smiled, adding, "I think because there are so many people, they are planning on letting them up a little early today. How would you like me to handle it?"

My mom and I laughed, shrugging simultaneously, and she said, "We trust you. Why don't you handle it?"

Nodding, I added, "Seems right."

Nurse Antonio folded his arms confidently, nodded his head, "I'm on it." He then raised his fist, pointing his finger up to the ceiling, declaring, "When Duty whispers low, 'Thou must.'" He then darted out of the room. Seconds later he leaned back into the doorway, "The youth replies, 'I can.'" And once again he was gone.

Every sentence was like watching a live performance. My mom and I exchanged similar expressions of wonder. Laughing, I said, "he's such an odd duck." After a brief pause, I added, "I love him so much already!"

There was no way we could have anticipated such an outpouring of love and support from seemingly my entire childhood community. Over fifty people were already there when the hospital opened that morning, and more continued to arrive throughout the day. Aside from my family and closest friends, everyone at my high school knew about my arrival as it was broadcast during homeroom the previous Friday. Incidentally, at my high school, they had been providing weekly, sometimes daily, morning updates since the initial tragedy. Even for those that didn't know me, I had become a local personality, known as "the boy who lost his father, and miraculously survived a plane crash." About six weeks earlier our school's homecoming was dedicated in my honor.

Anyone who attended Half Hallow Hills High School East on Monday, December 3, 1984, would forever remember it as "the date our institution closed due to a nonemergency and non-weather-related event." While I was only a high school junior, I had friends, and siblings of friends, in both the senior and sophomore classes. By nine-thirty a.m. there were already several hundred teenagers filling the hallways, lobby, and front entrance to the medical facility. For many of them it may have just been an excuse to cut class and skip school. For others, I'm certain that they were just curious and caught up in the excitement of the moment. Regardless, for the vast majority of people I saw that day, I know in my heart that they were there out of respect and love. And it was, is, and forever will be immensely appreciated.

Although Nurse Antonio had just arrived, my mom and I were already immeasurably grateful for his service. His flamboyant, charismatic personality was intoxicating. He was a born caretaker as well as being meticulously organized and authoritative. He orchestrated the day beautifully by having family and friends neatly line up in the hallway. And he was able to efficiently coordinate with hospital staff regarding the overflow in the lobby and entranceway. Being wonderfully structured and careful, he ushered them in groups of four, and ensured that everyone knew not to touch my bed.

Because of the sheer volume outside, he limited the visits to only five minutes each. Fascinatingly, the young people cooperated and waited patiently throughout the day. As the day pressed on it was evident that I didn't personally know two-thirds of the visitors. Additionally, by four o'clock in the afternoon it was obvious that more than half the crowd would be turned away, dissatisfied. It was incredibly touching that some of my nearest and dearest friends refused to leave and even snuck back into my room two and three times that same day. Again, that day was, is, and forever will be...immensely appreciated.

Allow me to entertain an overall positive and brief digression. Having the previous night to adjust my own programming, I was better prepared for the inadvertent negativity throughout the day. Similar to the previous day, when we had first arrived in New York, everyone visiting was unnervingly shaken. I on the other hand, having meditated the night before and for a couple of hours that morning, was emotionally secure, and at peace. Instead of being adversely affected by everyone's pity, sympathy, horror, and fear, I projected confidence and security. Amazingly, the transformative reactions were almost all similar. Loved ones would enter, experiencing an initial shock which typically triggered their pity and internal fear. The vast majority would leave comforted and assuaged by my stability, confidence and reassurance. Only they could tell you if they were consciously aware of their emotional metamorphosis.

Their initial response was warranted because, frankly, I was a mess. I was grateful that they had never previously witnessed such a tragedy. My body was so badly mangled that some of the teens merely peaked in through the hallway, too scared to enter. I barely resembled the young man many had remembered. Aside from my injuries, I had lost a third of my body weight and all muscle mass, weighing a gaunt eighty-two pounds. My skin tone was pale and colorless. My throat had a bulky plastic plug protruding out of a centered hole. There were tubes and wires affixed to my face, neck, chest, and arms. My hair was long, dry, straw-like, and frizzy having not been washed or cut since the accident. Worst of all was the eye-watering odor wafting from the infection raging in my rotting left leg.

All in all, their uniform emotional transformation was intoxicating and contagious. After experiencing my outwardly positive projections and fortitude, their sympathy and anxiety morphed into respectful admiration and inspiration. Unwittingly, most of them vocalized their own faulty programming by expressing thoughts like, "I have no idea how you are handling it so well." And "If it were me, I'd be hysterical." Some even hyperbolically took it to extremes, adding, "I couldn't handle the pain. I'd rather be dead." My external reaction was not an insincere facade. I was not merely "putting on a game face." After witnessing their alterations, I became ebullient! I empathically drew strength from each person I emotionally touched. Helping them, in turn, was helping me. Mitigating their fears was positively invigorating.

The outpouring of support was overwhelming. At the end of that first full visiting day in New York I was exhausted. Nurse Antonio was packing up to leave. I said, "Tony, thank you so much for all your help today. I'm confused though, you were with me all day. Don't you have other patients to take care of?"

As he packed his duffle bag, he explained, "I'm here for you. You're my only patient." He then handed me his bulging notebook of poems and pronounced, "Split the lark and you'll find the music." Opening the book to a dog-eared page, adding, "here, there's a whole section dedicated to Dickinson. I especially love the short ones. They are often the most profound. Happy reading and pleasant dreams, Laurence."

I was not used to that type of specialized service. It was incredibly reassuring and comforting having him there, eccentricities and all. A few minutes after his departure, my mother returned with a fresh cup of hot coffee, and as tired as I was we spent the next couple of hours reading random poems from Tony's book. To this day, I'm not confident if the shortest poems are actually the most profound, but they certainly were the easiest for me to understand. Cumulatively, they all seemed to have a powerful impact on me. As we immersed ourselves in the literature, I reflected on my mother, my family, my friends, and my newest friend Tony, and how blessed I truly was.

<hr />

On Tuesday, December fourth, Tony woke me up gently at seven o'clock in the morning. I was confused as to why my sleep had not been interrupted by the nursing staff checking my vitals every few hours. He explained, "You are scheduled for surgery today at seven thirty, which means you cannot eat anything. It also means you need your strength. There would be no reason to wake up early. So, I stood guard and made certain that they let you sleep." Then he handed me a small cup of water and two small sedative pills. "Here take these." He then raised his own glass of water and as I consumed the pills he exclaimed, "There's good ships and wood ships and ships that sail the sea, but the best ships are friendships so cheers to you and me." After a brief pause, he added, "Ayy, a simple Irish toast."

After we quickly drank our cups, he asked, "Did you sleep okay?"

"I did, and you?"

"Me? I always sleep like a log."

I gushed, "Tony, it's so nice having you here. That was the first uninterrupted night sleep I had since the accident. I'm used to being woken up every few hours by somebody poking, prodding, and checking something." My mom entered with two cups and a small bag.

Nurse Antonio graciously replied, "Not to worry. All that is going to change while I'm here. Good morning, Mrs. Kaldor, and don't you look lovely."

"Good morning, Nurse Tony, and thank you. Here, I brought you a hot cup of coffee and a muffin. Lau, did you sleep okay? Or are you nervous?"

"I'm okay. It was really wonderful seeing everyone yesterday. I was just telling Tony it was the first time I slept through the night without being interrupted. Thanks to him."

"I know, I've been here all night and Tony has been standing guard since the wee hours of the morning. I think he's planning on taking a break as soon as you go into surgery." My mother hadn't been home yet. She said that she couldn't leave until after my big surgery. "I cannot believe that you're not nervous. I'm a wreck. I didn't sleep a wink."

Trying to alleviate some of her anxiety, I said, "I'm really not nervous. Should I be?" After thinking about it, I asked, "Either of you have a pen?" My mom handed me the pen that was clipped to her newspaper crossword puzzle. I noticed something better on the countertop. "No-no, please give me that marker instead." I pulled off the covers, exposing my right leg. In big bold black capital letters, across my thigh, knee, and shin, I wrote, "NOT THIS LEG, AMPUTATE THE OTHER ONE," with arrows pointing to my left leg on top and bottom of the message. Tony and my mother laughed uncomfortably, both agreeing that it was a good idea.

Because of my mother's apprehension, I reflected on the surgery, the gravity, and permanence of the decision. She felt that we still had time and could continue to fight to save the leg. She suggested that we only remove the foot and ankle and then get a third opinion next week at another hospital. Ultimately the decision was mine, and I was ready, having made peace with the amputation. It was time. It was interesting though, that of the dozens of major surgeries I had endured thus far, this was the first that was removing something, as opposed to trying to repair it.

The sedatives were taking effect. I felt groggy and euphoric. Two orderlies arrived, and Nurse Antonio helped them transfer me to a portable gurney. Tony stuffed an extra rolled up blanket onto the cot, "Here, it gets cold in the recovery room after surgery." I was so impressed that he knew, and that he was taking such good care of me.

He then offered to give me Doc, but I pushed him back saying, "I think he'll be safer here. We don't want them to operate on him by mistake." He laughed and gave the monkey back to my mom.

As they wheeled me out, I saw my mom crying. I tried to reassure her, "Please don't worry. Everything will be okay. I promise, mom. I can do this." Even though she continued quietly sobbing, I could tell that my words and demeanor had a calming effect on her. It was becoming clear to me that one of the best ways to affect the outside world and specifically outside fear was simply to assuage it through my own confidence.

On the way down the various hallways, I made certain that everyone I passed saw the black ink message scribbled on my right leg. When they finally parked my gurney in the operating room under the lights, I pulled back my blanket and made certain that the nurses and anesthesiologist read my note as well.

I grabbed one of the nurse's arms and asked, "One quick question. Will I be able to play the violin after this?"

She paused and replied, "Sure, I don't see why not."

I quickly retorted, "Then Doctor Rosenthal is truly a master surgeon, because I could never play before." I heard groans and courtesy laughs from the other few staff members in the room. Regardless, my juvenile ego and dry wit were satiated. It was thrilling to no longer have my mouth wired shut. Thrilling for me, not so much for my audience. It was liberating being able to be obnoxiously silly once again. Where was my mom when I needed her most? She would have thought that was hysterical.

A few seconds later, Doctor Rosenthal entered the room wearing light green scrubs and gloves, covered from head to toe except for his eyes, and asked, "How are you feeling?"

"I'm good. Did you read my note?"

He looked down at my right leg, unamused, and said, "Cute. I get it. Because doctors make mistakes. Well, not this doctor." Then he patted my shoulder, calmly adding, "just relax, we're about to get started."

I interrupted, "One quick question. Do you think I'll be able to play the saxophone after this?"

Without hesitation, he replied, "Not if you couldn't before." Then, not missing a beat, remaining serious and unflinching, he nodded to the anesthesiologist, and asserted, "Just count back slowly from one hundred."

"One Hundred." I admit to being a little dejected that he wasn't amused by my note or my humorous anecdote. "Ninety-nine." But I shrugged it off, thinking, "Oh well, I guess you can't win them all. Ninety-eight." Then I thought, "I'll get him next time." I peacefully passed out, never reaching ninety-seven.

Waking up in the cold recovery room, of all the surreal experiences since the plane crash this was the most bizarre, but in a really good way. The searing and unending pain that consumed me had vanished. Although I was sedated, it was not a temporary numbness or euphoria. It was different. From the moment I awoke in the abyss, no matter how strong the pain medication had been, sadly, I had still felt some degree of tormenting anguish. Suddenly, it was all gone. I closed my eyes, searching the present for the pain. Only memories remained. It was incredible! Additionally, the pain that previously emanated from the multitude of severed nerve endings was also absent. The constant burning and stabbing feeling throughout my body had ended. The torture was finally over.

I opened my eyes, looking around the empty recovery room. I was alone, and I was cold. I reached down and grabbed the extra blanket, covering myself for warmth. I noticed that my leg was no longer in traction. The whole apparatus was missing. The small bed was noticeably spacious. I rolled from left to right and right to left. I flipped off the blanket covering my left leg. I was shocked, in spite of myself. It was yet another surreal experience. While I knew it would be gone, seeing it was astonishing. What was more interesting was that my overall feeling was...relief.

I examined my new situation. My entire left leg was only a stump wrapped in tan elastic stretchable bandages. I wiggled my left ankle and toes. I felt them. But visually, they weren't there. I lifted the stump up and down. I felt the coarse outer bandages, curious what it looked like underneath. I propped an extra pillow under my residual limb, covering it with the blanket, and then closed my eyes, waiting for an orderly. My relief was immeasurable, no longer being in pain. I just laid there on my back, wiggling my invisible toes.

I had been a prisoner of the abyss, tortured to the brink of insanity, and came out the other side. I chose life, making the decision to survive, not fully comprehending the scope, breadth, and burden it entailed. But having faith, renewed faith, receiving the knowledge and promise of a higher purpose, I accepted this monumental surgery as an affirmation, a turning point, liberating me by removing the debilitating pain. Moving forward, I possessed the tools to deal with future discomfort, outside influences, and the life trials ahead. I welcomed those challenges, without fear or apprehension, knowing that I would never give up, eternally protected within the hand of God. I eagerly accepted that my journey was ready to begin!

11

THE GIFT

My mother was perplexed to see me in such good spirits following the amputation. It was inconceivable that anyone could experience the trauma of limb removal and maintain a positive persuasion. In fairness, she also could not comprehend the level of contiguous pain I had been experiencing for the past several months. Regardless as to my testaments the pain level was incomprehensible. For her part she was still personalizing her grief, recently losing a spouse and witnessing the mutilation of her child. In projecting her heartache onto me, she was convinced that I must be in denial. Coincidentally, the new psychologist at Schneider's agreed, validating my mother's preconditioning. The only one who appeared to understand me was Nurse Antonio. We connected on a whole other level.

Doctor Rosenthal forcefully entered my room with the now familiar young male intern in his wake. Grandly, he bellowed, "Good morning, everyone. And how are we feeling?" He was clearly comfortable in his own skin and typically proud of his work. Without hesitation, he crossed to my bed, "Let's have a look."

"Good morning, Doc. I'm good." I pulled back the covers, elevating my residual limb. "I can't believe it. It's a little sore, but the shooting pain is all gone!"

My mother chimed in, "Good morning, Doctor." Antonio just nodded politely, arms folded, watching like a concerned lion.

Doctor Rosenthal swiftly unraveled the outer elastic bandage as well as the thick gauze underneath, discarding everything in a large plastic waste receptacle. Even though it wasn't immensely painful, I winced at the soreness of my stump. Doctor Rosenthal was not exceedingly gentle. "That's to be expected. It'll be tender for a little while. But that will get better in about a week or two when the swelling goes down." He sat on the bed in the space where my lower leg and foot should have been. And...that was another surreal experience. Carefully examining his handiwork, he continued, "It looks terrific. See, here," showing my mom and the intern. "Son, can you raise it again?" I raised it up. "Can you move it left and right.?" I oscillated it left and right. "Excellent!" He then turned to my mom, "There was no way to save the knee. It was all eaten away. However, the good news is that I was able to leave him a lengthy residual limb which will make a huge difference when he starts walking with a prosthesis. I cut only about an inch above the knee. And the best news is that we removed most of the infected area. I'm confident that with a strong antibiotic regiment we'll have it completely out of his system by next week." Exceedingly pleased with himself, he added, "We'll have you up and around in no time."

He got up, continuing, "You'll start physical therapy today. Just five and ten-minute intervals."

Nurse Antonio confidently interjected, "We can handle that. No problem."

Doctor Rosenthal added, "Next week we'll finally get you out of this bed." I observed that he didn't appear to be in his typical rush to leave. Perhaps he was genuinely concerned for my recovery and well-being or he just enjoyed our company. Or he was basking in the post-op glow of his brilliance. Regardless, it was nice having him in the room for an extra few moments.

I replied, "Sounds great. Doc, it's really weird. I can still feel my ankle and toes. I'm wiggling them right now."

"That's typical. It's called phantom sensation. But there's no pain, right?"

I replied, "No, it's sore, but it doesn't hurt. Actually, I feel great. A little weird. But great!"

Antonio interjected, "I've seen a lot of patients get horrible phantom pain after an amputation."

Doctor Rosenthal added, "It's all about the surgical incision. You cannot leave nerve endings open. A nice clean cut. Some doctors are butchers. The phantom sensation is perfectly normal. As far as your neural network is concerned you still have a foot."

Curiously, I asked, "When can I get bionic implants, like that guy on TV?" In a rare moment for me, I was not joking. I was dead serious.

"Sadly, we can't do that yet. That's just Hollywood. They have come a long way with prosthetics and orthotics. There's a doctor in Australia who is attempting to surgically attach a mechanical arm. And the military is always putting resources into R&D. Unfortunately, the technology is still years away." Seeing my mom's crestfallen expression, he expounded, "after making a full recovery there's no reason you cannot have a normal, full and productive life. We have counselors and therapists here who will come speak with you to help you temper realistic expectations regarding your recovery." He concluded, "Rest up. I'll be back to check on you in the morning."

"Thanks doc." Feebly attempting levity, I said, "Speaking of getting up and walking, I heard a doctor told this new amputee to walk five miles a day, for his health. Six months later the guy called his doctor collect and said, 'Hey doc can you help me. I feel great, but I'm lost in the middle of Missouri.'" The whole room was silent. Doctor Rosenthal just looked at me, nonplused and said nothing, exhaled deeply through his nose, and then turned to exit. I don't think he appreciated my deflection, preferring me to focus on his surgical procedure and professional advice.

My mother broke the silence, "Thank you so much, doctor. Have a good night and we'll see you tomorrow."

Stopping at the door he nodded and half-smiled at my mom. Responding to me, deadpan, "I'm glad your spirits are up. I'll see you tomorrow." And he and the intern walked out.

I reflected on his preconditioning. Most people are taught to guard their enthusiasm, expecting failure and accepting limitations. If I accepted that construct I would no longer be alive. People do not survive plane crashes. I interpreted the cautionary advice provided as being purely based on his predisposition. It had an immediate adverse effect on my mother because it comfortably spoke directly to her own faulty programming. Thankfully, I no longer existed in a universe with their limitations. Each moment was, and is, merely an opportunity to overcome obstacles.

Also, I vowed to tickle that man's funny bone.

The Story of Rehab

It was remarkable how much better I felt. In addition to being mostly pain free, I was also no longer suffering from chemical withdrawal symptoms. This provided ample opportunity for meditation, focusing on physical and emotional healing in between welcome visitations with family and friends.

Nurse Antonio was a blessing, alleviating my mother's burden, as he watched over me every day. Because he was in our private employ, he acted as liaison with the hospital and staff. Additionally, it afforded my mother a much-needed respite away from the hospital, allowing her to enjoy simple pleasures like sleeping at home in her own bed and taking nice long, hot, relaxing showers. Tony and I began physical therapy immediately. His positivity and optimism were contagious. We both believed that anything perceivable was attainable. It was tremendously comforting.

Almost a week after my amputation, six days to be precise, the hospital physical therapist came into my room with a metal walker and a pair of metal orthopedic forearm crutches. The physical therapist was in her late thirties, muscular, wearing green scrubs and white sneakers. I was taken by her portly build and oversized forearms. She resembled a classic cartoon sailor.

She greeted us with an awkward friendly enthusiasm, which I had grown accustomed to in the children's ward, "Hi, my name is Tammy. The kids here all call me Tam-Tam. I'll be here every day for physical therapy." Most of the support staff had a patronizing, overly sweet edge to their cadence as if they were on a Sunday morning kid's television show.

Doing my best to conceal any sarcasm, I smiled and courteously replied, "Hi Tam-Tam. Thanks, but I think we're good. I have Tony."

Her demeanor altered slightly, as if she were correcting a toddler while still maintaining her plastered smile, sternly replying, "Tony, is it? He can work with you as well. But it's my job to get you out of that bed." She was clearly queen frog of the physical therapy pond.

Without hesitation and trying to match her enthusiasm, I replied, "Great! I'm ready." I sat up quickly, genuinely eager to get started. She could see my sour expression concerning the equipment she brought in. I meekly asked, "Do I really need those?"

She folded her arms and made a fake frowny-face and spoke as though she was talking to a four year old, "Well, you can't be expected to hop everywhere. Can you?"

"No, but why not use regular looking crutches? Those devices are for invalids." I associated walkers with old people and the forearm crutches with the infirm. I know now that those negative stigmas were based solely on my ingrained societal preconditioning. They are incredibly effective rehabilitation tools that assist with mobility. Not to mention my immature, disrespectful and distasteful use of that word "invalid," meaning wholly unserviceable or useless. In retrospect, I still had a tremendous amount of reprogramming to do.

"You'll get used to them. I promise." Tammy positioned the walker next to my bed. I sat up and swung my right leg over the edge.

Nurse Antonio stood next to me with his arms extended as if he were spotting me, "Now take it easy and go slowly."

I didn't understand why Tony was suddenly being so cautious. I didn't know this woman at all, but I came to expect Nurse Antonio to be fearless. I slid off the bed excited to finally be upright. I had been confined to a mattress for three long months. The sensations that came with getting out of bed were euphoric. My naked foot touching the cold floor was exhilarating. However, when I reached for the walker I became lightheaded and began to pass out. Tony caught my shoulders while Tammy steadied the walker, grabbing my hands and forearms. They both eased me back up and into a seated position on the bed. Nurse Antonio laughed, "I told you, you're going to have to go slowly kiddo. We both know that 'to hit the mark, you must aim a little above it.'" As I laid back onto the pillow, catching my breath, he concluded, "But you also gotta remember...." He paused allowing me to compose myself.

"I know, I know. '...every arrow that flies feels the attraction of earth.' You really like that quote. And I know, I know, I'm the arrow, trying to fly. You reference that one several times a day."

"What can I say? Longfellow was profound. He's my physical therapy go-to. Everybody falls down. Everybody. So, what does he mean by this?"

"He means I should go slowly," I acknowledged.

"You got it! So go slowly." He patted my right leg affectionately. "And I'm proud of you for paying attention all week."

Tammy was utterly confused by our banter.

"I got so dizzy. What the hell just happened to me?" I asked, seated back on the bed, addressing both of them.

Tammy jumped in, authoritatively, "It's perfectly normal. You've been on your back for several months. Your equilibrium is out of whack. Take a minute and when you're ready we'll try it again, trooper."

Tony handed me a glass of water, "here, drink this." While I gulped it down, he said, "ready to go again?"

Tammy cautioned, "On second thought, maybe you should give it a few more minutes or even try again tomorrow."

I took a deep breath. "I got this." I slid off the mattress again, foot securely back on the floor. This time going slower, I steadied myself, still leaning against the side of the bed while holding the walker firmly with both hands. Again, I was lightheaded, but it was tolerable. Nurse Antonio held my shoulders and Tammy held the walker, both ready to catch me. I found my natural balance by adjusting the muscles in my foot. I was standing by myself on my one right leg. "I'm still a little dizzy but it's not that bad," I proclaimed.

Tammy said, "Okay. Let's just stand here for a few minutes and get comfortable being upright. You're doing great. That's pretty amazing for your first day. Can you get back into bed yourself or do you need help?"

I looked at Nurse Antonio and internalized, "That was quick," and, "That can't be it."

Tammy, seeing my confusion, added, "you have to take it slow. You don't want to overexert yourself there, trooper." Looking for support from Nurse Antonio, she added, "Come on, let's get him back into bed."

Nurse Antonio politely motioned for her to wait, then looked at me, "Are you the master and the captain?"

Tammy interjected, "Are you the what now?"

I was holding myself up almost exclusively with upper body strength, ensuring that I wouldn't fall, grunting through clenched teeth, "I am!" My resolve was palpable. I was still a little lightheaded but I was no longer dizzy. I added, "Is that Wordsworth or Kipling?"

Nurse Antonio laughed, warmly correcting me, "Close, it's from Henley's *Invictus*."

I exhaled and wailed a playful yet guttural sound of disappointment, and added, "I'll have to revisit that one tonight." To which Tony grinned approvingly.

Tammy, observing my refusal to be finished, backed away allowing Nurse Antonio to help me. She recognized our bond and yielded the space. He stepped closer. Then I motioned for him to wait as well. In my head I heard his voice reciting the words, "I am the master of my fate, I am the captain of my soul." I picked up the walker and moved it a few inches in front of me. Then, using my arms and one leg hopped towards it and stood inside the U-shaped device. Tammy was shocked and took another step backwards. Tony's voice echoed in my mind. I then repeated the procedure and hopped forward again. Tammy now looked concerned but moved out of the way as I replicated the same motion, hopping several paces forward and then right out of my hospital room doorway into the hall.

Tammy barked, "Hey, I think you should get back in here, trooper!"

I shouted to a few of the nurses down the hall at the nurse's station, "Hey everyone, look at me. I'm in the hallway!" A young couple walked past me with their nine-year-old son eating ice cream in a wheelchair . Apparently, he had his tonsils removed earlier that morning. The threesome appeared amused. I continued my *shtick*, "can you believe it? I came in here last week to get my tonsils out too, look what they did to me!"

The mom, playing along, said, "Oh my!" At least I think she was playing along. The little boy looked a little concerned.

I quickly chided, "Ah, I'm just kidding. That's what I do. I kid. I'm a kidder. This place is great, except the hospital charges an arm and a leg. Ha! Get it?" Peripherally, I noticed the family laughing at my antics. I winked at the kid and then turned, hopping with the walker back towards my room. I repeated, "An arm and leg. Did you hear that, Tony? I kill me!" Nurse Antonio was leaning against my bed, arms proudly folded, chortling and grinning from ear-to-ear like a famous fairytale feline. On my way back out of my room I shouted, "Hey Tam-Tam, let's see those invalid sticks you brought!" Tammy was awestruck by my exuberance. I hopped out of my room carrying the walker. As I passed Tammy, I explained "I am truly the master and the captain!"

Over the subsequent thirty minutes, Tony helped me learn to balance and navigate the crutches in a circle around my room. I wasn't completely proficient, but I was getting the hang of it. Tammy was awestruck. While I continued my crutch maneuvers in a figure eight, without looking up I said, "Tammy, why don't you just leave these crutches and the walker here in my room, if that's okay. Tony and I will work with them later."

Her demeanor lost all supercilious pretense. She shook her head, and for the first time spoke with a more normal voice, "I don't believe it. I've never seen anyone in your condition progress so quickly. Not after being on their back for as long as you have. Remarkable." Politely excusing herself, she announced, "Of course I'll leave these things here with you. I'll see you about the same time tomorrow." She wasn't annoyed. Even her smile seemed surprisingly genuine. She was sincerely impressed. Introspectively, accrediting my recent awakening and newfound awareness, I recognized her transformative reaction. I embraced her deficient preconceptions and merely displayed a little tenacity. Albeit, I did it in a very immature and silly way. But I did pull her out of her programming. Perhaps only a little. Perhaps only temporarily. Regardless, it felt good.

After Tammy left, Nurse Antonio and I sat on the end of my bed engaging in a quick heart-to-heart. I opened with, "That's why you can never give in to outside forces. You can never let them into your head."

Tony agreed, "Exactly. You create your own path."

We were echoing one mind, "You write your own future. Your own story. You never let anyone else censor it or edit it for you."

Gently patting my stump, he said, "And never give up." He reached over grabbing his book and opened it to a special page. "Guest sums it up best in *Don't Quit*."

And the surreal hits just kept on coming. It was almost dreamlike hearing those echoes of validation. We understood each other. The Universe had sent me the ideal caretaker. We spoke the same language. I exhaled in exasperation, "Am I always going to have to prove them wrong though? Just the thought of it seems exhausting."

"No, you should never work to prove them wrong. Ever! If you do, you're succeeding for the wrong reasons. You're letting their faulty conditioning affect your path. You achieve your success only for you and the betterment of mankind. Of course, you can prove them wrong. And you will every time. But that simply shouldn't be your motivation for accomplishing the things you will achieve."

Looking at his book, flipping through pages, intrigued, I quickly asked, "Who wrote that? Where did you get, 'faulty conditioning?'"

"That's funny. It's not from the classics. Or at least not as far as I'm aware. When I was a kid..." He hesitated. "Nah, you'll think it's stupid."

"Please. I have to know."

"Well, okay, I've never shared this with anybody. A voice in my head repeated that to me when I was young, a little younger than you are now. I was taking care of my mother who had cancer. The doctors told me that she was inoperable and had only a few months to live. Somehow, by the grace of God I nurtured her back to health. By the way, she's been living cancer free ever since. It's why I decided to work in the field of medicine. I just wanted to help people." He walked over to the window, gazing out, while orating, "That's not all. Like you, my dad passed away when I was kid. However, we were poor. Dirt poor. You know, we got our Christmas turkey from the church every year, poor. With my mother sick, I had to take care of my four other siblings, so medical school was off the table. *Capisce?* Being a nurse was my best option to help others. And I wasn't going to let other people's preconceptions stop me."

I was mesmerized by this man. "I'm so glad you listened to that voice." I jumped up, slid my foot back onto the floor, and said, "hand me those crutches again, will ya?"

Nurse Antonio coyly responded, "You got the walker next to you. Why don't you go get them yourself?" We both smiled at each other knowingly. He added, "For those of us that are enlightened, we're always going to be faced with other people's fear and conditioning. We just have to overcome it." He was speaking my language. In more ways than he ever could have imagined. I grabbed the walker, steadied myself, hopped over to the crutches and we got back to our therapy exercises.

The Story of My Reflection

Physical Therapy proved to be an interesting challenge facing both my programming and my resolve. Nurse Antonio was wonderful in creating a full tri-daily fitness routine for me. In addition to hopping around on crutches, he introduced clever ways of utilizing our medical space, accommodating sit-ups, dips, pull ups and push-ups. Surprisingly, my muscle tone was quickly returning. Within only a week of physical therapy I was proficient enough on crutches to manipulate myself around the hospital corridors. Exercising my freedom of mobility at night when Tony and my mother retired, I would traverse the outer hallway perimeter of my entire floor.

For a change of scenery, one night I decided to venture from the children's ward out into another wing of the hospital. I promised the on-call nurse not to amble far. She was amenable as I had developed an extremely pleasant, cordial friendship with all the nurses on my floor. I was one of the older, responsible, mature patients residing at the Children's hospital. "Well, as mature as one could be with a stuffed monkey," I thought. Regardless, I was trusted with my exploration. Across from my wing there was a long empty hallway that had just been renovated but wasn't open for patients yet. It made for the perfect long stretch to practice maneuvering, turning and speed.

After about thirty minutes of extensive practice, I stopped to catch my breath. By chance, I came to rest in front of a full-length floor-to-ceiling glass window. It was the first time since the accident that I observed my entire body in reflection. Thus far I had only seen my face in the bathroom mirror and the rest of me in small pieces with a small handheld mirror. I stared at my likeness. Horrified. The amputation had taken place almost two weeks earlier. This was the first time I was processing my deformity, and the permanence thereof. Oddly enough, in my mind the leg was still there. I could still wiggle my missing toes. And it was more than just the missing limb. The creature in the reflection was unrecognizable. I was still gaunt, pale, with a patched eye, a hole in my throat, stringy hair, and boney arms attached to handicapped metal sticks, designed for an invalid. Yeah, there was that word again, invalid. In-valid! I opened my hospital gown, exposing my chest zipper and scars. I was a disaster. No, not an invalid...I was a monster!

I began to cry. My right leg became weak. I tossed the crutches aside, crumbling to the floor. Disgusted, I glowered at the juvenile aberration. Dismayed. I was feeling sorry for myself, experiencing pity, similar to that of my visitors. I audibly sobbed, "This is how everyone else sees you." Then I suddenly became embarrassed yet relieved that my solitude was devoid of witnesses. I recomposed myself, sanguine that no one would ever learn of this moment of weakness. Ever. Augmenting time, I conjured a medley of images of myself participating in a variety of sports and athletic activities such as swimming, climbing, horseback riding, skydiving, running and even flying on a trapeze. I heard Tony's voice, "It's when things seem worst that you must not quit." I grimaced deeply into my own reflective eyes, wiping the moisture from my cheeks, intensely scowling, "Enough! Enough! Get up!" I resolved to figure out what poem that was as soon as I returned to my room.

Recomposing myself, I grabbed the crutches and steadfastly rose. Then, as if I were in a movie the reflection scolded me, "Let me tell you something, *schmuck!* If all you see are these superficial injuries, then you don't see me. You're better than this." The reflective image morphed, slowly ameliorating. It was me, aged slightly, in a suit, clean shaven. My eye patch was gone. My throat was healed, and I was standing somehow on two legs, without crutches. "Look at me. Look, at, me! The same way your family and friends have been drawing strength from your resolve, draw courage and confidence from mine. There's nothing you cannot do. This is who you are. This is your life. Now go live it!"

As I crutched back down the lengthy empty corridor, the conceptions of my athletic prowess shadowed me along both adjacent walls. Amazingly, some of the activities were being accomplished with only one leg, while in others I was somehow using two. Energized, I laughed out loud racing excitedly down the hallway watching myself expertly skiing. I mockingly joked, "Hey reflection, it's amazing that you can do that so well on one leg, considering you were a lousy skier on two." The reflective visualization turned his head, glared back at me, smirked, kicking up a huge wave of white powdery snow and then shot straight down the mountain, which only motivated me to crutch faster down the hallway.

I dashed back to my room, determined to conquer and overcome every obstacle, looking forward to my next encounter with a full-size reflective surface. After that day, with hubris, holding close my insecurities, I vowed to never prejudge and provide everyone else an opportunity to reveal their true nature, beyond their superficial surface. Steadfast in the knowledge that beyond the veneer, the totality of who we are exists here in the present.

~~~~~ ~~~~~

The First Interlude

The December holiday season was thankfully quiet and uneventful. Even still, I was fortunate to have at least a handful of visitors every single day during my stint in the New Hyde Park children's ward. Most days were spent meditatively healing, physically rehabilitating and joyfully visiting with family and friends. Overall, hospitalization was monotonously mundane. Similar to the "lipstick on a pig" metaphor, regardless as to how much you dress up a medical facility it's still a medical facility. Notwithstanding my surroundings and confinement, it was revitalizing and lovely having friends celebrate Hanukkah, Christmas and New Year's with me.

Fortunately, even the reparative surgical procedures were becoming infrequent, less arduous and routine. Most of them came with relatively ephemeral recoveries. For example, they removed my metallic chest-zipper and tracheotomy plug in a single tandem, minimally invasive, forty-five-minute procedure. On other occasions, under local anesthesia I had numerous metallic staples and plates removed from previously fractured bones which had subsequently healed. And the vast majority of those routine surgeries had minimal swelling and negligible soreness. All indications were that my internment was, with any luck, coming to an end.

During that period, the only noteworthy invasive operation was performed on my right eye in hopes of repairing the detached retina. Although it was an extremely rare and experimental technique, there was little downside. Sadly, the procedure failed and I suffered a total loss of vision in my right eye. With that finality came the realization that I had permanently lost my three-dimensional depth perception which, at this point, was merely one more thing to accept and process.

One of my most heartfelt memories as a patient occurred on New Year's Eve when a family member and one of my closest friends snuck in a bottle of champagne and hid in my room after visiting hours. Although I couldn't consume the alcohol, staying up most of the night watching televised global celebrations and laughing was pure medicine. Unlike my Florida isolation with my mother, at the Long Island Jewish medical facility in New York I had logged over two thousand visits from hundreds of people in only six weeks, all of which remain in my heart and my memory. Reflecting on them is a personalized reminder of their importance to my overall recovery.

Just before the Christmas holiday Doctor Rosenthal began making plans for my transition in January from in-patient to out-patient. It was truly the conclusion of my detention. The light at the end of the tunnel. I was finally going home. However, out-patient care dictated that I would still be required to return for at least another dozen reparative surgeries and scores of follow-up visits. Accepting the present, rehabilitation and complete amelioration would take time.

On Monday, January fourteenth, nineteen eighty-five, I was discharged and was headed home. My causal and relaxed departure from the New York Children's hospital stood in stark contrast to my harried exit from the Florida medical facility. In preparation, most of my things – gifts, toys, cards and personal affects – had already been shuttled to my home which was only about a thirty-minute drive without traffic. The only, and I mean only, dour sentiment regarding my departure was the inevitable expiration of Nurse Antonio's exclusive services. Our bond had solidified over those six weeks. I could not imagine having to go through that without him. I was forced to accept the solitary consolation that our insurance allowed him to come out to our house bi-weekly for physical therapy. Even that was only covered for another three months. On his own initiative, outside the scope of his employment, Tony volunteered to follow us home, making certain that I settled in safely. He was amazing.

It was an exceptionally frigid winter and we had just experienced a modest snowstorm delivering several feet of snow blanketing Long Island and the whole tri-state area. Despite my extensive practice indoors upon dry hospital floors, crutching through mounds of snow and treacherous patches of ice was a tad daunting. My lack of enthusiasm was exacerbated by outside fearful influences. Before my exit I received unsolicited advice from almost everyone at the hospital. Their trepidations and apprehensions were incessantly shared regarding my transition home. Tammy even suggested that I take a wheelchair home and, "not even risk the elements." All in all, the potentially hazardous outdoor obstacles, no matter how precarious, were invariably easier to navigate than the bombardment of negative projections and fear-laden anxieties.

This was another lesson I had to learn. Continually reassuring people that I was fine, confident and secure could have otherwise become a full-time occupation. Recognizing this, I concluded that it was not my job to reassure or convince others of anything, but merely to lead by poised example. With each interaction I grew stronger. We all said our goodbyes, hugging and extending warm heartfelt wishes. Then I packed up my crutches and was ready to finally go home.

※※※※

The Story of the Icy Steps

Arriving at my childhood home the first challenge did not disappoint. Our house boasted a long, two-hundred-fifty-yard, inverted, steep and curved driveway, that was rendered unusable by our automobile due to the recent snowfall. Therefore, we had to park at the top, curbside, and walk down. We all got bundled up, prepared for the brutal cold, and exited my mother's car. The scenery was captivating. I slowed the progression of time in order to take it all in. The picturesque leafless tree branches were covered in majestic white lines of powder. Five-foot white packed icy piles created by city snowplows lined the gutters. Observing my chilled breath as it gently wafted from my mouth, I reflected on countless fond memories playing in those piles during my childhood.

As we stood outside the parked car, initially Tony asked, "Ay, nothing to be embarrassed about. Would you like me to carry you down? As we discussed, snow and ice can be tricky on crutches. And those steps will be slippery. You don't need to be a hero on your first day home. And you know you don't need to impress me."

After visualizing and contemplating the luxury of being carried, I knew this was something that eventually required mastery. And over the coming weeks and months, throughout the rest of the winter, Nurse Antonio wouldn't be here daily to assist. As the saying goes, there was no time like the present.

Masking my trepidation with false bravado, I nodded and joked, "Who are you, Tam-Tam?" Quickly adding, "I got this. Master and captain, remember?" As I began maneuvering the crutches slowly, taking extremely small hop-steps, I could feel the instability. The entire experience was an allegory for overcoming moments of terror. I closed my eyes and drew upon my revelations regarding rational fear. There was a very real possibility that I could slip, fall and seriously injure myself. Regulating my breathing, getting centered, inhaling and exhaling slowly, I reminded myself that, "while caution is warranted success is often achieved through baby-steps." Despite the teeth-chattering cold, I took as many breaks as were necessary working my way down the upper portion of the driveway at a sloth's pace.

The entire time, Tony was guiding me, making certain that I didn't fall. As we continued down and his confidence grew, he provided me a wider berth. Observing my vigilantly gradual pace, he recognized that I knew better than to fall and re-injure my fresh, still healing wounds. After what felt like an eternity, gazing back, I satisfyingly took in the top third of the driveway behind me. We stopped at a staircase that offered a shortcut down to my house, bypassing the steepest and most treacherously icy section of the driveway. The steep narrow shortcut, covered in fresh snow, appeared almost as dangerous. I asked Nurse Antonio, "What do you think Robert Frost would say?"

We both laughed knowingly and considered my options – the long steep icy driveway, versus the narrowly inclined, slippery railroad tie steps, rocks and tree branches. They both presented their own challenges. The thirty-two steps, connecting directly to our portico and covered front entrance were narrow and steep, making it more difficult for him to assist me. While the driveway, being much wider, facilitated Tony's help, but it was four times the distance and contained an extremely hazardous incline. Both were not simplistic descents, especially on crutches.

Nurse Antonio sent my mother trudging down the snowy steps ahead of us, assuring her that he would help me. He knew that she was in pain, suffering from extremely bad circulation and that she would truly appreciate the warmth our home provided. Furthermore, he convinced her that she could watch us from our kitchen window below and always come back out if necessary.

We stood at the top step, in the bitter cold, for at least ten minutes. Looking down at my house and my mom already inside the kitchen, Tony asked, "Okay kiddo, I'm freezing. What's it going to be?"

I said, "Well, you know how way leads to way, don't you?" Then I slowly started forward.

Standing securely on the step just beneath me, looking up, seeing my terrified expression, he smiled, "Come on. You can do this. Go slow. This is your house, and these stairs are not going anywhere. You have to learn to do this eventually. Relax, I'm here if you get wobbly."

A feeling of dread wrenched my stomach, yet I knew that inaction was not an option. I proceeded slowly. I lowered the crutches gently onto the first step and gingerly applied my body weight. Nurse Antonio's hands were open, arms extended, spotting me. I felt the right crutch begin slipping on a patch of ice under the snow. My heart raced. I saw myself tumbling down fracturing my neck. I pulled back, regaining my balance. Antonio grabbed me making certain I remained upright. Looking at the path ahead I re-envisioned the long tumble and multitude of injuries that would accompany falling. Not a pretty prospect at all. "Okay," I conceded, "maybe this is a bad idea. Can you help me down?"

I was stupefied when Nurse Antonio, my friend, turned and headed down the stairs without me. "Nope, you're on your own, Laurence!" And he marched down the stairs, knees high in the deep snow. On his way, without turning back to me, raising his right hand high, he proclaimed, "And by the way, it's not Frost, it's Henley. No, no, no, I take that back. Correction, it's not Henley. This moment calls for Lord Tennyson. You got this Laurence. You got this! I'll see you inside." He wasn't kidding. He just left me there. I was awestruck as he went all the way down, kicked the snow off his wet shoes and entered the house. I meekly stood there, freezing, looking down at the hazardous decline and at my mom and Antonio looking up at me from our kitchen window.

I tried again to put both crutches on the next step only to feel them slip. The boot encasing my right foot was also unsteady. I pulled back and regained my composure and balance on that top step. This was obviously a test. A lesson. They wouldn't let me freeze to death. They wouldn't allow me to injure or kill myself. But they expected me to work this out. Nice! I was affixed to that step, and I was alone, terrified, cold and wet. Feeling sorry for myself, the invalid, I started to cry. Not giving up I tried planting the right crutch onto the step below. I became infuriated as it again frustratingly sank into the icy powder. I lost my balance, leaned terrifyingly forward and then thrust myself backwards, falling hard onto my rear-end. My cotton sweatpants were not waterproof. I was then drenched and cold, and wallowing in self-pity. Sitting in the snow I shouted, flailed my arms like a child, pounded the snow, cursed and continued to cry.

Inside our kitchen my mother desperately pleaded with Nurse Antonio to help me. But he reasoned with her emphatically, "No, Mrs. Kaldor. We have to let him do this." Ultimately, she relented knowing he was right. "Laurence needs this. Trust me, I'd never let anything bad happen to that kid. I may have provided him the inspirational words of the classic laureates, but he has incorporated them into his idiom." Nurse Antonio proudly concluded, "He's strong. Stronger than you may think. Confident. He can do anything he puts his mind to. You just have to let him do it. Don't ever, ever, hold him back."

Sitting in the snow, freezing, I contemplated all my lessons and insights. My fear was rational. It was a dangerously steep and icy incline. Falling would likely result in serious injury. And no one was coming to help me. Instinctually, I knew Nurse Antonio was teaching me a lesson and it was one I had to learn. It was the hospital hallway reflection all over again. Speaking to myself aloud, I actually laughed, "Oh man, I should never have told him about that story, and that I got over it on my own. I'm such an idiot." Looking around, taking it all in, observing myself in the snow...I understood the lesson. That moment was emblematic of my new life going forward and all of life's obstacles ahead of me. And just then my inner voice echoed, "Made weak by time and fate." Unexpectedly, it wasn't Tony's voice I heard, it was my own inner voice reciting the poetry, and it wasn't a whisper. It was strong, bold and confident. I picked myself up, leaned on the crutches and balanced on my right leg. I felt the muscles in my foot working overtime to keep me upright. I repeated the opening phrase, doing my best to conjure up the rest of the words, "Made weak by time and fate." As I lodged the crutches into the snow this time, they both sank, never hitting solid ground and I fell hard on my right shoulder, face planting into the icy powder. I cursed and screamed in frustration. Internally, I regained my composure, focusing I remembered, "Made weak by time and fate...but strong in will. But strong in will!" I then augmented reality so that I could visualize myself getting to the bottom. I was incorporating all my new tools along with the classic inspirational refrain, which was reverberating in my head.

Interestingly, after thoroughly exploring the present, I concluded that there was no scenario where I successfully made it down by myself on those crutches without getting hurt. It became a lesson about hubris and humility. My ego. And there it was. I had to get over myself. And with that, I immediately knew the solution and continued aloud, "To strive..." I grabbed the crutches and inched down the steps on my butt. "To seek..." sliding every few feet, completely immersed in the frosty precipitation. "To find..." I was doing it. I was getting down and very quickly, I might add. Resolutely, I concluded, "...and not to yield!" At first, I felt silly. But that passed quickly. Ultimately, all that mattered was accomplishing my task, getting safely to the bottom. I then heard my familiar whisper, "...and not to yield." As I neared the end of the descent I shouted triumphantly, "...and not to yield! Never!"

Reaching that final step, I rose, dusted myself off and crutched slowly to the front door where Antonio and my mother greeted me with a warm embrace and an even warmer cup of hot cocoa. Tony helped me take off my wet clothes, while my mother wrapped me in a dry, soft towel and rubbed my hands briskly. She said, "None of this is going to be easy." Then she jokingly prodded, "I wanted to help you out there. He wouldn't let me."

"That's so true, she did want to help. I wouldn't let her. I knew you would figure it out."

My mother and I simultaneously replied, "I wasn't so sure," prompting us all to have a good laugh.

"Well, I didn't doubt you for a second," Tony said. Adding, "Piece of cake. eh?"

I sarcastically chided, after a short exhale, "Yeah, piece of cake," looking back up and out the window at the steps and my imprint in the snow.

Nurse Antonio asked, "You feel pretty good about yourself, don't you?"

Sipping my hot cocoa, enjoying the warmth the cup provided my fingers, still slightly shivering, I responded, "I feel cold and wet. And I'm certain my backside is all bruised. I could have broken my neck you know." After a brief pause, adding, "And yeah, it feels pretty darn good."

Tony pulled a notebook out of his backpack. It resembled his poetry book except it was new, flat and not bursting at the seams. As he handed it to me, he said, "Life is going to present you with those same icy, snow-covered steps every day. I have no doubt that you're going to persevere the exact same way you did today. One step at a time." He flipped through the first few pages, showing me, "I started you with a few of my favorites. Filling the rest in is going to be up to you." He held the book tight as I grabbed it, not letting go, adding, "Never yield!" And we both smiled as he gently released his end.

Admiring the first few pages and all the blank ones, I nodded and echoed his sentiment, "Never give up!"

Nurse Antonio was absolutely correct as I would revisit the memory of that "struggle with the icy steps" during my strenuous, often difficult recovery and, at times, throughout the rest of my life. After those three short months of rehabilitation ended, I only saw Antonio a few more times over the remainder of the year. In the fall he moved out of state, got married and opened his own physical therapy business. A couple of years after that he relocated his practice to Italy, where his wife is from, so they could start a family. Sadly, we had lost touch over the years. I will forever owe him an invaluable debt of gratitude. I am truly blessed to have received validation from our shared insights and more so for his camaraderie, friendship and love.

The Story of Natalie

My arduous two-year physical recovery came with many opportunities for constructive emotional growth. Possibly my grandest and most dramatically conditioned evolution was regarding vanity and superficiality. On the one hand, I began to accept the positive inspirational effect my survival had on people which paved the way for wonderful lasting friendships. On the other hand, those were all platonic friendships. It was exceedingly difficult to perceive that my marred, frightful and permanently disfigured appearance would ever attract a romantic partner or mate. I seriously questioned whether anyone would ever love me in that way. Surviving, overcoming adversity and even thriving academically were all respected and attractive traits. However, being physically, amorously, and passionately attractive was a different matter entirely. Aesthetically, I was still a monster. I questioned my positive premonitions regarding my future family, believing that they were nothing more than delusional fantasies.

My own mother, members of my family as well as several close friends contributed similar reservations that due to my permanent injuries and outward appearance, I would likely have to settle romantically. I should be prepared. They were imposing and projecting their own material superficialities and insecurities onto me. For my own protection. Despite my newfound ability to craft my own historiography visualizing a loving wife and family, my engrained faulty programming was susceptible to the bombardment of their negativity. I let them project their fear onto me. They wore me down. My self-confidence in that specific regard waned and was ultimately shattered.

I was then provided a serendipitous gift. A miraculous infusion of insight, companionship and affection. It came wrapped in the package of a close friend, Natalie, with whom I had maintained a special childhood connection. She was innocent, slim, about my height, blonde flowing hair, an endearing smile and the warmest brown eyes. She was intelligent, no, brilliant, talented and clever, and most of all we made each other laugh. Before the plane crash we were too young to date. However, we often exchanged innocuous, sweet, juvenile flirtations. Since my hospitalization in New York, I was amazed at how attentive she was, even more so after my transition home to outpatient care. She was no longer a child. She had become a vivacious young woman. I refused to tempt, or torture myself with impossibilities, convinced my feelings were still innocent. I was in serious denial.

As the months dragged on and visitations from family and friends dissipated, she remained a fixture. She was also a tremendous help to my mother. Her outpouring of warmth and affection for me and my family was incomprehensible and boundless. I convinced myself that our sweet childhood flirtations had blossomed into a healthy, solid, mature relationship whereby she had quickly become my best friend and confidant. And, due to my extremely low self-image, perceiving myself a monstrosity, I was absolutely certain that her affection for me was sincere, albeit familial, friendly and innocent.

THE GIFT

My insecurity, childish fears and faulty wiring prohibited honesty. Objectively observing her through the eyes of a healthy post pubescent male, it was evident that we were no longer children. She was still slender but developing womanly curves. She was sexy and sultry, while maintaining a tomboyish charm, like a young Katharine Hepburn. The truth was that my corrupted circuitry prohibited credence that a young woman like that could ever be romantically interested in a revulsion like me. I simply wasn't good enough. I wasn't worthy. I would have to settle on being her friend.

One spring afternoon, we were relaxing at my kitchen table seated next to each other finishing a snack discussing my gratitude for her company and assistance. It started off as a casual conversation that we already had many times. What made that one different was that I confided in her my fears regarding my low self-image and never finding true love. Before I could finish my sentence she leaned over and kissed me gently on the lips. It wasn't passionate, but rather "matter of fact." She was confident. I was confused.

"What was that for?" I asked.

"What was that for?" She pulled away, feeling rejected. "Well, I'm sorry. I thought you needed it. And I wanted to." Receiving my negative, confused response only magnified her rejection which quickly manifested into annoyance. She stood up. "I didn't mean to...I just thought..." She exhaled, still uncertain about my reaction, "Was it that bad?" It didn't dawn on me for a second that we were both awkward teenagers with our own insecurities.

Pouting, I nastily said, "I don't need your pity. You're too good a friend. I can't handle that from you. Not you!" Talk about faulty programming. A beautiful young woman just kissed me for the first time and that was my reaction.

She crossed to the opposite side of the table, facing me. Her annoyance exploded into anger. "You are such a jerk! I don't pity you. Actually, I think you're an idiot. You know what? I take that back. I do pity you. I do. I feel really sorry for you. But not because of your injuries. I feel sorry for you because you're an idiot!"

Never underestimate how inefficient your programming makes you. Even more confused, I replied, "Why are you so angry?" After a brief pause, I added, "I don't know what to say."

She let out an even louder guttural cry of irritation. She was incensed! She quickly paced for a moment in a semi-circle and then stormed out. Then she stormed back in. Then back out. Then she returned, shaking her balled up fists inches from my face in utter frustration. "You don't have to say anything. Look moron, I don't see all of this," waving her hands wildly, referring to my face, body, and stump. "How long have I known you? You're a beautiful person. You're kind, intelligent and funny. You have a huge heart and all kinds of inner strength that most people would kill for. Actually, you're the bravest person I know. And believe it or not, I think you're kind of cute. Even if you are the biggest freaking idiot in the world. The biggest!"

Then I pulled her close. She pushed me away holding up her index finger in my face, "Don't!"

"Come here." Gently tugging on her shirtsleeve I tried again.

She pulled her sleeve loose and re-raised her index finger, "No! Don't you touch me!" Even though I was no longer touching her, or restraining her in anyway, she remained only a few inches from me.

I reached out for her shoulders, trying to pull her face a little closer to facilitate a kiss. She pulled away again, but only a couple of inches, "Ewe, why would I kiss such a horrible monster, idiot-jerk-face?"

I gently pulled her close so that we were nose to nose, "I'm sorry." She fought me less. "I am so sorry." She leaned in and we kissed. It was amazing. It wasn't familial. It wasn't long, sloppy or salacious. It was soft and tender. It was love. I thought to myself, "How is this possible?" I was a monster. She was adorable. She was brilliant and sexy. What in the world would she want with a monstrosity like me?

She got up, still a little annoyed, pacing, "You know, I had a crush on you in junior high and I thought you weren't interested in me. But then, over the next couple of years we became better friends. And I was happy with that. It was enough. It was fine." She paused, exhaling while her anger softened, "But when we all got the news of your plane crash...When I got the news...the news that I almost lost you. I thought about you every day while you were struggling to survive in Florida." Her voice crackled as she began to cry. "I would concentrate every day, hoping to send you strength through telepathy. I cannot tell you how many nights I cried myself to sleep. There were so many nights that your mom would put the phone next to your ear. You couldn't talk. You were barely conscious. I used to listen to you sleep. I missed you so much." She tenderly cradled my face in her hands, "I missed my friend." We just stared into each others eyes touching foreheads, and she softly repeated, "I missed my friend."

Like an idiot, all I could say was, "Wow."

"Wow?" She blinked rapidly and slightly fluttered her head in irritation. "Really? Wow? That's all you can come up with?" She exhaled again. I half smiled, uncomfortably and shrugged my shoulders. She sniffled, then let out a single chuckle, wiping the water off her face and her nose, "You're a real jerk-face, you know? A colossal idiot."

"Yes, I am," I admitted, as I pulled her back affectionately and kissed her.

Drying her eyes she added, "I don't know what I would have done if I had lost you." She gently punched my chest with her fist and repeated the sentiment, "I can't believe I almost lost you." Then playfully adding, "I can't believe I care."

We tilted our foreheads together again looking deeply into each other's eyes, I whispered, "I love you!"

She smiled, wiped her nose, rose, pivoted and walked away. Half-turning back, one hand on her hip, confident and recomposed, she coyly jousted, "I know you do." Smirking and laughing knowingly, she sauntered out of the room. Man, was she sexy.

We went into the living room, snuggled into an embrace and spent the rest of the afternoon curled up on the couch watching television.

We loved each other very much. And we still do. She was, is, and will always be one of my most treasured friends. Although we dated briefly throughout high school we knew that our personalities were, and are, too similar to maintain a serious romantic relationship. Years later, I was honored and thrilled to attend her wedding, and soon thereafter, watch her two amazing children grow into magnificent adults. Our families remain close friends to this day.

Natalie was instrumental in reprogramming my self-image. From that day forward I no longer felt like a monster. Furthermore, that awakening magnified my conditioning and how shallow, superficial and materialistic I was. Everyone is valid. Everyone has worth. We all matter. We are all important. Natalie's open affection and honesty helped reinforce my insights, providing me a foundation of self-confidence that would endure. She also validated my premonitions, my future chapters. While others questioned the veracity of my visualizations, after Natalie I began accepting them as gospel. It would still take a few years but eventually I learned, I re-programmed myself, to trust them. And I would eventually embrace true love with my future best friend and create an incredible family, just as I had prophesized. Never settling! Never giving up!

The Story of Responsibility

I had spent the winter, spring and summer of nineteen eighty-five being homeschooled and privately tutored in hopes of physically returning to class in the fall and starting my senior year with my peers. My high school building was enormous. The campus hosted over fifteen hundred students, on a scenic twenty-acre wooded property, containing a sprawling array of classrooms with lengthy corridors and a plethora of steps. A disabled person's nightmare.

Anticipating issues of tardiness relating to traversing the school on crutches, or eventually on a prosthetic limb, my mother and I visited Doctor Rosenthal to discuss special medical accommodations excusing my inevitable unpunctuality. Doctor Rosenthal rejected this idea outright. He sat me down and simply said, "No." In response to my disappointment, shock and dismay, he explained, "Life can be unfair. It wasn't fair that you were in an accident and lost your leg.

However, life throws people curve balls all the time. I'm not doing you any favors giving you an excuse to be late. An excuse to be lazy. Your disability is permanent. Yes, you will always have to try harder than the other guy. Yeah, you may have to get up earlier, move faster and even miss the chance to stand around chatting in the hallways. However, you will get to your classes on time. Actually, as a matter of fact, you'll learn to be early."

His speech was presented bluntly and matter of fact. I pleaded, "But won't there be occasions when I can't get there on time? When the distance is just too far away?" He just sat there allowing his silence to be my answer.

To my chagrin, I could tell he had my mother sold. She was smiling and nodding approvingly. Everyone was against me. I was alone on this one.

I tried to pull a little guilt and manipulation out of my pocket. "What if I fall? You know, because I'm rushing."

He smugly responded, "You'll get yourself up. And you'll still get yourself there on time. Oh, and if you're planning on falling often, I strongly suggest wrapping yourself in some padding. Or maybe getting yourself a helmet." To which my mother had the nerve to laugh into her hand. He wasn't finished. "Son, in all candor, your life will be harder and more difficult than it is for your friends. It will even be brutally challenging at times. Just getting dressed in the morning will be a chore. Hopping into the shower will not be quick or easy. So, you'll have to get up earlier. You'll learn to move faster. You'll be stronger. You're no longer like everyone else. You're going to have to be better. No excuses. No, I'm not going to give you one."

Falling back on levity, I said, "You know, if you write me the tardy slip it will really give me a 'leg up' on the other kids." I oscillated a beat between both of their expressions back and forth. No reaction. Silence. Strike one. I looked at my mom and shrugged, as if to say, "come on, you're my best audience." But no. She made a lemon face, closed her eyes, looked down and shook her head negatively. Then I tried, "Okay, I give up. I guess I don't have 'a leg' to stand on. Do I?" Again, no reaction. Crickets. Strike two. Clearly not knowing when to quit, waving my stump from left to right, I repeated, "Get it? Don't have a leg to stand on. Eh? Eh?"

"Yeah, we get it," my mother interjected trying to save me. She looked at me still waving my stump back and forth pathetically trying to get attention. She just exhaled exacerbated, turned and walked out, saying, "Bye Doctor Rosenthal. And thank you. We'll see you in a few months. Come on Lau."

Doctor Rosenthal got up, and said, "Take care. See you in a few months." He shook my hand, hardily, like a man and walked over to his desk, sat down and scribbled a few notes into my open file. In retrospect, no one had ever shaken my hand with that much respect before.

Since I was still in the room, I was still at the plate. I knew I couldn't hit the fast ball, so I decided to swing at a high one, "What do you call a guy with no legs?" He just looked me. I answered, "Neil." He exhaled, raised an eyebrow and continued scribbling. Strike three? No, I'd swear I connected, catching a piece of that one...foul tip. I quickly continued, "What about a guy with no arms and no legs at your front door?" After a quick beat I answered, "well, you call him Matt." This time he looked up at me from his desk, stone faced. Ayy, he didn't laugh and he didn't smile. But he did look up. I'm calling that one another foul.

He picked up his pocket voice recorder that he used to make notes and brought it closer to his mouth as if he was going to speak. He had heard enough and he was showing visible signs of annoyance, sternly adding, "I have to get back to work."

As I exited, crutching slowly, over my shoulder I said, "If you throw Matt in the water..." I paused and then swung for the bleachers with, "Well, now you call him Bob!" Dah, nothing! Strike three, I was out, game over. Thanks folks, drive home safely as you exit the park.

Doctor Rosenthal, nonplused, put his recorder down, got up and said, "Comedy is not for everyone kid. I'll show you out." As I exited, crutching past the threshold, he said to me, "Next time you might want to try jokes that aren't a hundred years old. For example, what do you call a woman with one leg?" I turned, eyes wide. I shrugged. I was in disbelief and actually held my breath in anticipation. Completely deadpan and straight-faced, he delivered, "Eileen." It took me a few seconds, and then I smiled and uttered a solitary laugh. My smile grew as I embraced our shared moment of humor.

He began closing his office door, looking down at me, adding, "What do you call the same girl if she happens to be Asian?" Seconds before the door closed completely, he smirked, totally nailing it with, "Irene." The door slammed shut. I heard him chuckle on the other side, "He, he-he!" He did it. He smacked one completely out of the park. He had a sense of humor after all. Okay, it wasn't my bat or even my swing, but I did get it out of him. And a victory is a victory to be relished all the same.

Doctor Rosenthal remained my orthopedist for the next few years until I moved to California. Although I only knew him for an extremely short period his prudence had a profound impact on my life and my recovery.

During the car ride home that day my mother and I reflected on the serious subject matter discussed at the visit. She echoed his sentiment, agreeing wholeheartedly. The wisdom was undeniable. From that moment on I accepted my ambulatory disability as a gift, persistently and steadfastly driving me forward to my fullest potential, always striving to become the best version of myself. All my life I would have to work harder. And I would never, ever give up! Thank you Doctor Rosenthal.

The Story of David

Throughout the first couple of years after the plane crash, I was continually seeking validation similar to that received by my experience with Natalie. Validation that my insights and visualizations were genuine and not fantasies, delusions or hallucinations. Frankly, I was looking for signs. Inexplicable corroboration from a Higher Power. Amazingly I received them all the time. Perhaps they were always offered yet my faulty preconditioning had me closed off to them. And they often arrived when I least expected them and through the most surprising and unexpected messengers. My experience with David was no different.

It was the end of August, nineteen eighty-five, eleven months after the plane crash and only one week after I had seen Doctor Rosenthal. I was back in Long Island Jewish Medical Center having a minor surgical procedure that was expected to only take about thirty minutes, which meant I didn't even have to stay overnight. Having fasted since dinner the previous evening, I checked into the hospital at five-thirty in the morning with expectations of a quick surgery at eight o'clock, hoping to be home just after lunchtime. However, soon after we arrived, my doctor was called into an emergency surgery that took precedence over my procedure. Therefore, we had to wait.

Just after the nurse gave us the news, my mom said, "I'm so sorry honey. I was going to wait until they took you into surgery. But I'm starving. I'm going to run down to the cafeteria and get some breakfast."

I sarcastically replied, "Nice! I thought we were in this together."

My mom patted me on the shoulder and tried to make light of my hunger and childish frustration, "You thought wrong kid. I love you, but I'm hungry. You're on your own." Then she added, "Besides there's no reason both of us should suffer. Right?" Noticing that my sense of humor was absent, she lovingly paused and sincerely said, "You've had to do this before. Just drink water, it will settle the hunger pangs." Then she tried one more time, "And don't think about food. Think about...going to the movies."

"You're not helping," I said. "Now I want a hot buttery popcorn and a pretzel. Ay, just go! Enjoy your breakfast while you know your son is here starving. And on your way back see if we can get an ETA on how long I'll be delayed." I sat up and sipped my water through a straw.

"You got it, kiddo."

While we were talking, a young teenager about my age was wheeled in. He easily got up, unassisted, and walked to the other bed in the room, parallel and adjacent to mine, climbed in and laid down. The nurse exited with the chair. Next to him was a metal stand on wheels with a bag of fluid hanging on it. He was tethered to the bag of fluids by a long plastic tube plugged into his forearm. "If he could walk why was he wheeled in?" I thought to myself. Observing him distracted me from my hunger.

My mom gave me a kiss and said, "I love you, Lau. Just hang in there." Then she looked at the other kid and said, "Hello, young man." He smiled and waved. As she walked out, she added, "It's nice, you'll have company. He can help you keep your mind off...you know, that stuff you're not supposed to be thinking about." And she was gone.

After a moment of silence, the teen spoke, "Tough break."

"Excuse me?"

"I was listening. They delayed your surgery. It's a tough break. I've been there. Waiting is a pain in the you know what. But the fasting is brutal."

"Yeah, it's the worst! Hi, I'm Laurence."

"David. What are you in for?"

I spoke harmonically, being playful, "Oh, minor surgery. They have to close this hole in my throat. It had been opened so long it refuses to close on its own. Stupid hole." He chuckled, which may have been a courtesy laugh, but I'll take it. I asked, "Why the wheelchair? You seem fine walking on your own."

David explained, "I just got out of surgery." He lifted up his shirt reveling a huge patch of taped gauze covering his stomach and chest. "You know, standard procedure, they don't let you walk back from the recovery room."

"Huh," shaking my head affirmatively. "I thought it was only the guys without legs that they didn't let walk back. Silly me." Then I added, "I've been there." I lifted my shirt revealing the multitude of scars on my chest. "Wait a sec. It's so early. You're done already?"

He looked over at the clock on the wall. "Yeah, look at that. I was only gone for about forty-five minutes. In-and-out. They just needed to look around."

"Look around? What did you swallow something?"

"Yeah. Cancer."

"Holy shit!" I paused. "Cancer." I paused again. "That's serious. That sucks."

"Tell me about it. I've had it since I was five. It went away for a few years but decided to come back this summer. Wasn't that nice of it?"

I shivered as chills ran through me. Becoming solemn, I said, "How bad?"

"That's why we're here. In May they removed a golf ball-sized tumor and they've been giving me this treatment for the past few months. We're hoping for good news today."

"I'll bet. Don't sweat it. I'm sure the news will be good. You look great."

I wasn't patronizing him or joking. He looked terrific. He was well built, tall, athletically fit, muscle-toned, bulky arms and legs, broad shoulders, freckles, a warm smile and a full head of thick wavy hair. He didn't resemble any of the other cancer patients that I had observed at Schneider's when I was a resident.

He looked around taking stock, "I feel okay. I just get tired so easily. How'd you lose the leg? Car accident or dirt bike?"

"Neither, shark attack!" His eyes popped open. I quickly corrected the record, "I'm only kidding. It was a plane crash. But everyone always guesses car or motorcycle accident. I'm just trying out new material."

"I get that. Everyone always gets so quiet and uncomfortable when I mention cancer." Then he pointed at my stump, "But you don't really need to embellish. Surviving a plane crash is no joke. Holy shit! A plane crash. Man, that's unlucky!"

Without hesitation, I couldn't contain my excitement and responded, "Right?" I was so impressed that someone finally understood that.

And then he even completed the thought, "Yeah, lucky people land their planes." We nodded silently in agreement as his parents walked in with a doctor.

David offered, "Mom, Dad, this is Laurence. He survived a plane crash." They both smiled at me, nodded hello politely and grabbed the curtain surrounding David's bed, enclosing all four of them inside. They then proceeded to have a private conversation which I was able to overhear. While the curtain provided visual privacy it did little to muffle sound.

His father began, "David, the doctor has something to tell you."

THE GIFT 265

After a brief pause the doctor said, "It's not good news. The cancer has metastasized and spread to all your major organs. It's... it's like a mesh spider web. It's everywhere." While the doctor was speaking, I could hear his mother audibly sobbing.

"Okay, so what's the plan? What are we going to do?" David calmly responded.

The doctor speaking compassionately and softly said, "It's inoperable. There's nothing we can do. I'm so sorry." The doctor began to cry quietly. "David, I am so sorry."

I had been a patient now for almost an entire year and that was the very first time I had heard a doctor audibly cry. Listening, my eyes watered.

David appeared to be the only one not choked up. He asked, "Give it to me straight. How long?"

The oncologist answered, "It's pretty advanced. I've rarely seen it this bad. It could be months. It could be weeks. Once the organs fail it will be quick." The doctor partially opened the curtain to exit. "I have to go get you a few things to take home but I'll see you in my office tomorrow."

Confused, David inquired, "I'm going home?"

The doctor just shrugged. Then the dam burst, tears began pouring down his face. He couldn't find his voice. He was barely audible, "There's no reason to keep you. You'll be much more comfortable at home, with your family. There's nothing I can do. There's...nothing I could do. I'm so sorry." Then the doctor walked out, drying his eyes with a handkerchief from his coat pocket. His father walked over to console his mother. He then pulled the curtain back farther, put his arm around her shoulder, and then he also began to weep. I was not used to seeing grown men crying. Tears rolled down my face as well. I wiped my eyes and picked up a magazine, pretending to read it.

His mom said, "Honey, we have to speak to the nurse. Your clothes are in your duffle bag. Get dressed. We'll be back in a few minutes to collect you." They were both pale and stammered out of the room like zombies.

David looked over at me. I dropped the magazine and blurted out, "Holy shit dude. Holy shit!"

"You heard, huh?"

Sitting up facing each other, we hung our legs off the bedsides. I couldn't believe how calm he was. I asked, "How are you doing? This is huge!"

"I'm okay. I guess. A little sad."

I uncomfortably laughed, "A little sad? You think? I'd be freaking out!"

David shrugged and then casually pulled his shirt over his head. "I guess it's different when it happens to you. I couldn't imagine being in a plane crash. Let alone surviving."

And then it hit me like a ton of bricks. I was treating David the same way everyone else was treating me. Our roles were reversed. I was thinking, "Better you than me." I was internalizing dying of cancer. He was dealing with it, accepting it and being strong.

As he pulled his jeans on, he commented, "I suppose it's all the way you look at it. I've had cancer since I was little. They didn't expect me to live as long as I have. When the cancer went into remission everyone else was overjoyed. For me it was just another day. Same thing happened when it came back in May. Everyone around me panicked. For me, just another day." He shrugged again and slipped on his sneakers.

"Wow! You're amazing! Your attitude is amazing." He was my new hero!

Then he drove a stake through my heart, piercing me with my own words, "let me guess, if it happened to you, you couldn't take it. Right?"

Awash in validation, recognizing my initial misperception, I sincerely corrected him, "Nuh-nuh-nuh-nuh, no, I was actually going to tell you that I'm sorry for projecting my crap onto you. And to let you know how grateful I am to have met you." After a beat I added, "I am truly sorry you have cancer though."

While tying his laces he said, "I've never asked anyone this before, because, you know…I was afraid they would think the cancer patient has gone nuts. But…have you ever heard voices?"

"What kind of voices?" I asked. "And no, I don't think you're crazy. Go on." Before I was impressed, then I became captivated by that young man.

He sat back leaning against the headboard and a couple of pillows with his left leg dangling over the side of the bed and one shoelace still undone, "When I first learned about my cancer I was overwhelmed with thoughts about life, love and appreciation. It wasn't exactly a voice but an idea. A clear impression, an internal echo, a message, that every day was a gift. To be treasured." We both just let his comment hang in the air. After a few silent seconds he asked, "Crazy right?"

I shook my head, "No, not crazy at all." I couldn't believe what I was hearing.

"I don't know what compelled me to share that," David continued. "I can't explain it, but I knew you would understand."

I smiled, nodding, "More than you can imagine."

David lifted his left foot onto his bed. Tying his laces he said, "Since then, I've been at peace. I don't live in fear of pretty much anything. All of this was borrowed time. And I enjoyed every day. Every moment of every day, as if it were all there was." With his shoes neatly tied, he slid his feet onto the floor. "I mean, what choice did I have?"

A nurse entered with a wheelchair followed by his mother, "Honey, your dad will meet us around front with the car. Let's go." To me she politely smiled, "it was very nice meeting you."

I replied, "Nice meeting you too." To David I said, "If it makes you feel any better, I'm starving."

As he was being wheeled out, he retorted, "It doesn't. But, if makes you feel any better, I'm going to go home and have a huge late breakfast. Stack of pancakes, this big! I'll be thinking about you. Every bite."

I laughed, "I bet you will." I rolled off my bed and hopped over to him without crutches, "Here's my number. Let's stay in touch." I handed him a torn out piece of the magazine with my name and home telephone number scribbled on it.

He waved goodbye with the paper in his hand. "I'll call you this weekend." And following his mother the nurse rolled him out.

Reflecting on my meeting with David, I was humbled and troubled by the ease with which I resorted back to my faulty conditioning. That encounter served as a cautionary reminder that I would always be challenged by my unerasable upbringing. Since my initial software could not be deleted, I would always be working to rewrite it. To reprogram it. But my past would always be my past and it would always be with me. The communication from David, a sign, was yet another surreal experience, almost unbelievable. I was overcome with joy and satisfaction that my insights were once again validated. I received the message loud and clear. I was also impressed with how pristinely he articulated it. I thought to myself, "If I ever chronicle it I hope to do it justice." I also appreciated David's message to be a charge, and I therefore dedicated my life to appreciating my own gift and sharing the knowledge with as many other people as I could so that they could best appreciate theirs.

Incidentally, my procedure that day was postponed because my doctor had lost his patient after a four-hour marathon surgery. We merely had to reschedule for the following week. While I was disappointed to have to wait, I was thrilled to get to eat.

David and I did keep in touch. However, his condition rapidly declined and six weeks later he passed away. I further dwelled on our chance meeting. The fact that I was only in the hospital for a few hours. If my surgery had occurred as scheduled I would never have met David. Even if my doctor would have simply rescheduled when he was initially called away I never would have met David. Everything was meant to be. David's strength and words of validation were a gift. David's friendship was a gift. David was a gift and he will always be with me in the present.

The Second Interlude

Within the subsequent eight months I completed my outpatient care and had endured over one hundred surgeries. During the middle of my senior year in high school I received my first prosthetic leg. By June, nineteen eighty-six I was able to walk without crutches or a cane on stage, receiving my diploma on time and with my peers. Academically, I then proceeded on to college, graduate school, law school and film school. Industriously, I have been honored with several illustrious careers replete with excitement and fulfillment. Socially, I have been blessed with the most intelligent, beautiful, and wonderful wife, most spectacular daughters, and supportive close friends. Perhaps I have been the recipient of a little luck after all.

※※※※

The Story of Nurse Vanessa

Two years after graduating law school, in nineteen ninety-eight, I took a trip to Jacksonville Memorial Hospital to surprise some old friends. I called ahead, making certain that everyone was scheduled to work and would be there during my trip. When I arrived, the receptionist was kind enough to provide me a guest pass while maintaining my visit's secrecy. I raced up to the Intensive Care Unit on the second floor, burst out of the elevator and headed straight for the nurse's station. I was smartly decked out in a new suit and proudly walking on my new high-technology prosthetic limb. Stepping off the elevator I eagerly searched left and right to no avail.

Fortunately, it was a quiet afternoon at the hospital. There were two nurses behind the counter – a seasoned heavy-set redhead, seated closest to me and another, younger, fair skinned brunette with a similar build standing a little farther away. As I approached the dark-haired nurse, she said, "Yes, we can help you."

I whispered, doing my best to maintain the secrecy of my mission, "I'm looking for Nurse Vanessa. The receptionist in the lobby said she was up here. I'm an old friend. I just came by to surprise her. If it's not too much trouble, can you page her for me?"

The seasoned nurse seated closest to me interjected, "That's not necessary. She's just back there. I saw her a few seconds ago, going to get a cup of coffee. Melody, can you run back and tell Vanessa she has a visitor." The younger nurse nodded and went into a private lounge behind the counter. The seated nurse then asked me in a patronizing, yet playful whisper, "And who might we say is visiting?"

I leaned onto the counter, proud of my return, "My name is Laurence. I was a patient here fourteen years ago. But please don't tell her. I want her to be surprised."

She responded full throated no longer whispering, "Did you say fourteen years ago? Oh dear." Then she immediately picked up her phone, pressed an intercom button on the main panel, covered the bottom mouthpiece with her hand and quietly muttered something inaudible into the receiver. I couldn't hear her conversation. Regardless, I was too eager to see Nurse Vanessa to pay much attention anyway. Inside I was bouncing up and down with anticipation. I was replaying the last time I had seen her face, over and over, in my mind.

Nurse Melody returned with a tall, young, attractive Caucasian nurse with high cheek bones and horn-rimmed glasses. The nurse said, "Hi I'm Nurse Vanessa, I was told you came to see me. How can I help you?"

"You're not..." I paused, reading her name tag. It read, "Nurse Vanessa."

From behind me I heard a familiar deep, unforgettable, masculine voice say, "He doesn't know." I turned quickly around and saw Doctor Johnson and Nurse Kelley, both with solemn and serious expressions. They had both aged, but it was unmistakably them. They each broke their seriousness and half-smiled at me. However, there was something heavy underneath.

Nurse Kelley broke the silence by lunging at me, pulling me close and giving me an immensely warm bearhug. Then she pulled back, holding both my hands tightly, "Mmm-mmm, look at you. As I live and breathe. The miracle child returns...a man!" And her eyes welled up with water, adding, "oh, pardon me." She turned and took a few steps over to the counter, grabbing a handful of tissues, quickly patting the moisture just under her eyes.

I reached out my hand which was met by Doctor Johnson's, "It's so good to see you doc. They told me you had surgery later today. I'm so glad I caught you."

"It's really nice to see you, son."

"I just wanted to come and thank you all in person. You know, for saving my life and all."

"You're most welcome. But as I told you over ten years ago, it's our job." He looked me up and down, grinning and said, "I'm glad to see you're looking so well. You've come a long way from the first time you were here." He smiled and then surprised me by pulling me in for a heartfelt embrace, patting me several times on the back.

I then asked, "So, where's my Nurse Vanessa? And don't tell me it's her day off."

Everyone just stood there uncomfortably looking at me. Doctor Johnson took a deep breath, exhaled, and said, "Nurse Vanessa Allen was hit by a drunk driver three...three and a half years ago while she was walking home."

I covered my mouth with my left hand, "Oh my God."

"She didn't suffer," he added.

I looked down at the floor, shaking my head, "Oh my God. That can't be. We were writing to each other. Oh crap. Has it been that long. I guess I lost track of time with school, bar exams, work..."

The nurse seated at the counter interjected, "As soon as you told me that you were here fourteen years ago, I caught the confusion and called them."

Nurse Kelley took me by the hand, leading me behind the desk to a corner of the counter where there was a small shrine erected to Nurse Vanessa Allen. I scanned the entire memorial. Next to a large framed glossy photograph of

Nurse Vanessa was a collage of pictures of her family and various hospital staff. In the upper corner was a picture of me, in traction, propped up, smiling and being gently bookended and hugged by Nurse Vanessa and Nurse Kelley, each leaning in on opposite sides of my bed. Nurse Kelley pulled off the picture and gave it to me, "She worked here for eighteen years. You're the only patient she ever kept a picture of. She'd want you to have it."

Pressing the photo to my chest, I said, "she'll always be a part of me. You all will." I stared at the picture, reflecting on Nurse Vanessa's intoxicating smile. The lesson could not have been clearer regarding the preciousness of every moment. Every gift. Say everything you want to say to people while you have the opportunity. Cherish every moment with your loved ones. Cherish every gift.

Doctor Johnson interjected, "Come, let's grab a cup of coffee and catch up. I have about an hour before surgery. My, it's good to see you, son."

Nurse Kelley looked back at the seated nurse, "Melody, please cover my patients. They're all resting right now. And we won't be long." Nurse Melody nodded and smiled.

As we sat in the lounge, sipping our tasty, caffeinated beverages I was thrilled to learn that things with Nurse Kelley, Doctor Johnson and their respective families were going exceedingly well. However, we spent most of that hour exchanging wondrous yarns about Nurse Vanessa, and heartedly laughing, repeatedly. Although we haven't kept in touch over these long years, Doctor Johnson and the nursing staff remain among my most treasured gifts.

The Moral of the Story

Over these past decades I have met every challenge head on, one step at a time. I often tell people that I still have fear, I simply don't let it inhibit me in any way. I do not superficially pre-judge anyone, diligently continuing to rewrite my shallow, materialistic preconditioning. And while I am constantly challenged by my faulty wiring (which I acknowledge will always be with me), as well as contending with unlimited outside forces (which may always be at play), I work meticulously, embracing and overcoming them, finding solace in the universal truth. Lastly and proudly, I receive and accept every gift, appreciating and cherishing every aspect of each and every one of them.

Regarding all the physical activities that others had said I could not do because of my debilitating limitations or lack of physical prowess – like waterskiing, snow skiing, sky diving, tennis, racquet ball, rock climbing, hiking, running, martial arts, and piloting – after enjoying them all and more, I humbly advise you to, "Never give up!"

To those who were concerned that I had suffered debilitating brain damage, well...the jury is still out. But, after graduating high school, college, graduate school, law school, and film school on time and with my peers, I humbly advise you to, "Never give up!"

To those who cautioned me to settle regarding my career because certain things are out of reach for most people, but especially for folks with disabilities – like writing, producing and directing an independent film; working in Hollywood; acting on a television show; becoming a domestic violence litigator and trial attorney; volunteering for years as a City Prosecutor; and sitting for over a decade on the bench as a volunteer California Superior Court Judge Pro Tem, – after experiencing them all, I humbly advise you to, "Never give up!"

To those fearing that I would have difficulty finding true love, or needing to lower my expectations and romantically settle, after over fourteen years of marriage to the most amazing wife imaginable, raising two brilliant daughters that I could not be prouder of, – I humbly advise you to, "Never give up!"

To those who still believe that people do not survive plane crashes, I strongly and humbly suggest you question your preconditioning. To everyone else I encourage you to seriously challenge your programming too, hoping to humbly inspire you to live your life to the fullest and "Never, ever, give up!"

"The Gift"

"The Gift" is the present. "The Gift" is the past. "The Gift" is the future. "The Gift" is giving. "The Gift" is receiving. "The Gift" is accepting. "The Gift" is awareness. "The Gift" is the plane crash. "The Gift" is the pain. "The Gift" is the pleasure. "The Gift" is the suffering. "The Gift" is the joy. "The Gift" is the humor. "The Gift" is the insight. "The Gift" is the journey. "The Gift" is my wife. "The Gift" is my children. "The Gift" is my grandchildren. "The Gift" is my great grandchildren. "The Gift" is my extended family. "The Gift" is my friends. "The Gift" is my eternal gratitude. "The Gift" is you. "The Gift" is me. "The Gift" is all of us. "The Gift" is every moment. "The Gift" is truth. "The Gift" is life. "The Gift" is love. "The Gift" is my Spirit Guide. "The Gift" is God. Appreciate "The Gift!"

The beginning!

Epilogue

I truly hope you enjoyed the beginning of my journey. Thank you so very much for taking the time to experience it with me. While it is my desire to be both inspirational and entertaining, it is also my sincerest hope that you will be able to utilize the allegories from my experiences to enhance your own life with an individualized appreciation of the present, "The Gift!" If any aspect of my story ultimately has a positive impact on you, then I have succeeded in what I set out to do, and all my trauma, torment and suffering were not in vain. Please take that to heart, I do mean that sincerely. If you save one life you save the universe. I am eternally grateful for the opportunity to share this extremely personal period of my life with you.

LITERARY LICENSE

I would be remiss if I didn't point out my use of "literary license" at times during this lengthy allegory. Specifically, because I put so much emphasis on the "truth." And with even more specificity on the "objective truth." Ultimately, the overall allegory is objectively true regarding "my story of survival, recovery and enlightenment," and "my experiences regarding the Gift." Therefore, I was being objectively truthful to the overall work. However, during the long exploration creating this book I realized that there were simply too many nurses, doctors and close friends to mention and that doing so would be a distraction, a dilution, and a disservice to the overall message. For creative literary purposes or legal reasons, when I was objectively certain to remain true to the integrity of the story, certain attributes, names, anecdotes, conversations and even people were either omitted, embellished, altered or meshed together. Also, some characters' names and identities have been fictionalized, masked or omitted to protect and preserve their privacy.

To any members of the medical profession or any of my childhood personal friends or family that were inadvertently omitted I respectfully hope you don't feel slighted in any way. Please know that I love, respect and appreciate you, more than you could ever possibly imagine. You contributed positively to my journey. And if I had the ability to make this work marketable, legible and entertaining in unlimited length and duration I would have personally and individually included and thanked you. Hopefully you know how much you mean to me.

Additionally, there are two specific people that are relevant to the overall plane crash and recovery allegory that were intentionally omitted because, unfortunately, their "life rights authorization" could not be obtained. Therefore, they will be included now, to the limited extent that I can, in the efforts of full disclosure and objective truth. First, there was a third person in the plane with my father and I when we crashed. He was a young teenage friend of mine. He too survived the plane crash along with me. Fortunately, he was not ejected from the plane like I was and was found alive and coherent amongst the wreckage. He was rescued with me by the emergency helicopter crew and was released from the hospital after about a week following the crash, while I was still unconscious – living in my subconscious. Therefore, I could not have firsthand knowledge of the events that included him in the immediate aftermath of the crash, or even the month that followed. He was released from the hospital before I regained full consciousness. Unfortunately, personal injury litigation following the plane crash impeded our friendship and we lost touch. He was not omitted from the story out of malice or oversight but intentionally because of legal restrictions and limitations mentioned above. I have nothing but love and the utmost respect for him and wish him well. As a personal homage to him, I'm including a private joke and reference to "the bloody finger." To which only he will know and still think is hysterical. He and our childhood friendship will always be with me in the present. Furthermore, his omission in no way affected the overall allegory, my experiences during recovery or my insights regarding "The Gift."

The other glaring omission from the allegory is my sister. She too was not omitted from the story out of malice or oversight but intentionally because of similar legal restrictions mentioned above. She was attending college at the time of the crash. She came to Florida to be with me and to keep our mother company. She was incalculably supportive to both my mother and I throughout my recovery. While she didn't suffer the physical pain that I endured because she was not in the plane with us, she very likely suffered substantial emotional trauma from the loss of her father and witnessing her younger brother's brutal struggles. I can only imagine what she went through. Her personal loss and pain were most likely devastating and cannot be minimized. I love my sister very much, always have, always will. And I am immensely grateful for the time she spent with me in the hospital and during my recovery. However, obtaining the necessary and appropriate legal permissions were not practical in my creation of this work. And similarly, her omission from the work in no way affects my overall allegory, my experiences during recovery or my insights regarding "The Gift."

CLOSING THOUGHTS

This book has been almost forty years in the making. It has been a cathartic experience, to say the least. In closing, I'll leave you with a few final thoughts that encapsulate my overall message.

First, from *Ulysses*, by Alfred Tennyson,
"...we are;
One equal temper of heroic hearts,
Made weak by time and fate, but strong in will
To strive, to seek, to find, and not to yield."

And second, from *Don't Quit*, by Edgar A. Guest,
"Success is failure turned inside out...
And you can never tell how close you are
It may be near when it seems so far.
So stick to the fight when you're hardest hit
It's when things seem worst that you must not quit."

And lastly, from my personal favorite *Invictus*, by William Ernest Henley,
"It matters not how strait the gate,
How charged with punishments the scroll,
I am the master of my fate,
I am the captain of my soul."

THE GIFT

It is my genuine honor to have you on this journey with me.

Please always remember —

It's your story. Do not let anyone else write it for you.

Always question, challenge and when necessary re-write your programming.

Never give up!

And throughout every moment of every moment, above all else...

...appreciate "The Gift."

ABOUT THE AUTHOR

Laurence N. Kaldor has had, and continues to have, an extraordinary life. He is a driven attorney and had the honor of serving over twelve years as a volunteer California Superior Court Judge Pro Tem. He has also had the privilege of serving several years as a volunteer prosecutor. In his spare time, he volunteered over twenty years as a litigator fighting for victims of domestic violence in New York and California. In the entertainment industry he has enjoyed a career as a multi-award-winning independent feature filmmaker, as well as a producer, director, actor, stand-up comic, author, and screen writer.

He is most proud of his intelligent, magnificent, and beautiful wife and partner, as well as his two extraordinarily gifted, talented, and gorgeous daughters. His wife has a successful and fulfilling career as a policy research analyst. She is his rock! And, as her biggest fan, he is beyond impressed with her abilities and talents. Together they have raised and nurtured their daughters who are flourishing under their guidance. They also have the joy and pleasure of spending their days homeschooling and interacting with their children. Laurence could not be more grateful for his family or more satisfied with his life! Each day he and his family aspire to be the best versions of themselves, always at the service of others.

As a child he dreamed of joining the Air Force to serve his country, as his father had done in the Air National Guard. However, in 1984 at just 16 years old, he experienced a devastating airplane crash that would dramatically alter the course of his life. Against all odds, he survived. And yet only after confronting death, did he learn how to truly live.

This is his story, told in his own words, and in his own voice.

Made in the USA
Middletown, DE
16 February 2025